BARRON'S

COMPREHENSIVE

POSTAL
EXAM
473/473-C

JERRY BOBROW, Ph.D.
Executive Director
Bobrow Test Preparation Services

Programs at major universities, colleges, school districts,
and county offices of education throughout California

Award-winning educator, lecturer, consultant, and author of more
than 30 nationally known test preparation books

Contributing Author and Consultant
Michele Spence, B.A.
Author, Educator, Senior Editor

BARRON'S

W

Acknowledgments

I would like to thank my family: my wife, Susan; my daughter, Jennifer; and my sons, Adam and Jonathan, for their continuing moral support.

I would also like to thank an outstanding writer, contributor, and close friend, Michele Spence, for her major contributions to this book.

Finally, my thanks go to Barron's Educational Series acquisitions editor, Wayne Barr, J.D., for offering me this project and to Barron's editor Kathleen Ganteaume, for her hard work and diligence in helping make this project a success.

TEST
351.3
POSTAL
2006

All inquiries should be addressed to:
Barron's Educational Series, Inc.
250 Wireless Boulevard
Hauppauge, New York 11788
www.barronseduc.com

Library of Congress Catalog Card No. 2006040108

ISBN-13: 978-0-7641-3412-8
ISBN-10: 0-7641-3412-4

Library of Congress Cataloging-in-Publication Data
Bobrow, Jerry.
   How to prepare for the comprehensive postal exam, 473/473-C / by Jerry Bobrow.
     p. cm.
   Includes index.
   ISBN-13: 978-0-7641-3412-8
   ISBN-10: 0-7641-3412-4
     1. Postal service—United States—Examinations, questions, etc. 2. Postal service—United States—Study guides. I. Title: Comprehensive postal exam, 473/473-C.
   II. Title.

HE6499.B628 2005
383'.1076—dc22

2006040108

PRINTED IN THE UNITED STATES OF AMERICA

9 8 7 6 5 4 3 2 1

CONTENTS

Preface

We know that getting a top score on the Postal Examination 473/473–C is important to you. And we can help!

As a matter of fact, for the last thirty-one years we have assisted more than *two million* test takers in successfully preparing for many types of important exams ranging from graduate exams to civil service tests to teacher preparation exams. Our regular preparation programs at more than 15 universities and colleges, as well as our many special programs for school districts, county offices of education, industries, and civil service agencies, have helped us develop strategies, techniques, and materials to help you do your best.

Our easy-to-use *Comprehensive Postal Exam 473/473–C* gives you your key to success by focusing on

What to Expect

What You Should Know

What to Look For

What You Should Do

We give you lots of strategies and techniques along with plenty of practice problems and tests.

If you want to do your best on the Postal Examination 473/473–C, follow our study plan and step-by-step approach to success!

Good luck,
Jerry Bobrow, Ph.D.

Part I

INTRODUCTION

HOW TO USE THIS BOOK

This book presents a careful breakdown and analysis of each of the question types on Postal Examination 473/473–C. These examinations are given for the jobs of City Carrier (473–C) and Mail Processing Clerk, Mail Handler, and Sales, Service, and Distribution Associate (473). Examinations 473 and 473–C are actually the same, but the designation 473–C is used when the City Carrier position is specifically being filled.

Take advantage of the many benefits included in this book—insight, analysis, strategies, and lots of practice.

First, carefully check the format chart on page 5 to become aware of the question types, number of questions, and time allotments.

Second, carefully read each of the sections. You will learn techniques and strategies to apply to each question type. Carefully work the practice exercises that follow. As you apply the strategies, you will build speed and accuracy. Once you have thoroughly read each of the sections and completed the practice exercises, then,

Third, turn to Part III, the six full-length practice exams. Take the first practice exam using the time limits given. When you finish, correct your test and analyze your answers. Notice the kinds of mistake you make and work at understanding why you are making them. Then focus on eliminating these mistakes as you review the sections and take the second practice test. Again, correct your test and analyze your answers. Continue this process until you have completed and analyzed all six exams.

This timed practice is vital to becoming comfortable with time pressure on the actual test. You will build up speed, accuracy, and endurance so that you can work at an efficient and effective pace throughout the complete exam.

GETTING THE MOST OUT OF YOUR STUDY TIME

Check off each step after you complete it.

Before You Begin

☐ 1. Find a quiet work space—one with good light, a clean, flat surface on which to work, and no distractions.

☐ 2. Have the proper materials: sharpened number 2 pencils with good erasers and an alarm clock or kitchen timer (one easily set for time limitations).

☐ 3. Set aside numerous regular time periods for study. Many short periods (of, say, 1 to 2 hours each) are better than a few very long periods (for example, 5 to 6 hours each).

☐ 4. Learn to make notes in this study guide: Circle or underline or write notes in the margin about points or items you think are important. Use Post-it notes to mark places in this book and help organize your studying.

1

☐ **5.** Read the Postal Examination information materials available at your local post office or online at *www.usps.com*. "Test 473 Orientation Guide for Major Entry-Level Jobs" (Publication 60-A) is an outstanding source available free online.

☐ **6.** Read Questions Commonly Asked, page 2.

☐ **7.** Look over the Format of the Exam and Scoring, page 5.

☐ **8.** Review Description of the Test, page 5.

☐ **9.** Carefully read each section in Part II: Working Toward Success, starting on page 9.

☐ **10.** Work each practice exercise following the analysis for each part of the exam.

☐ **11.** Strictly following time allotments, take Practice Examination 1, pages 87–126. Check your answers and analyze your results.

☐ **12.** Review your weak areas in Part II: Working Toward Success.

☐ **13.** Strictly following time allotments, take Practice Examination 2, pages 127–166. Check your answers and analyze your results.

☐ **14.** Strictly following time allotments, take Practice Examination 3, pages 167–206. Check your answers and analyze your results.

☐ **15.** Review your weak areas as necessary.

☐ **16.** Continue taking as many practice exams as you have time to complete and review. Follow the strict time allotments.

- Practice Examination 4, pages 207–246.
- Practice Examination 5, pages 247–286.
- Practice Examination 6, pages 287–326.

☐ **17.** Carefully read Are You Ready? page 327.

QUESTIONS COMMONLY ASKED

Q: What is test 473 about?

A: Test 473 is open to the public to meet the staffing needs for the positions of City Carrier, Mail Processing Clerk, Mail Handler, and Sales, Services, and Distribution Associate. This test helps identify individuals with the important experience, abilities, and personal characteristics necessary for the positions mentioned.

Q: What is the difference between test 473 and test 473–C?

A: Nothing. The two tests are identical. The designation 473 is used when the test is given for all four entry-level positions: City Carrier, Mail Processing Clerk, Mail Handler, and Sales, Services, and Distribution Associate. When the test is given specifically to fill the position of City Carrier, it is labeled 473–C.

Q: Do I need to pay to take the test?

A: No. You don't have to pay anyone to take a Postal Exam.

Q: Do I need to pay for information about job vacancies or employment opportunities with the Postal Service?

A: No. You never have to pay for this information. It is free from your local Postal Service or on the Internet at *www.usps.com/employment*.

Q: Where do I look for announcements of tests for entry-level jobs?
A: Test dates are publicized widely on the Postal Service Internet home page *www.usps.com/ employment*; on bulletin boards in Post Offices and in local, federal, and state municipal buildings; in newspaper, radio, and television advertisements; at state employment offices; and through community organizations.

Q: How do I schedule myself to take the test?
A: During the open registration period appearing on the test announcement, you can schedule yourself by calling the toll-free telephone number provided on the Internet at *www.usps.com/ employment*.

Q: How will I know when and where to take the test?
A: At least one week before the test date, the Postal Service will mail you a package telling you when and where to report for the test. You will also receive an admission pass, applicant instructions, and sample questions.

Q: What type of questions or items are on the test?
A: Test 473 is composed of four parts: Part A: Address Checking; Part B: Forms Completion; Part C: Section 1—Coding, and Section 2—Memory; Part D: Personal Characteristics and Experience Inventory. These will be analyzed and discussed in great detail in the Working Toward Success section.

Q: What score do I need to qualify?
A: The basic rating range is from 70 to 100, and you need a minimum score of 70 to qualify.

Q: What happens if I get a passing score?
A: If you get a passing score on the test, you are off to a good start and are qualified to continue in the hiring process, but you are not guaranteed a job with the Postal Service.

Q: Are there any other requirements?
A: Yes. You must be at least 18 years old (or at least 16 years old if you are a high school graduate), and you must be a U.S. citizen or permanent resident alien. You must also have a basic competency in speaking and reading English and must be registered with the Selective Service System (by the time you reach your eighteenth birthday) if you are a male born after December 31, 1959. A drug screen is also a requirement. There may also be minimum acceptable standards for vision, physical ability, dexterity, and driving ability, depending on the job for which you are applying. Check with the personnel office of your local Post Office.

Q: Is there any preference given to veterans?
A: The Veteran's Preference Act of 1944 requirements may add points to the basic rating, and there may be other preferences.

Q: What materials should I bring with me on the day of the test?
A: You should bring several specially sharpened number 2 pencils with good erasers, your admission pass, picture identification, and the employment application or any other materials sent to you in the scheduling package. Be sure to wear comfortable clothes and dress in layers, which will enable you to adapt to different temperature conditions (for example, a sweater in case the building is cold).

Q: Should I guess on the test?

A: Be careful; different parts of the test are scored differently. Know which sections penalize you for incorrect answers.

- If you don't know an answer on Part B: Forms Completion, you should fill in a guess because no points are deducted for wrong answers on this part. So, yes, **you can guess on Part B**.
- If you don't know an answer on Part A: Address Checking and Part C: Coding and Memory, guess only if you can eliminate one or more choices. Because a third of a point is deducted for each incorrect answer, **don't guess blindly on Parts A and C**.
- Because Part D is a Personal Characteristics and Experience Inventory, you should not guess. Just answer honestly to the best of your ability. So, no, **don't guess on Part D**.

Q: How should I prepare?

A: Learn as much as you can about the exam. Know the sections and the skills necessary to do well on these sections. Spend consistent, quality time learning the techniques presented in this book. Practice them at home under timed testing conditions.

A QUICK LOOK AT THE EXAMINATION PROCESS

1. **The Postal Service announces examination openings.** Test dates are publicized widely on the Postal Service Internet home page *www.usps.com/employment*; on bulletin boards in Post Offices and local, federal, and state municipal buildings; in newspaper, radio, and television advertisements; at state employment offices; and through community organizations.

2. **If you are interested in applying for City Carrier, Mail Handler, Mail Processing Clerk, or Sales, Services, and Distribution Associate, you should apply for test 473.** Test 473–C is used when City Carrier is the only opening to be filled. During the open registration period listed on the test announcement, you can schedule yourself by calling the toll-free telephone number provided or the Internet at *www.usps.com/employment*.

3. **At least one week before the test date, the Postal Service will mail you a package telling you when and where to report for the test.** You will also receive an admission pass, applicant instructions, and sample questions.

4. **You take test 473 or 473–C.**

5. **The National Test Administration Center scores your test.**

6. **If you pass the test (a score of 70 or higher), you will receive a notification from the Postal Service of your eligible rating and your name will be placed on the appropriate hiring register.** Your name will appear in numerical order from high to low scores and will include any veteran's preference points.

7. **If you fail the test (a score below 70),** you will be sent notification from the Postal Service of your ineligible rating and will not receive further job consideration under this examination announcement.

FORMAT, DESCRIPTION, AND SCORING

Format

Test Section	Number of Items	Time Allowed
Part A Address Checking	60	11 minutes
Part B Forms Completion	30	15 minutes
Part C Section 1—Coding	36	6 minutes
Part C Section 2—Memory	36	7 minutes
Part D Personal Characteristics and Experience Inventory	236	90 minutes

Description of the Test

Part A: Address Checking
On this part you are asked to determine whether two addresses are the same.

Part B: Forms Completion
On this part you are asked to identify information for correctly completing different types of postal forms.

Part C: Section 1—Coding
On this part you are asked to identify the correct code to be assigned to an address.

Part C: Section 2—Memory
On this part you are asked to memorize codes to be assigned to a range of addresses.

Part D: Personal Characteristics and Experience Inventory
On this part you are asked to assess personal characteristics, tendencies, or job-related experiences associated with performing effectively as a Postal Service employee.

Scoring

Part A: Your score is based on the number of items answered correctly minus one-third of the number of items answered incorrectly. Because of this penalty for wrong answers, **it is not to your advantage to guess blindly**. Guess only if you can eliminate one or more choices.

Part A: Address Checking

Enter the number you got right: _____

Enter the number you got wrong
(not including those left blank): _____

Divide the number wrong by 3
(or multiply by 1/3): _____

Subtract this answer from the number right: - _____

Raw Score _____

Part B: Your score is based on the number of items answered correctly. There is no penalty for wrong answers or guessing. **Never leave a question without at least marking a guess.** As a matter of fact, with one minute left in the section, stop where you are, fill in your guesses to finish the section, and then if time permits, go back and continue working.

Part B: Forms Completion

Enter the number you got right
(no penalty for guessing): Raw Score _____

Part C (Sections 1 and 2): Your score is based on the number of items answered correctly minus one-third of the number of items answered incorrectly. Because of this penalty for wrong answers, **it is not to your advantage to guess blindly.** Guess only if you can eliminate one or more choices.

Part C: Coding and Memory

Enter the number you got right: _____

Enter the number you got wrong
(not including those left blank): _____

Divide the number wrong by 3
(or multiply by 1/3): _____

Subtract this answer from the number right: - _____

Raw Score _____

Part D: Your score is based on your responses to the items in this section. An actual scoring formula is not available.

Part D: Personal Characteristics and Experience Inventory

Scoring system not given.

PREPARING YOUR PENCIL POINTS

Many sections on the Postal Examination are high speed—that is, you'll have to work very quickly in order to complete them. So any time wasted in filling in the answers on your Answer Sheet is valuable time lost.

In filling in the circles on your Answer Sheet, notice how a well-sharpened pencil requires more pencil strokes than one with a less sharp point. Therefore, prepare your pencils to meet the task at hand, which is not fine writing, but filling in circles with bold, dark strokes as quickly as possible. If your pencil point is too sharp, you'll take many more strokes to fill in the circle, thus wasting time. If the point is too dull, your pencil strokes may mark outside the circle. So, as you practice doing the tests in this book, learn exactly how much of a point you need to most efficiently fill in the Answer Sheet circles. Then, before you leave home for the test center on the day of the exam, prepare all your pencils with just the amount of sharpening that works best.

This advice may seem simplistic, but you would be surprised how much time you can save by having your materials properly prepared.

FILLING IN THE ANSWER SHEET

It is important that you fill in the circles on the Answer Sheet correctly. If you don't, they could be counted as wrong answers.

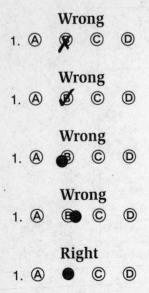

And remember, if you change an answer, **be sure you erase the first answer completely.** If the scoring machine counts more than one answer penciled in for a question, that answer will be marked wrong.

MARKING IN THE TEST BOOKLET

Some of the strategies mentioned in this book are based on your being allowed to mark in the test booklet. The actual directions state that unless instructed otherwise for a specific part of the exam, you may make notes or write in your test booklet. The specific part of the exam they are referring to is the Memory section of Part C, where you are not allowed to make notes.

Because this policy of allowing marks in the test booklet is a new policy, the examiner may not be familiar with the change and may ask you to stop marking. Simply point to the directions at the bottom of the first page that allow you to mark in the test booklet unless instructed otherwise for a specific part of the exam.

When you fill in your answers on the Answer Sheet, keep in mind that you are not allowed to make extra marks or notes on the Answer Sheet—only in the test booklet.

Part II

WORKING TOWARD SUCCESS

HOW TO USE THIS SECTION

The following section will introduce you to Postal Examination 473/473–C by pointing out:

- **What to expect**
- **What you should know**
- **What to look for**
- **What you should do**

This section emphasizes important test-taking techniques and strategies and how to apply them to the different question types.

Read this section very **carefully**. **Underline** or **circle key techniques**. **Make notes** in the margins to help you understand the strategies and question types.

Part A: Address Checking

WHAT TO EXPECT

The Address Checking part is 11 minutes long and contains 60 multiple-choice questions. That gives you only about 5 to 6 seconds to answer each question. Therefore you must work extremely quickly and accurately in order to complete this part.

On this part of the exam you are to determine whether two addresses are the same or different. You will be given a **Correct List** that contains addresses and ZIP codes and a **List to Be Checked**. This **List to Be Checked** should be the same as the **Correct List**, but it may contain some errors.

- Expect the following choices to be above the **Correct List** and the **List to Be Checked**.

A. No Errors	B. Address Only	C. ZIP Code Only	D. Both

- Expect the **Correct List** to be in boxes on the left with the *Address* in one box and the *ZIP Code* in another.
- Expect the **List to Be Checked** to be in boxes on the right with the *Address* in one box and the *ZIP Code* in another.

	Correct List			List to Be Checked	
	Address	*ZIP Code*		*Address*	*ZIP Code*
1.	9411 Tangelo Street Fontana, CA	92335		9011 Tangelo Street Fontana, CA	92353
2.	190 Bell Canyon Rd. Bell Canyon, CA	91307-4232		190 Bell Canyon Rd. Dell Canyon, CA	91307-4232

- Expect some **Lists to Be Checked** to have no errors, that is, to have no differences from the **Correct List**.
- Expect some **Lists to Be Checked** to have an error somewhere in the *Address*—numbers, street, P.O. box, city, or state. On occasion, there may be two errors in the *Address*, but that doesn't change the answer.
- Expect some **Lists to Be Checked** to have an error in the *ZIP Code* or the four-number extension when given.
- Expect some **Lists to Be Checked** to have an error in both the *Address* and the *ZIP Code*.
- Expect two sample exercises on the actual exam. One sample exercise will be 2 minutes long and have a few samples, whereas the second sample exercise will be 2 minutes long and have ten samples.

WHAT YOU SHOULD KNOW

- You should know that the answer choices will be the same for all questions.
- You should know that you will be comparing numbers, abbreviations, and words in addresses and ZIP codes.
- You should know that on this part *Address* means street number, street name, P.O. box, compass direction, apartment number, street abbreviation, city, and state.
- You should know that *ZIP Code* means the five-number ZIP code and any four-number extension if given.

WHAT TO LOOK FOR

Look for some of the common types of errors. They include transposing, changing, adding, and deleting.

Transposing (Order Reversals)

Sometimes the order of two letters or two numbers is reversed. For example, "37" may be transposed to "73"; "ae" may be transposed to "ea"; "NM" may be transposed to "MN."

See if you can spot the order reversals.

A. No Errors	B. Address Only	C. ZIP Code Only	D. Both

Correct List

	Address	ZIP Code
1.	3738 Main St. Neavitt, MD	21652
2.	14 Glenmaelin Ave. Akron, OH	45155-3231
3.	1213 Center Ct. Hicksville, NY	11801

List to Be Checked

	Address	ZIP Code
1.	3738 Main St. Neavitt, MD	21625
2.	14 Glemnaelin Ave. Akron, OH	45155-3231
3.	1213 Centre Ct. Hicksville, NY	11081

Did you spot the order reversals?

Correct List

	Address	ZIP Code
1.	3738 Main St. Neavitt, MD	216**52**
2.	14 Gle**nm**aelin Ave. Akron, OH	45155-3231
3.	1213 Cent**er** Ct. Hicksville, NY	11**80**1

List to Be Checked

	Address	ZIP Code
1.	3738 Main St. Neavitt, MD	216**25**
2.	14 Gle**mn**aelin Ave. Akron, OH	45155-3231
3.	1213 Cent**re** Ct. Hicksville, NY	11**08**1

- In sample 1, only the ZIP codes are different: 216**52** and 216**25**. So the correct answer is C—ZIP Code Only.
- In sample 2, only the addresses are different: Gle**nm**aelin and Gle**mn**aelin. So the correct answer is B—Address Only.
- In sample 3, the addresses are different: Cent**er** Ct. and Cent**re** Ct., and the ZIP codes are different: 11**80**1 and 11**08**1. So the correct answer is D—Both.

Changing (Replacing)

Sometimes all or part of a town, street number, or address has been changed. For example, Ct. may have been changed to Ln.; Riverwalk may have been changed to Riverview; 91364 may have been changed to 91524.

See if you can spot the changes.

A. No Errors	B. Address Only	C. ZIP Code Only	D. Both

<table>
<tr><td colspan="3" align="center">Correct List</td><td colspan="2" align="center">List to Be Checked</td></tr>
<tr><td></td><td>Address</td><td>ZIP Code</td><td>Address</td><td>ZIP Code</td></tr>
<tr><td>4.</td><td>56418 Ringward Ln.
Carson City, NV</td><td>89434-1735</td><td>56478 Ringward Ln.
Carson City, NV</td><td>89434-1735</td></tr>
<tr><td>5.</td><td>2319 Snow Rd.
Buyck, MN</td><td>55920</td><td>2319 Snow Rd.
Boyck, MN</td><td>55920</td></tr>
<tr><td>6.</td><td>543 W 3rd Street
Dannebrog, NE</td><td>68831</td><td>543 W 2nd Street
Dannebrog, ME</td><td>68031</td></tr>
<tr><td>7.</td><td>321 Wrangler Road
Ringold, OK</td><td>74754</td><td>321 Wrangler Road
Ringold, OK</td><td>74734</td></tr>
<tr><td>8.</td><td>12 Woodley Place
Cumberland, ME</td><td>04021-9382</td><td>12 Woodman Place
Cumberland, ME</td><td>04021-9381</td></tr>
<tr><td>9.</td><td>9342 Packard Dr.
Hadley, MA</td><td>01035</td><td>9342 Packard Dr.
Harper, MA</td><td>01035</td></tr>
<tr><td>10.</td><td>73113 W. Califa
Culleoka, TN</td><td>38451-3316</td><td>73113 W. Carter
Culleoka, TN</td><td>38451-3316</td></tr>
<tr><td>11.</td><td>1515 Moisk Street
Ibapah, Utah</td><td>84034</td><td>1515 Mosk Street
Ibapah, Utah</td><td>64044</td></tr>
</table>

Did you spot the changes?

	Correct List		List to Be Checked	
	Address	*ZIP Code*	*Address*	*ZIP Code*
4.	564<u>1</u>8 Ringward Ln. Carson City, NV	89434-1735	564<u>7</u>8 Ringward Ln. Carson City, NV	89434-1735
5.	2319 Snow Rd. B<u>u</u>yck, MN	55920	2319 Snow Rd. B<u>o</u>yck, MN	55920
6.	543 W. **<u>3rd</u>** Street Dannebrog, **<u>NE</u>**	68<u>8</u>31	543 W. **<u>2nd</u>** Street Dannebrog, **<u>ME</u>**	68<u>0</u>31
7.	321 Wrangler Road Ringold, OK	747<u>5</u>4	321 Wrangler Road Ringold, OK	747<u>3</u>4
8.	12 Wood**<u>ley</u>** Place Cumberland, ME	04021-938<u>2</u>	12 Wood**<u>man</u>** Place Cumberland, ME	04021-938<u>1</u>
9.	9342 Packard Dr. **<u>Hadley</u>**, MA	01035	9342 Packard Dr. **<u>Harper</u>**, MA	01035
10.	73113 W. **<u>Califa</u>** Culleoka, TN	38451-3316	73113 W. **<u>Carter</u>** Culleoka, TN	38451-3316
11.	1515 M**<u>ois</u>**k Street Ibapah, Utah	<u>8</u>40<u>3</u>4	1515 M**<u>os</u>**k Street Ibapah, Utah	<u>6</u>40<u>4</u>4

In sample 4, only the addresses are different: 564<u>1</u>8 and 564<u>7</u>8. So the correct answer is B—Address Only.

In sample 5, only the addresses are different: B<u>u</u>yck and B<u>o</u>yck. So the correct answer is B—Address Only.

In sample 6, the addresses are different: 543 W **<u>3rd</u>** Street, Dannebrog, **<u>NE</u>** and 543 W **<u>2nd</u>** Street, Dannebrog, **<u>ME</u>**, and the Zip codes are different: 68<u>8</u>31 and 68<u>0</u>31. So the correct answer is D—Both. Notice that there are two differences in the address, but as soon as you spot one difference in the address, move on to check the Zip code.

In sample 7, only the Zip codes are different: 747<u>5</u>4 and 747<u>3</u>4. So the correct answer is C—Zip Code Only.

In sample 8, the addresses are different: Wood<u>ley</u> and Wood<u>man</u>, and the ZIP codes are different: 04021-938<u>2</u> and 04021-938<u>1</u>. So the correct answer is D—Both.

In sample 9, only the addresses are different: **<u>Hadley</u>** and **<u>Harper</u>**. So the correct answer is B—Address Only.

In sample 10, only the addresses are different: **<u>Califa</u>** and **<u>Carter</u>**. So the correct answer is B—Address Only.

In sample 11, the addresses are different: M<u>ois</u>k and M<u>os</u>k; and the ZIP codes are different: <u>8</u>40<u>3</u>4 and <u>6</u>40<u>4</u>4. So the correct answer is D—Both.

Adding and Deleting (Missing or Extra Numbers or Letters)

In some cases a letter or number may have been added or dropped. For example, in 1245 Folke Hills the "e" may have been deleted, leaving 1245 Folk Hills; in 726 Sill Rd. a "1" may have been added, resulting in 7261 Sill Rd.; in Mullinville an "l" may have been deleted, leaving Mulinville. This double-letter (or double-number) type of error can be difficult to spot.

See if you can spot the additions or deletions.

| A. No Errors | B. Address Only | C. ZIP Code Only | D. Both |

Correct List

	Address	ZIP Code
12. *B*	9302 Dannmar Rd. St. Paul, MN	55401-1121
13. *B*	374 Hawthorn Pkwy. Little Rock, AR	72259
14. *B*	5412 Seaport Ln. Vero Beach, FL	33408-6215

List to Be Checked

Address	ZIP Code
9302 Danmar Rd. St. Paul, MN	55401-1121
374 Hawthorne Pkwy. Little Rock, AR	72259
54112 Seaport Ln. Vero Beach, FL	33408-6215

Did you spot the additions or deletions?

Correct List

	Address	ZIP Code
12.	9302 Da**nnm**ar Rd. St. Paul, MN	55401-1121
13.	374 Hawthor**n** Pkwy Little Rock, AR	72259
14.	5**41**2 Seaport Ln. Vero Beach, FL	33408-6215

List to Be Checked

Address	ZIP Code
9302 Da**nm**ar Rd. St. Paul, MN	55401-1121
374 Hawthor**ne** Pkwy Little Rock, AR	72259
5**411**2 Seaport Ln. Vero Beach, FL	33408-6215

In sample 12, a letter has been deleted in the address only: Da**nnm**ar and Da**nm**ar. So the correct answer is B—Address Only.

In sample 13, a letter has been added only in the address: Hawthor**n** and Hawthor**ne**. So the correct answer is B—Address Only.

In sample 14, a number has been added only in the address: 5**41**2 and 5**411**2. So the correct answer is B—Address Only.

No Errors (Item Exactly the Same on Both Lists)

- Look for some questions to have no errors. The **Correct List** and the **List to Be Checked** are identical.

A. No Errors	B. Address Only	C. ZIP Code Only	D. Both

	Correct List		**List to Be Checked**	
	Address	*ZIP Code*	*Address*	*ZIP Code*
15.	16812 Kramer Rd. Dayton, Ohio	45423	16812 Kramer Rd. Dayton, Ohio	45423
16.	P.O. Box 93 Big Ridge, AZ	86999-2972	P.O. Box 93 Big Ridge, AZ	86999-2972

Notice that in samples 15 and 16, the **Correct List** and the **List to Be Checked** are exactly the same. The correct answer for samples 15 and 16 is A—No Errors.

WHAT YOU SHOULD DO

Memorize the answer choices because they will always be the same.

A. No Errors	B. Address Only	C. ZIP Code Only	D. Both

You may wish to use a memorization technique such as:

A is none
B is add
C is ZIP
D is both

A—none   B—add   C—ZIP   D—both

- Because you have 60 questions to answer in 11 minutes, you must work quickly. Memorizing the choices will help you work quickly.
- Keep focused. This takes practice.
- Use a plan of attack.
- Once you find a mistake in one part, mark it and move on to the next part.
- Because there is a penalty for guessing, don't guess blindly.
- The practice sets at the end of this chapter and the full-length practice tests will help you build up speed and endurance.
- You may wish to short yourself slightly on time (30 seconds to 1 minute) when you take the first few practice tests. This will help you get used to working at a fast pace.
- Look for the common types of errors mentioned earlier.

- As you practice, you can also develop your own techniques to use along with those mentioned.
- Use effective techniques to find the differences. Try the following techniques as you practice, and determine which one works best for you.

Use Your Hands

One technique is to use one of your hands to help compare the lists. Try this technique to see if it works for you. If you are right-handed, use the index finger and the pinky finger on your left hand as guides to compare the lists. Fold down the middle fingers. Keep your pencil in your right hand to mark the page and your answer sheet. (If you are left-handed, put the pencil in your left hand and use the fingers on your right hand as a guide.) This method looks like this:

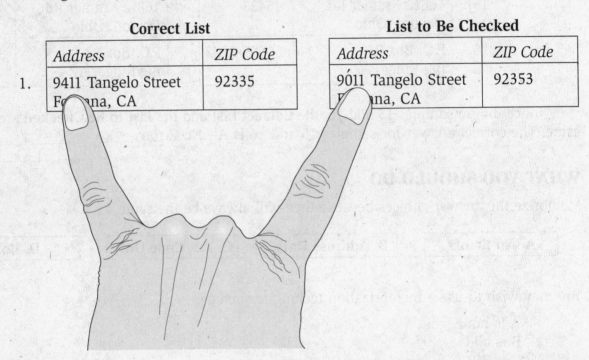

Correct List			**List to Be Checked**	
	Address	*ZIP Code*	*Address*	*ZIP Code*
1.	9411 Tangelo Street Fontana, CA	92335	9011 Tangelo Street Fontana, CA	92353

Notice that the pinky finger on your left hand is lined up with the address numbers in the **Correct List**, and the index finger is lined up with the address number in the **List to Be Checked**. As you move your hand to the right, you can quickly compare the items in the boxes. As soon as you spot an error in the address box, put a small mark next to it and slide your hand over to check the ZIP codes.

You should have spotted that the **Correct List** has 9411 as the address number and the **List to Be Checked** has 9011. Make a small mark as shown and move your hand (guide) to the ZIP Code box.

16

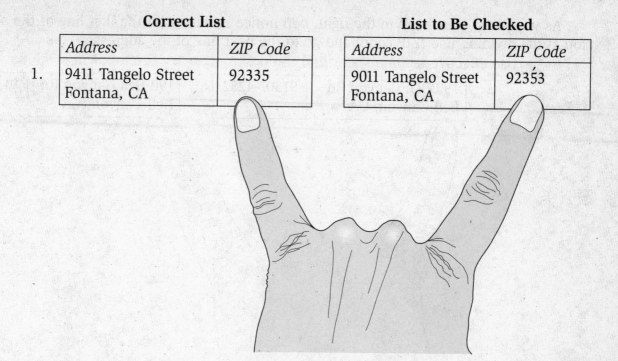

	Correct List		**List to Be Checked**	
	Address	*ZIP Code*	*Address*	*ZIP Code*
1.	9411 Tangelo Street Fontana, CA	92335	9011 Tangelo Street Fontana, CA	92353

Notice that the ZIP codes are different—923**35** and 923**53**. Make a quick mark and notice that there are errors in both the address and the ZIP code; so fill in D (for Both) on the answer sheet.

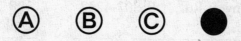

Move on quickly to the next question.

Note: As soon as you spot an error in the address, you immediately know that the answer is either B—Address Only or D—Both.

2.	190 Bell Canyon Rd. Bell C▨yon, CA	91307-4232	190 Bell Canyon Rd. Dell▨yon, CA	91307-4232

As you move your hand to the right, you notice no errors on the first line of the address, so stop at the dividing line (ZIP code) and go to the next line of the address.

| 2. | 190 Bell Canyon Rd
Bell Canyon, CA | 91307-4232 | 1̦90 Bell Canyon Rd
Dell Canyon, CA | 91307-4232 |

As soon as you notice the error—**B**ell and **D**ell—make a simple mark and move your hand to compare the ZIP codes.

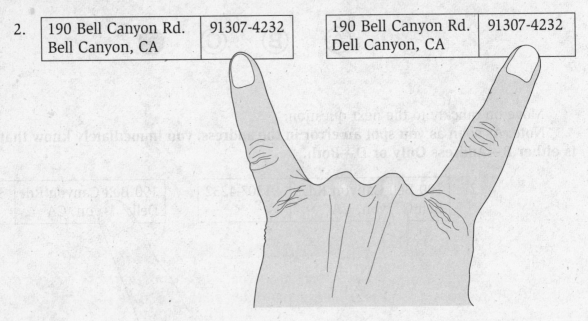

| 2. | 190 Bell Canyon Rd.
Bell Canyon, CA | 91307-4232 | 190 Bell Canyon Rd.
Dell Canyon, CA | 91307-4232 |

Because there are no errors in the ZIP codes, fill in B (for Address Only) on your answer sheet.

DIVIDE AND CONQUER

Another technique to find the differences is to divide each question into parts, and checking each part individually, quickly scan across to determine if the corresponding parts are similar or different. For example, using this technique, you would first check the street numbers and name:

<table>
<tr><td colspan="2" align="center">Correct List</td><td colspan="2" align="center">List to Be Checked</td></tr>
<tr><td>Address</td><td>ZIP Code</td><td>Address</td><td>ZIP Code</td></tr>
<tr><td>43572 Southridge Dr.
Seattle, WA</td><td>98104</td><td>43572 Southridge Dr.
Seattle, WA</td><td>98104</td></tr>
</table>

Quickly scan and check these.

43572 Southridge Dr.   **43572 Southridge Dr.**

Then check the city and state.

Seattle, WA   **Seattle, WA**

And finally, check the two ZIP Codes.

98104   **98104**

In this case, there were no differences, so you would mark answer A (for no errors) on your answer sheet.

If you decide to use this method, keep in mind that you should still mark the errors as soon as you spot them and move on once you spot an error.

PRACTICE, PRACTICE, AND MORE PRACTICE

Most of all, practice. Once you find techniques that work comfortably for you, your ability on this section will improve as you practice finding differences. The more you practice, the faster you'll go and the more accurate you'll get.

PART A: ADDRESS CHECKING PRACTICE SETS

WARMING UP

Practice Set 1—12 items

For the following 12 items, compare the address in the **Correct List** with the address in the **List to Be Checked**. Determine if there are **No Errors** (answer A), an error in the **Address Only** (answer B), an error in the **ZIP Code Only** (answer C), or an error in **Both** (answer D). For this practice exercise, give yourself a time limit of 2 minutes.

A. No Errors	B. Address Only	C. ZIP Code Only	D. Both

	Correct List		**List to Be Checked**	
	Address	*ZIP Code*	*Address*	*ZIP Code*
1.	4480 E Country Club Dr. Yuma, AZ	85365	4480 E Country Club Ln. Yuma, AZ	85365
2.	P.O. Box 2505C San Rafael, CA	94913	P.O. Box 2505C San Rafael, CA	94193
3.	1392 McCasland Road Ashtabula, OH	44004-5149	1392 McCasland Road Ashtabula, OR	44004-5149
4.	8616 NW 116th Way Gainesville, FL	32607-3396	8616 NW 116th Way Gainesville, FL	62607-3396
5.	5871 Indian Pointe Rd. Walterville, OR	97489-6163	5871 Indian Pointe Rd. Walterville, OR	97489-6163
6.	3078 Idyll Acres Lane Westmoreland, TN	37186	3078 Idyll Acres Lane Westmore, TN	37186
7.	872 N Cardinal Ct. Palatine, IL	60074	892 N Cardinal Ct. Palatine, IL	60073
8.	10800 Horseshoe Trl. Bossier City, LA	71112	10800 Horseshoe Trl. Bossier City, LA	77112

	Correct List		**List to Be Checked**	
	Address	*ZIP Code*	*Address*	*ZIP Code*
9.	35819 S Nc Highway 109 Lexington, NC	27292-5575	35819 E Nc Highway 109 Lexington, NC	27292-5575
10.	7214 Interstate 45 S Conroe, TX	77385-4840	7214 Interstate 45 S Monroe, TX	77385-4804
11.	7457 Sadberg Rd. Gerrardstown, WV	88205-0832	7457 Sadberg Rd. Gerrardstown, WV	88205-0832
12.	3235 Bradmore Ave. West Bloomfield, MI	48324	3235 Bradenton Ave. West Bloomfield, MI	48324

Practice Set 1 Answers

	Correct List		List to Be Checked	
	Address	*ZIP Code*	*Address*	*ZIP Code*
1. **B**	4480 E Country Club **Dr.** Yuma, AZ	85365	4480 E Country Club **Ln.** Yuma, AZ	85365
2. **C**	P.O. Box 2505C San Rafael, CA	94**913**	P.O. Box 2505C San Rafael, CA	94**193**
3. **B**	1392 McCasland Road Ashtabula, **OH**	44004-5149	1392 McCasland Road Ashtabula, **OR**	44004-5149
4. **C**	8616 NW 116th Way Gainesville, FL	**3**2607-3396	8616 NW 116th Way Gainesville, FL	**6**2607-3396
5. **A**	5871 Indian Pointe Rd. Walterville, OR	97489-6163	5871 Indian Pointe Rd. Walterville, OR	97489-6163
6. **B**	3078 Idyll Acres Lane Westmor**eland,** TN	37186	3078 Idyll Acres Lane Westmor**e,** TN	37186
7. **D**	872 N Cardinal Ct. Palatine, IL	6007**4**	8**9**2 N Cardinal Ct. Palatine, IL	6007**3**
8. **C**	10800 Horseshoe Trl. Bossier City, LA	7**1**112	10800 Horseshoe Trl. Bossier City, LA	7**7**112
9. **B**	35819 **S** Nc Highway 109 Lexington, NC	27292-5575	35819 **E** Nc Highway 109 Lexington, NC	27292-5575
10. **D**	7214 Interstate 45 S **C**onroe, TX	77385-48**40**	7214 Interstate 45 S **M**onroe, TX	77385-48**04**
11. **A**	7457 Sadberg Rd. Gerrardstown, WV	88205-0832	7457 Sadberg Rd. Gerrardstown, WV	88205-0832
12. **B**	3235 Brad**more** Ave. West Bloomfield, MI	48324	3235 Brad**enton** Ave. West Bloomfield, MI	48324

BUILDING SPEED

Practice Set 2—24 items

For the following 24 items, compare the address in the **Correct List** with the address in the **List to Be Checked.** Determine if there are **No Errors** (answer A), an error in the **Address Only** (answer B), an error in the **ZIP Code Only** (answer C), or an error in **Both** (answer D). For this practice exercise, give yourself a time limit of 4 minutes.

A. No Errors	B. Address Only	C. ZIP Code Only	D. Both

	Correct List		List to Be Checked	
	Address	*ZIP Code*	*Address*	*ZIP Code*
1.	4835 N Buncombe Rd. Florence, SC	29506	4835 N Buncombe Rd. Florence, SC	29506
2.	2484 Merritt Pkwy. Reading, PA	19609-0944	8424 Merritt Pkwy. Reading, PA	19609-0944
3.	80661 S Klein Ave. Oklahoma City, OK	73139-1273	8061 S Klein Ave. Oklahoma City, OK	73139-1273
4.	6980 136th Ave. NE Bismarck, ND	58501	6980 136th Ave. NE Bismarck, ND	38501
5.	3925 Hawthorne Rd. Apt. 39 Waltham, MA	02451-1156	3925 Hawthorne Dr. Apt. 39 Waltham, MA	02451-1066
6.	818 Ambrose St. Providence, RI	02904-2028	818 Amboy St. Providence, RI	02994-2028
7.	5914 W 137th Pl. Burnsville, Minnesota	55337	5914 W 137th Pl. Burnside, Minnesota	55337
8.	3937 NW 197th Lane Opa Locka, FL	33055	3937 NW 197th Lane Opa Locka, FL	33055
9.	3350 E Tanglewood Ln. Tacoma, WA	98404	3350 E Tanglewood Ln. Tacoma, WA	94804
10.	40411 Beardsley Ave. Stratford, CT	06615-9444	40411 Beardsley Ave. Stratford, VT	06615-9444

	Correct List		**List to Be Checked**	
	Address	*ZIP Code*	*Address*	*ZIP Code*
11.	6233 G St. NW Washington, DC	20037-0265	6233 G St. NW Washington, DC	20037-0265
12.	Rt. 5 Box 581 Yucca Valley, CA	92284-7376	Rt. 5 Box 581 Yucca Valley, CA	92284-7376
13.	5098 N US Hwy 89 Van Buren, AR	72956	5098 N US Hwy 89 Van Buren, AR	72967
14.	4008 Marble Arch Way Alexandria, VA	22315-0128	4008 Mable Arch Way Alexandria, VA	22315-0128
15.	9931 Turnagain Bluff Ave. Anchorage, AK	99515-3780	9931 Turnagain Bluff Ave. Anchorage, AK	90515-3780
16.	63622 Mineral Wells Hwy. Weatherford, Texas	76088	63632 Mineral Wells Hwy. Weatherford, Texas	76088
17.	4120 Sunrise Ln. Milledgeville, TN	38359	4120 Sunrise Ln. Millerville, TN	88539
18.	25906 Ave. B NE North Charleston, SC	29405-0886	25906 Ave. D NE North Charleston, SC	29405-0886
19.	6396 Green Bush Dr. Cranston, RI	02921-1009	6396 Green Briar Dr. Cranston, RI	02922-1009
20.	5257 Highway MM Wellersburg, PA	19567	5257 Highway MM Wellersburg, PA	19567
21.	7824 Robbins Cres. Apt. 1773 New Rochelle, NY	10801	8742 Robbins Cres. Apt. 1773 New Rochelle, NY	10611
22.	4808 S 41st Ter. Bellevue, NE	68147	4808 W 41st Ter. Bellevue, NE	68147
23.	5034 Cyclamen Sq. West Jordan, Utah	84084-0138	5034 Cyclamen Sq. East Jordan, Utah	84084-0138
24.	44631 472nd Ave. Sioux Falls, SD	57108	44631 472nd Ave. Sioux Falls, SD	88108

Practice Set 2 Answers

<table>
<tr><th colspan="2" align="center">Correct List</th><th colspan="2" align="center">List to Be Checked</th></tr>
<tr><td>Address</td><td>ZIP Code</td><td>Address</td><td>ZIP Code</td></tr>
<tr><td>1. A 4835 N Buncombe Rd.
Florence, SC</td><td>29506</td><td>4835 N Buncombe Rd.
Florence, SC</td><td>29506</td></tr>
<tr><td>2. B 2484 Merritt Pkwy.
Reading, PA</td><td>19609-0944</td><td>8424 Merritt Pkwy.
Reading, PA</td><td>19609-0944</td></tr>
<tr><td>3. B 80661 S Klein Ave.
Oklahoma City, OK</td><td>73139-1273</td><td>8061 S Klein Ave.
Oklahoma City, OK</td><td>73139-1273</td></tr>
<tr><td>4. C 6980 136th Ave. NE
Bismarck, ND</td><td>58501</td><td>6980 136th Ave. NE
Bismarck, ND</td><td>38501</td></tr>
<tr><td>5. D 3925 Hawthorne Rd. Apt. 39
Waltham, MA</td><td>02451-1156</td><td>3925 Hawthorne Dr. Apt. 39
Waltham, MA</td><td>02451-1066</td></tr>
<tr><td>6. D 818 Ambrose St.
Providence, RI</td><td>02904-2028</td><td>818 Amboy St.
Providence, RI</td><td>02994-2028</td></tr>
<tr><td>7. B 5914 W 137th Pl.
Burnsville, Minnesota</td><td>55337</td><td>5914 W 137th Pl.
Burnside, Minnesota</td><td>55337</td></tr>
<tr><td>8. A 3937 NW 197th Lane
Opa Locka, FL</td><td>33055</td><td>3937 NW 197th Lane
Opa Locka, FL</td><td>33055</td></tr>
<tr><td>9. C 3350 E Tanglewood Ln.
Tacoma, WA</td><td>98404</td><td>3350 E Tanglewood Ln.
Tacoma, WA</td><td>94804</td></tr>
<tr><td>10. B 40411 Beardsley Ave.
Stratford, CT</td><td>06615-9444</td><td>40411 Beardsley Ave.
Stratford, VT</td><td>06615-9444</td></tr>
<tr><td>11. A 6233 G St. NW
Washington, DC</td><td>20037-0265</td><td>6233 G St. NW
Washington, DC</td><td>20037-0265</td></tr>
<tr><td>12. A Rt. 5 Box 581
Yucca Valley, CA</td><td>92284-7376</td><td>Rt. 5 Box 581
Yucca Valley, CA</td><td>92284-7376</td></tr>
<tr><td>13. C 5098 N US Hwy 89
Van Buren, AR</td><td>72956</td><td>5098 N US Hwy 89
Van Buren, AR</td><td>72967</td></tr>
<tr><td>14. B 4008 Marble Arch Way
Alexandria, VA</td><td>22315-0128</td><td>4008 Mable Arch Way
Alexandria, VA</td><td>22315-0128</td></tr>
</table>

		Correct List		List to Be Checked	
		Address	*ZIP Code*	*Address*	*ZIP Code*
15.	C	9931 Turnagain Bluff Ave. Anchorage, AK	99515-3780	9931 Turnagain Bluff Ave. Anchorage, AK	90515-3780
16.	B	63622 Mineral Wells Hwy. Weatherford, Texas	76088	63632 Mineral Wells Hwy. Weatherford, Texas	76088
17.	D	4120 Sunrise Ln. Mill**edge**ville, TN	**38359**	4120 Sunrise Ln. Mill**er**ville, TN	**88539**
18.	B	25906 Ave. **B** NE North Charleston, SC	29405-0886	25906 Ave. **D** NE North Charleston, SC	29405-0886
19.	D	6396 Green **Bush** Dr. Cranston, RI	02921-1009	6396 Green **Briar** Dr. Cranston, RI	02922-1009
20.	A	5257 Highway MM Wellersburg, PA	19567	5257 Highway MM Wellersburg, PA	19567
21.	D	**7824** Robbins Cres. Apt. 1773 New Rochelle, NY	10**8**01	**8742** Robbins Cres. Apt. 1773 New Rochelle, NY	10**6**11
22.	B	4808 **S** 41st Ter. Bellevue, NE	68147	4808 **W** 41st Ter. Bellevue, NE	68147
23.	B	5034 Cyclamen Sq. **West** Jordan, Utah	84084-0138	5034 Cyclamen Sq. **East** Jordan, Utah	84084-0138
24.	C	44631 472nd Ave. Sioux Falls, SD	**57**108	44631 472nd Ave. Sioux Falls, SD	**88**108

BUILDING ENDURANCE

Practice Set 3—36 items

For the following 36 items, compare the address in the **Correct List** with the address in the **List to Be Checked**. Determine if there are **No Errors** (answer A), an error in the **Address Only** (answer B), an error in the **ZIP Code Only** (answer C), or an error in **Both** (answer D). For this practice exercise, give yourself a time limit of 6 minutes.

A. No Errors	B. Address Only	C. ZIP Code Only	D. Both

	Correct List		List to Be Checked	
	Address	*ZIP Code*	*Address*	*ZIP Code*
1.	3546 W La Donna Dr. Tempe, AZ	85283	3546 W La Donna Dr. Tempe, AZ	85283
2.	2864 State Road AA 109G North Weymouth, MA	02766-9928	2864 State Road AA 110G North Weymouth, MA	02766-9988
3.	291 El Terra Rd. Lynnville, TN	38359-5514	291 El Tierra Rd. Lynnville, TN	38359-5514
4.	4833 S Williams Lake Road White Lake, MI	48386	4833 S Williams Lake Road White Lake, MI	48368
5.	5967 Morthland Drive Valparaiso, Indiana	46383-7567	5967 Northland Drive Valparaiso, Indiana	46383-7567
6.	4398 Calle Guillermina Bayamon, PR	00957	4398 Calle Guillermina Bayamon, PR	00957
7.	5335 52nd Ave. N Saint Petersburg, FL	33709-4541	5335 32nd Ave. N Saint Petersburg, FL	33309-4541
8.	58616 Bruce Park Ave. Ext. Greenwich, CT	06830-1131	58616 Bruce Park Ave. Ext. Greenwich, CT	06830-1131
9.	1458 SW Heritage Ct. Beaverton, Oregon	97006	1458 SW Heritage Ct. Beaverton, Oregon	97706
10.	28917 US Hwy. 395 Victorville, CA	92394-6051	28971 US Hwy. 395 Victorville, CA	92394-6051

	Correct List		**List to Be Checked**	
	Address	*ZIP Code*	*Address*	*ZIP Code*
11.	7764 S Westtown Cir. Wahpeton, ND	58075-7613	7764 S Westtown Cir. Wahpeton, ND	58075-7113
12.	6675 Susquehanna St. Binghamton, NY	13901	6675 Susquehanna Ave. Binghamton, NY	13901
13.	Post Office Box 55438 Norristown, PA	19404	Post Office Box 55438 Norriston, PA	09404
14.	59988 Road 237A Cheyenne, WY	82009-9602	59988 Road 237A Cheyenne, WY	82900-9602
15.	3910 Ledges Lowland Loop Biddeford, ME	04005	3910 Ledges Lowland Loop Biddeford, ME	04505
16.	554 Chevelle Ct. Apt. 5066R Anderson, IN	46012-9988	554 Chevelle Ct. Apt. 5066R Anderson, TN	46012-9988
17.	4705 Hodencamp Rd. Thousand Oaks, CA	91360-0106	4705 Hodencamp Rd. Thousand Oaks, CA	91360-0109
18.	2233 129th Pl. SE Renton, WA	98056-0431	2233 129th Pl. SE Renton, WA	98056-0431
19.	2109 Olentangy Dr. Akron, OH	44333-5153	2109 Oldentandy Dr. Akron, OH	44333-1553
20.	8050 Hwy ZZY Cumberland, NC	28331	8050 Hwy ZZY Cumberland, NC	28331
21.	36011 Cinco Park Rd. Katy, TX	77450-0002	36011 Cinco Park Rd. Katy, TX	77452-0002
22.	76285 Old Government Rd. Mobile, AL	36695-6252	76285 Olde Government Rt. Mobile, AL	36695-6252
23.	5425 58th St. Kenosha, WI	53144	5452 58th St. Kenosha, WI	53144
24.	7569 Foote W Hwy. Burlington, WV	26710	75669 Foote W Hwy. Burlington, WV	22710
25.	2087 Flatwoods Pt. Rd. Centerpoint, IN	47840	2087 Flatwoods Pl. Rd. Centerpoint, IN	47840

	Correct List		**List to Be Checked**	
	Address	*ZIP Code*	*Address*	*ZIP Code*
26.	2569 Greenup Street Covington, KY	41011-8965	2569 Greenup Street Covington, KY	41011-8965
27.	6614 42nd St. SE Everett, WA	98203-7296	6614 42nd St. SE Everett, WA	98513-7296
28.	19394 Tallowood Dr. Wichita, KS	67230-2146	19394 Tallwood Dr. Wichita, KS	72230-2146
29.	6172 County Hwy. 54 Brattleboro, VT	05301	6172 County Hwy. 54 Battleboro, VT	05311
30.	5336 Thrushridge Dr. Newry, SC	29665	5336 Thrushridge Dr. Newberry, SC	29665
31.	6861 Burchfield St. Genesee, PA	17104	6861 Burchfield St. Genesee, PA	17014
32.	9914 Pidgeon Ln. Des Moines, IA	50313	9914 Pidgeon Ln. Des Moines, IA	50313
33.	1086 W Emporia Ave. Ponca City, OK	74601-6111	1086 W Emporium Ave. Ponca City, OK	74601-6111
34.	3404 W Jefferson Manor Kokomo, IN	46901-0450	3404 N Jefferson Manor Kokomo, IN	46901-4450
35.	974 Mountview Ct. Englewood, OH	45322-2001	974 Mountview Ct. Bentwood, OH	45322-2001
36.	4252 Rubles Point N Buckingham, IL	60917	4252 Rubles Point N Buckingham, IL	60917

Practice Set 3 Answers

	Correct List		List to Be Checked	
	Address	*ZIP Code*	*Address*	*ZIP Code*
1. **A**	3546 W La Donna Dr. Tempe, AZ	85283	3546 W La Donna Dr. Tempe, AZ	85283
2. **D**	2864 State Road AA 1**09**G North Weymouth, MA	02766-99**2**8	2864 State Road AA 1**10**G North Weymouth, MA	02766-99**8**8
3. **B**	291 El **Te**rra Rd. Lynnville, TN	38359-5514	291 El **Tie**rra Rd. Lynnville, TN	38359-5514
4. **C**	4833 S Williams Lake Road White Lake, MI	483**8**6	4833 S Williams Lake Road White Lake, MI	483**6**8
5. **B**	5967 **M**orthland Drive Valparaiso, Indiana	46383-7567	5967 **N**orthland Drive Valparaiso, Indiana	46383-7567
6. **A**	4398 Calle Guillermina Bayamon, PR	00957	4398 Calle Guillermina Bayamon, PR	00957
7. **D**	5335 **5**2nd Ave. N Saint Petersburg, FL	33**7**09-4541	5335 **3**2nd Ave. N Saint Petersburg, FL	33**3**09-4541
8. **A**	58616 Bruce Park Ave. Ext. Greenwich, CT	06830-1131	58616 Bruce Park Ave. Ext. Greenwich, CT	06830-1131
9. **C**	1458 SW Heritage Ct. Beaverton, Oregon	97**0**06	1458 SW Heritage Ct. Beaverton, Oregon	97**7**06
10. **B**	289**17** US Hwy. 395 Victorville, CA	92394-6051	289**71** US Hwy. 395 Victorville, CA	92394-6051
11. **C**	7764 S Westtown Cir. Wahpeton, ND	58075-7**6**13	7764 S Westtown Cir. Wahpeton, ND	58075-7**1**13
12. **B**	6675 Susquehanna **St.** Binghamton, NY	13901	6675 Susquehanna **Ave.** Binghamton, NY	13901
13. **D**	Post Office Box 55438 Norris**town,** PA	**1**9404	Post Office Box 55438 Norris**ton,** PA	**0**9404
14. **C**	59988 Road 237A Cheyenne, WY	82**009**-9602	59988 Road 237A Cheyenne, WY	82**900**-9602

	Correct List			List to Be Checked	
	Address	*ZIP Code*		*Address*	*ZIP Code*
15. **C**	3910 Ledges Lowland Loop Biddeford, ME	04**0**05		3910 Ledges Lowland Loop Biddeford, ME	04**5**05
16. **B**	554 Chevelle Ct. Apt. 5066R Anderson, **IN**	46012-9988		554 Chevelle Ct. Apt. 5066R Anderson, **TN**	46012-9988
17. **C**	4705 Hodencamp Rd. Thousand Oaks, CA	91360-010**6**		4705 Hodencamp Rd. Thousand Oaks, CA	91360-010**9**
18. **A**	2233 129th Pl. SE Renton, WA	98056-0431		2233 129th Pl. SE Renton, WA	98056-0431
19. **D**	2109 Ol**en**tangy Dr. Akron, OH	44333-**5**153		2109 Ol**den**tandy Dr. Akron, OH	44333-**1**553
20. **A**	8050 Hwy ZZY Cumberland, NC	28331		8050 Hwy ZZY Cumberland, NC	28331
21. **C**	36011 Cinco Park Rd. Katy, TX	7745**0**-0002		36011 Cinco Park Rd. Katy, TX	7745**2**-0002
22. **B**	76285 **Old** Government **Rd.** Mobile, AL	36695-6252		76285 Ol**de** Government **Rt.** Mobile, AL	36695-6252
23. **B**	54**25** 58th St. Kenosha, WI	53144		54**52** 58th St. Kenosha, WI	53144
24. **D**	7**569** Foote W Hwy. Burlington, WV	**2**6710		7**5669** Foote W Hwy. Burlington, WV	**2**2710
25. **B**	2087 Flatwoods **Pt.** Rd. Centerpoint, IN	47840		2087 Flatwoods **Pl.** Rd. Centerpoint, IN	47840
26. **A**	2569 Greenup Street Covington, KY	41011-8965		2569 Greenup Street Covington, KY	41011-8965
27. **C**	6614 42nd St. SE Everett, WA	98**203**-7296		6614 42nd St. SE Everett, WA	98**513**-7296
28. **D**	19394 Tal**low**ood Dr. Wichita, KS	**6**7230-2146		19394 Tal**lw**ood Dr. Wichita, KS	**7**2230-2146
29. **D**	6172 County Hwy. 54 **Bra**ttleboro, VT	053**0**1		6172 County Hwy. 54 **Ba**ttleboro, VT	053**1**1

		Correct List		List to Be Checked	
		Address	*ZIP Code*	*Address*	*ZIP Code*
30.	**B**	5336 Thrushridge Dr. Newry, SC	29665	5336 Thrushridge Dr. Newberry, SC	29665
31.	**C**	6861 Burchfield St. Genesee, PA	17104	6861 Burchfield St. Genesee, PA	17014
32.	**A**	9914 Pidgeon Ln. Des Moines, IA	50313	9914 Pidgeon Ln. Des Moines, IA	50313
33.	**B**	1086 W Emporia Ave. Ponca City, OK	74601-6111	1086 W Emporium Ave. Ponca City, OK	74601-6111
34.	**D**	3404 **W** Jefferson Manor Kokomo, IN	46901-**0**450	3404 **N** Jefferson Manor Kokomo, IN	46901-**4**450
35.	**B**	974 Mountview Ct. **Engle**wood, OH	45322-2001	974 Mountview Ct. **Bent**wood, OH	45322-2001
36.	**A**	4252 Rubles Point N Buckingham, IL	60917	4252 Rubles Point N Buckingham, IL	60917

Part B: Forms Completion

WHAT TO EXPECT

The Forms Completion part is 15 minutes long and contains 30 multiple-choice questions. You will be given about five different Postal Service forms with about six questions relating to each form. You will have about 30 seconds to answer each question, so you must work fairly quickly and accurately in order to complete this part. Don't get stuck on any one question. Because there is no penalty for guessing on this part, if you get stuck, just take a guess and move on.

On this part of the exam you are to identify the information needed to correctly complete forms. You will be given a Postal Service form with numbered items and questions referring to some of the items.

- Expect about five different Postal Service forms in this part.
- Expect about six questions relating to each form.
- Expect the form to be next to or across from the questions that relate to it.
- Expect the form and the items in it to be easy to see.

WHAT YOU SHOULD KNOW

- You should know that on the actual test you will be given a 2-minute sample exercise with a few questions.
- You should know that this short sample exercise will not be scored.
- You should know that each scored question on the exam is of the same value.
- You should know that there is no penalty for guessing.
- You should know some of the common question types.

WHAT TO LOOK FOR

Look for some of the common question types. Some of the common types with introductions and explanations follow.

Questions 1 through 6 are based on the following form.

CERTIFIED MAIL RECEIPT

For Domestic Use Only
No Insurance Coverage Provided

1. Postage	$
2. Certified Fee	$
3. Return Receipt Fee (Signature of Receiver of Mail Required)	$
4. Restricted Delivery Fee (Signature of Receiver of Mail Required)	$
5. Total Postage and Fees	$

7. Postmark Here

6. Mail Sent To

6a. Name _____

6b. Street, Apt. No., or PO Box No. _____

6c. City, State, ZIP _____

The "Correct Entry" Question

This type of question specifies a particular box or line on the form and gives you a list of possible entries. You must choose the entry (the information) that is correct for that box or line.

1. Which of these would be a correct entry for Box 3?
   A. "James Butterfield"
   B. "$2.25"
   C. "6039 Oak Drive"
   D. A checkmark

Answer

3. Return Receipt Fee (Signature of Receiver of Mail Required)	$

34

The correct answer is B. Notice that the answers can include both the exact information you might enter (which is in quotation marks) and types of entries such as checkmarks or signatures. For these questions, you should immediately circle or underline the box or line number mentioned, Box 3 in this question. Then find Box 3 on the form. On this form, Box 3 is for the Return Receipt fee. You'll see that a dollar amount is needed here. Only one dollar amount is given in the answers, in answer B. Fill in B for question 1 on your answer sheet. Notice that the amount of money given in the answer is not important. You will never be asked to choose between two answers that both have dollar amounts. You only need to find the answer that *is* an amount of money.

The "Where Would You Indicate" Question

These questions don't give you a list of possible entries from which to choose but instead give you an item of information and ask you to choose the correct box or line listed in the answer choices. There are several ways this type of question might be asked.

2. Where would you indicate the total postage and fees?
   A. Box 1
   B. Box 3
   C. Box 5
   D. Box 7

Answer

5. Total Postage and Fees $ _____

The correct answer is C. This question could also be phrased, "Where would you enter the total postage and fees?" Circle or underline "total postage and fees" in the question. Box 5 is labeled "Total Postage and Fees," so answer C is correct. Notice that Box 1 (answer A) is labeled "Postage," but Box 1 doesn't include fees, so it can't be the correct answer.

A Variation of This Question Type

3. Postage for this mail is $5.32. Where would you indicate this?
   A. Box 1
   B. Box 3
   C. Box 5
   D. Box 7

Answer

1. Postage $ _____

The correct answer is A. Circle or underline "postage." As you scan the boxes, you'll see that "Postage" is listed first, in Box 1. You don't need to take the time to look at any of the other boxes. Choose answer A for Box 1. This question could also be phrased, "Where would you enter $5.32."

4. Where would you indicate that the mail has been sent to Dorothy Jones?
   A. Box 7
   B. Line 6a
   C. Line 6b
   D. Line 6c

Answer

6a. Name _____

The correct answer is B. This question is basically the same as question 2, although its phrasing is slightly different. You're still being asked to find the appropriate box for a particular piece of information, in this case, the name of the person to whom the mail has been sent, sometimes referred to as the "addressee," in these questions. Circle or underline "sent to Dorothy Jones." Notice that it's important to understand that "sent to" is part of the information. On this form, there is only one place in which a name can be entered, so the answer must be Line 6a, answer B. But on more complicated forms, there may be other places for names, for example, the name of the sender or the name of the Post Office. So you need to be sure you notice *everything* that's being asked for: in this case, not just a name, but the name of the receiver of the mail.

The "EXCEPT" Question

These questions ask you to choose a box in which you could ***not*** correctly enter a particular type of information.

5. A dollar amount would be a correct entry for all of the following EXCEPT which one?
   A. Box 2
   B. Box 4
   C. Box 5
   D. Box 7

Answer

```
7. Postmark
   Here
```

36

The correct answer is D. Here you must find the one box that would *not* be an acceptable place for entry of a dollar amount, an amount of money. Circle or underline "dollar amount" and "EXCEPT." Box 7 is for a postmark, so answer D is correct. You could not correctly enter a dollar amount in Box 7. As soon as you find the box or line in which you *could not* put a dollar amount, choose that answer. There is no need to check the remaining answers because there is only one correct answer for each question.

The "How Would You" Question

The "how would you" type of question gives you a task to be completed (that is, entering information on the form) and asks how you would go about doing it.

> 6. How would you indicate that the mail is being sent to Eagle River, Alaska 99577?
> A. Enter "Eagle River, Alaska 99577" in Box 7
> B. Enter "Eagle River, Alaska 99577" on Line 6a
> C. Enter "Eagle River, Alaska 99577" on Line 6b
> D. Enter "Eagle River, Alaska 99577" on Line 6c

Answer

6c. City, State, ZIP _____

The correct answer is D. This is the same task as in the "where would you indicate" questions, although in this case, the action you would take (entering) is mentioned along with the box or line number. Circle "sent to Eagle River, Alaska 99577." The place on this form for the city, state, and ZIP code the mail is being sent to is Line 6c, answer D.

MAIL FORWARDING CHANGE OF ADDRESS ORDER

1. Change of address for (check one)

    1a. ❑ Individual   1b. ❑ Entire Family   1c. ❑ Business

17. Official Use Only

17a. Zone/Route ID Number

2. Is this move temporary? (check one)

    2a. ❑ Yes   2b. ❑ No

17b. Date Entered on Form 3982

17c. Clerk/Carrier Endorsement

3. Start Date	**4. If the move is temporary, list date to discontinue forwarding.**

5. Name
5a. Last Name   5b. First Name and Middle Initial

6. If Business Move, Print Business Name

PRINT OLD MAILING ADDRESS BELOW

7. OLD Street Address or PO Box

8. OLD City	**9. OLD State**	**10. OLD ZIP Code**

PRINT NEW MAILING ADDRESS BELOW

11. NEW Street Address or PO Box

12. NEW City	**13. NEW State**	**14. NEW ZIP Code**

15. Print and sign name: 15a. Print: _____ 15b. Sign: _____	**16. Date Signed**

Although the following types of questions are quite similar to those above, and ask for the same types of information, they have a slightly different look and may be more complex.

The "Multiple-Answer" Question

These questions have not just one item in each answer choice, but two or possibly more.

7. This customer is moving from Orlando, Florida, to Racine, Wisconsin. Where should "Racine, Wisconsin" be entered?
   A. Box 7 and Box 9
   B. Box 8 and Box 9
   C. Box 12 and Box 13
   D. Box 13 and Box 15

Answer

12. NEW City

13. NEW State

The Correct answer is C. This is a more time-consuming question because you must deal with looking at more than one box, but you can save yourself time. Circle or underline "to" and "Racine, Wisconsin." It's important to realize that this is the *new* city and state. Once you realize that, you can look *only* at the section of the form labeled "Print *New* Mailing Address Below." You immediately know that answers A and B are wrong because the boxes they list aren't in this section of the form. So now you need to check only answers C and D. But when you check answer C, you can see it is correct because Box 12 and Box 13 are for the city and state. So answer C is correct, and you don't need to check answer D.

Another "Multiple" Question

8. If only one person is moving and the move is temporary, how would the customer indicate this?
   A. Put a checkmark on Line 1a and Line 1c
   B. Put a checkmark on Line 1a and Line 2a
   C. Put a checkmark on Line 1a and enter a date in Box 3
   D. Put a checkmark on Line 2a and enter a date in Box 3

---

1. Change of address for (check one)

    1a. ❑ Individual   1b. ❑ Entire Family   1c. ❑ Business

---

2. Is this move temporary? (check one)

    2a. ❑ Yes   2b. ❑ No

The correct answer is B. Circle or underline "one person" and "temporary." You need to find the correct procedure for noting *both* of these things. You can see that all these options are in the first three boxes of the form. The quickest way to answer this question is to first find the place that indicates that only one person is moving, which is Line 1a, where you would check "Individual" (one person). Then notice where you would indicate a temporary move. You would check Line 2a. Now find the answer that contains Line 1a and Line 2a. While this may seem to be a long procedure, in fact it is very quick. In this case, checking each answer might not take a great deal longer because the correct answer is B, the second one down. But if the correct answer were farther down, answer C or D, you would be taking unnecessary time in checking each one.

The "None of the Above" or "All of the Above" Question
These questions have D as their answer, either "None of the above" or "All of the above."

None of the Above

    9. Where would you indicate the ZIP code of the old address?
       A. Box 6
       B. Box 9
       C. Box 14
       D. None of the above

Answer

---

10. OLD ZIP Code

The correct answer is D. Circle or underline "ZIP code" and "old." Find the section for the old address. Now find within that the section for the ZIP code, Box 10. Quickly scan the answers. Box 10 is not listed, so the answer must be D, None of the above. Notice though that just because "None of the above" appears as an answer, it is not necessarily the *right* answer.

All of the Above

    10. The customer is moving from Charlotte, North Carolina, to Nashville, Tennessee. Where would you enter "North Carolina"?
       A. Box 8
       B. Box 9
       C. Box 13
       D. All of the above

Answer

---

9. OLD State

The correct answer is B. Circle or underline "from" and "North Carolina." In this case, "All of the above" is *not* the correct answer. First check Box 8. Box 8 is labeled "Old City," not "Old State," so Box 8 is wrong. If one choice is wrong, the answer *can't* be "All of the above." Now, you need to find the one correct answer of the remaining two, B and C. When you check answer B, you will see that it's correct. Box 9 is the place for the old state.

The More Complex Questions

These questions may be in any of the forms mentioned but generally give you more information to deal with, which may be more confusing or may take extra time.

    11. Kevin Danson is moving to Chicago, Illinois, on January 2, but will return March 15. Where should this customer fill in his name and his return date?
       A. Box 3, Box 5, and Box 15
       B. Box 5 and Box 15
       C. Box 4, Box 5, and Box 15
       D. Box 5, Box 15, and Box 16

> **4. If the move is temporary,**
> **list date to discontinue forwarding.**

> **5. Name**
>
> 5a. Last Name

> **15. Print and sign name**
> 15a. Print: _____
> 15b. Sign: _____

The correct answer is C. Circle or underline "name" and "return date." In doing so, you'll realize that the other information ("Chicago, Illinois" and "January 2") are extra information that you don't need to answer this question. In fact, even the return date itself is extra information. You don't need to know the date. You just need to know where it goes. The customer's name goes in Box 5 (both 5a and 5b) and in Box 15, where he should print and sign his name. His return date goes in Box 4 (the move is temporary if he is returning). Even if you don't immediately see that the name must also go on the bottom of the form, in Box 15, you can answer this question correctly if you realize that Box 4 and Box 5 must be filled in because the only answer that contains both is answer C.

A Variation

12. What should the customer do to indicate that his family is moving as well as his home-based business?
    A. Enter the business name and address in Box 6
    B. Check Line 1c and enter the business name in Box 5b
    C. Check Line 1a and Line 1c and enter the business name in Box 6
    D. Check Line 1b and Line 1c and enter the business name in Box 6

> **1. Change of address for** (check one)
>
> 1a. ❏ Individual   1b. ❏ Entire Family   1c. ❏ Business

> **6. If Business Move, Print Business Name**

The correct answer is C. This is a complicated question simply because you must deal with several items at once. For this sort of complex question, it is best to first determine for yourself how to indicate the given items rather than trying to check each answer, which can be confusing. In this case, circle or underline "family" and "home-based business." In checking Box 1, you'll see that the customer would have to check both Line 1b, for "Entire Family," and Line 1c, for "Business." Now, before you go any further, quickly scan the answers to see where both Line 1b and Line 1c appear. In this case, only one answer includes both these lines, answer C. So that *must* be the correct answer. If two answers contained these lines, you'd have to go on to look at the third item in each answer (here, Box 5b or Box 6), but in this case you don't have to. In fact, the customer would fill in Box 6 with the business name.

WHAT YOU SHOULD DO

- Scan the form quickly.
- Don't memorize the form.
- Note some of the common items in the forms.
- Underline what is being asked.
- Check all the choices.
- Be careful to match the questions with the numbers.
- Practice, practice, practice.

PART B: FORMS COMPLETION PRACTICE SETS

WARMING UP

Practice Set 1—6 questions

Questions 1 through 6 are based on the following form.

DOMESTIC RETURN RECEIPT	
SENDER: Complete this section	**CARRIER:** Complete this section on delivery
1. Article Addressed to: 　1a.　Name _____ 　1b.　Street _____ 　1c.　City _____ 　1d.　State _____ 　1e.　ZIP Code _____	**4. Signature of receiver of mail:** 　　X _____
	5. This signature is that of (check one) 　5a.　Addressee ____ 　5b.　Addressee's Agent ____
2. Service Type Requested: 　2a.　Certified Mail ____ 　2b.　Registered Mail ____ 　2c.　Insured Mail ____ 　2d.　Express Mail ____ 　2e.　C.O.D. ____	**6. Is delivery address different from Item 1?** 　6a. Yes ____　　6b. No ____
	7. If "Yes" is checked in Box 6, enter delivery address below.
3. Restricted Delivery 　(Extra Fee) 　3a. Yes ____　3b. No ____	

1. Which of these would be a correct entry for Box 4?
   A. "Danielle Morgan"
   B. "28694"
   C. A signature
   D. A checkmark

2. Which of these would be a correct entry for Line 1c?
   A. "Danielle Morgan"
   B. "Tampa"
   C. "Florida"
   D. "U.S.A."

3. How would the sender indicate that he or she wants the mail to be insured?
   A. Put a checkmark on Line 1e
   B. Put a checkmark on Line 2b
   C. Put a checkmark on Line 2c
   D. Put a checkmark on Line 3a

4. If a fee is charged for all services in Box 2, what service would require an extra fee?
   A. Certified Mail
   B. Registered Mail
   C. Express Mail
   D. Restricted Delivery

5. The sender should complete all of the following EXCEPT which one?
   A. Box 1
   B. Box 2
   C. Box 3
   D. Box 4

6. The article is addressed to 6839 Palmetto Street, but the carrier actually delivers it to 2953 Seaside Avenue. Where should "2953 Seaside Avenue" be entered?
   A. Box 1
   B. Box 6
   C. Box 7
   D. None of the above

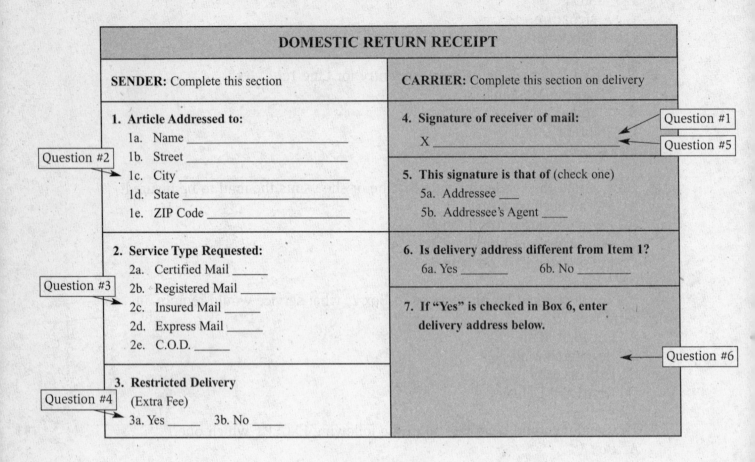

1. **C** Box 4 is for the signature of the receiver of the mail.
2. **B** Line 1c requires the city of the person the article is addressed to.
3. **C** Insured mail is listed on Line 2c.
4. **D** Box 3 says that an "Extra Fee" is required for Restricted Delivery.
5. **D** The sender would not complete Box 4. Notice that Box 4 is in the shaded section of the form, beneath the instructions that the carrier should complete this section. This box is for the signature of the receiver of the mail.
6. **C** If the delivery address is different from the address on the mail, the delivery address should be entered in Box 7.

BUILDING SPEED

Practice Set 2—12 questions

Questions 1 through 6 are based on the following form.

Delivery Notice/Reminder/Receipt
1. Sorry we missed you.
1a. Today's Date _____ 1b. Sender's Name _____
2. Delivery
2a. _____ We will redeliver the item   2b. _____ Please pick up the item at the Post Office.
3. Check type of item

3a. _____ Letter
   3b. _____ Large envelope, magazine, catalog, etc.
   3c. _____ Parcel
   3d. _____ Restricted Delivery
   3e. _____ Perishable Item
   3f. _____ Other:

4. If delivery confirmation is required, check type of mail service.

4a. _____ Express Mail
   4b. _____ Certified Mail
   4c. _____ Recorded Delivery
   4d. _____ Registered Mail
   4e. _____ Insured Mail
   4f. _____ Return Receipt
   4g. _____ Delivery Confirmation

5. If article requires payment check type(s) and note total payment amount.
5a. Postage Due _____ 5b. COD _____ 5c. Customs Fee _____   5d. Total Amount Due $ _____
6. Final Notice: Article will be returned to sender on this date: _____

1. You could enter a checkmark on all of the following EXCEPT which one?
   A. Line 1b
   B. Line 2b
   C. Line 3d
   D. Line 5b

2. Where would you indicate that the mail is a letter?
   A. Line 2a
   B. Line 3a
   C. Line 4a
   D. Line 5a

3. There is a customs fee due on this mail. Where would you indicate this?
   A. Line 3f
   B. Line 4d
   C. Line 4g
   D. Line 5c

4. How would you indicate that the mail is an insured parcel?
   A. Put a checkmark on Line 3b and Line 4e
   B. Put a checkmark on Line 3c and Line 4d
   C. Put a checkmark on Line 3c and Line 4e
   D. Put a checkmark on Line 4e and Line 5b

5. Where would you enter the addressee's name?
   A. Line 1a
   B. Line 1b
   C. Box 6
   D. None of the above

6. Where would you indicate that the item is Express Mail?
   A. Line 3d
   B. Line 3f
   C. Line 4a
   D. Line 5c

Questions 7 through 12 are based on the following form.

CUSTOMS DECLARATION			
1. Sender's Name and Address	**2. Sender's Customs Reference (if any)**		
	3. Insured Number		
	4. Insured Amount		
	5. Sender's Instructions in Case of Nondelivery		
	5a. ❏ Treat as Abandoned		
	5b. ❏ Return to Sender (return charges at sender's expense)		
	5c. ❏ Redirect to address below:		
6. Addressee's Name and Address	**7. Addressee's Telephone/Fax/Email (if known)**		
8a. Description of Contents	8b. Quantity	8c. Weight	8d. Value
		8e. Total Weight	8f. Total Value
9. Check One: 9a. ❏ Airmail/Priority 9b. ❏ Surface/Nonpriority			
10. Check One: 10a. ❏ Gift 10b. ❏ Documents 10c. ❏ Commercial Sample 10d. ❏ Returned Goods 10e. ❏ Other			
11. Date and Sender's Signature			

7. Which of these would be a correct entry for Box 4?
   A. "$200"
   B. "52986"
   C. "10"
   D. A checkmark

8. Where would the sender indicate that the item is a gift?
   A. Box 2
   B. Box 8a
   C. Box 9b
   D. Box 10a

9. This package contains antique glassware. Where would you indicate this?
   A. Box 4
   B. Box 8a
   C. Box 8b
   D. Box 10c

10. If the item is to be returned to the sender, who will pay the return charges?
    A. The addressee
    B. The sender
    C. The Post Office
    D. None of the above

11. If the package contains 10 antique glasses, each valued at $20, for a total of $200, where would "$200" be entered?
    A. Box 4
    B. Box 8d
    C. Box 8f
    D. Box 10e

12. How would you indicate that the items in the package weigh a total of 6 pounds?
    A. Enter "6" in Box 4
    B. Enter "6" in Box 8a
    C. Enter "6" in Box 8c
    D. Enter "6" in Box 8e

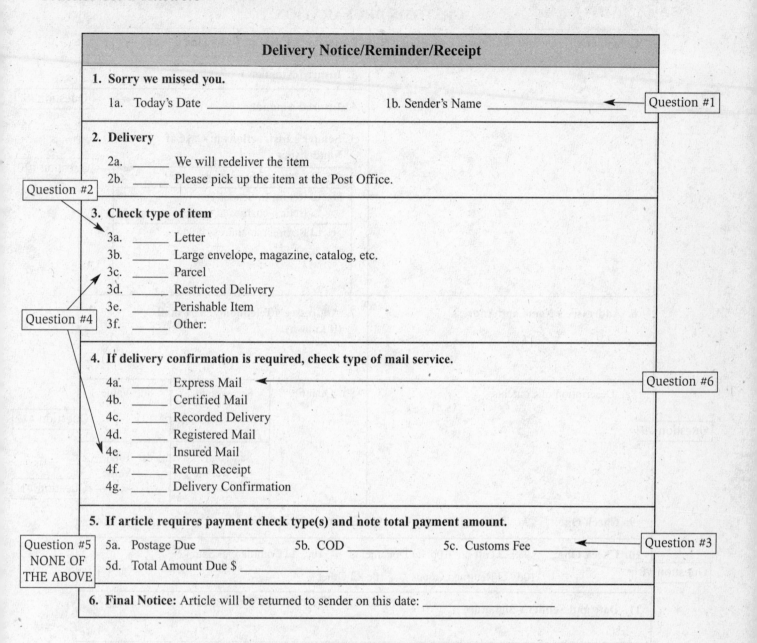

Delivery Notice/Reminder/Receipt

1. Sorry we missed you.

   1a. Today's Date _____   1b. Sender's Name _____ ← Question #1

2. Delivery

   2a. _____ We will redeliver the item
   2b. _____ Please pick up the item at the Post Office.

Question #2 →

3. Check type of item

   3a. _____ Letter
   3b. _____ Large envelope, magazine, catalog, etc.
   3c. _____ Parcel
   3d. _____ Restricted Delivery
   3e. _____ Perishable Item
Question #4   3f. _____ Other:

4. If delivery confirmation is required, check type of mail service.

   4a. _____ Express Mail ← Question #6
   4b. _____ Certified Mail
   4c. _____ Recorded Delivery
   4d. _____ Registered Mail
   4e. _____ Insured Mail
   4f. _____ Return Receipt
   4g. _____ Delivery Confirmation

5. If article requires payment check type(s) and note total payment amount.

Question #5
NONE OF
THE ABOVE
   5a. Postage Due _____   5b. COD _____   5c. Customs Fee _____ ← Question #3
   5d. Total Amount Due $ _____

6. Final Notice: Article will be returned to sender on this date: _____

1. **A** The sender's name, not a checkmark, should be entered on Line 1b.
2. **B** Line 3a should be checked if the mail is a letter.
3. **D** Line 5c should be checked if there is a customs fee.
4. **C** To indicate that the mail is a parcel, check Line 3c. To indicate that the mail is insured, check Line 4e. So the correct answer is C.
5. **D** There is no box for the addressee's name (only for the sender's name). So the correct answer is D, None of the above.
6. **C** Express Mail is noted on Line 4a.

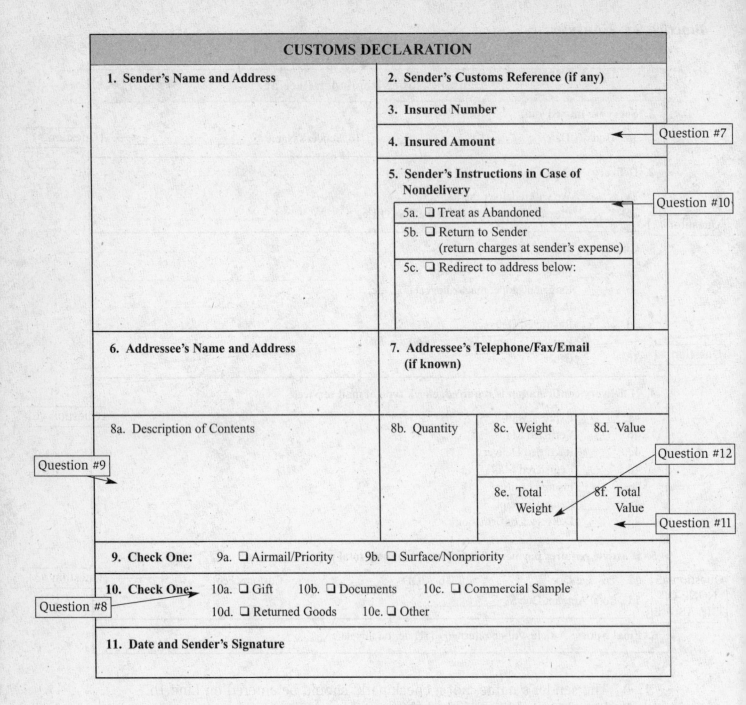

CUSTOMS DECLARATION

1. Sender's Name and Address	2. Sender's Customs Reference (if any)
	3. Insured Number
	4. Insured Amount ← Question #7
	5. Sender's Instructions in Case of Nondelivery ← Question #10
	5a. ❏ Treat as Abandoned
	5b. ❏ Return to Sender (return charges at sender's expense)
	5c. ❏ Redirect to address below:
6. Addressee's Name and Address	7. Addressee's Telephone/Fax/Email (if known)

8a. Description of Contents	8b. Quantity	8c. Weight	8d. Value
Question #9		8e. Total Weight	8f. Total Value
		Question #12 ↗	Question #11 ←

9. Check One: 9a. ❏ Airmail/Priority   9b. ❏ Surface/Nonpriority

10. Check One: 10a. ❏ Gift   10b. ❏ Documents   10c. ❏ Commercial Sample
Question #8 →   10d. ❏ Returned Goods   10e. ❏ Other

11. Date and Sender's Signature

7. **A** Box 4 is for the insured amount, a dollar amount, such as in answer A.
8. **D** "Gift" can be checked in Box 10a.
9. **B** The "Description of Contents" is entered in Box 8a.
10. **B** In Box 5b, "Return to Sender" can be checked. Beneath that box in parentheses is "return charges at sender's expense."
11. **C** The total value of the package is $200. The total value is entered in Box 8f.
12. **D** The total weight of the items goes in Box 8e.

BUILDING ENDURANCE

Practice Set 3—18 questions

Questions 1 through 6 are based on the following form.

Authorization to Hold Mail	
To Be Completed by Customer	*To Be Completed by Post Office*
Postmaster: Please hold mail for: 1. **Name (s)**	7. **Date Received**
	8. **Clerk**
	9. **Carrier**
	10. **Route Number**

2. **Address**
   2a. Street/apartment/suite number
 	
   _____
   2b. City _____
   2c. State _____
   2d. ZIP Code _____	

3. **Beginning Date**	
4. **Ending Date**	

5. **Instructions**
   5a. _____ Please deliver all accumulated
        mail and resume normal delivery on
        the ending date shown above.
   5b. _____ I will pick up all accumulated
        mail when I return.	

6. **Customer Signature** _____	

1. Where would the customer indicate that he or she wishes the held mail to be delivered?
   A. Box 3
   B. Box 4
   C. Line 5a
   D. Box 6

2. Which of these would be a correct entry for Box 8?
   A. "Tina Franklin"
   B. "6/8/06"
   C. "59"
   D. A checkmark

3. Which of these would be a correct entry for Line 2c?
   A. "04843"
   B. "6902 Dock Avenue"
   C. "Camden"
   D. "Maine"

4. How would the customer indicate that the mail will be held beginning on September 12?
   A. Enter the date in Box 3
   B. Enter the date in Box 4
   C. Enter the date in Box 5
   D. Enter the date in Box 7

5. The ZIP code for this Post Office is 04843. Where would this be indicated?
   A. Line 2d
   B. Box 9
   C. Box 10
   D. None of the above

6. The Post Office will complete all of the following EXCEPT which one?
   A. Box 6
   B. Box 7
   C. Box 8
   D. Box 10

Questions 7 through 12 are based on the following form.

Domestic Insured Parcel Receipt
(not for international mail)

1. **Parcel Addressed for Delivery at**

   1a. Post Office _____

   1b. State _____

   1c. ZIP Code _____

2. **Postage** $ _____

3. **Insurance Fee** $ _____

4. **Special Delivery Fee** $ _____

5. **Special Handling Fee** $ _____

6. **TOTAL FEES** $ _____

7. **INSURANCE COVERAGE**

   $ _____

8. **Postmark of Mailing Office**

9. **Check all that apply for this parcel.**

   9a. _____ Fragile   9b. _____ Liquid   9c. _____ Perishable

10. **Sender: Enter name and address of addressee on the reverse and read information regarding insurance coverage and claims.**

7. Where would you indicate the ZIP code of the Post Office of the addressee?
   A. Line 1e
   B. Line 1c
   C. Box 8
   D. Box 9

8. The Special Handling Fee is $3.25, and the Special Delivery Fee is $3.00. Where would you enter "$3.00"?
   A. Box 4
   B. Box 5
   C. Box 6
   D. Box 7

9. The package contains fruit, which will rot if not delivered on time. Where would you indicate this?
   A. Box 1
   B. Box 5
   C. Line 9a
   D. Line 9c

10. You could enter a checkmark on each of the following EXCEPT which one?
    A. Line 1a
    B. Line 9a
    C. Line 9b
    D. Line 9c

11. Where would you indicate the postage on this parcel?
    A. Box 1
    B. Box 2
    C. Box 6
    D. Box 7

12. There is no insurance on this parcel. How would this be indicated?
    A. Enter a dollar amount in Box 3 and Box 6
    B. Enter a dollar amount in Box 3 and Box 7
    C. Leave Box 3 and Box 6 blank
    D. Leave Box 3 and Box 7 blank

DOMESTIC MAIL OR REGISTERED MAIL INQUIRY
To Be Completed by Customer

1. Mailer Information			2. Addressee Information		
1a. First Name	1b. Middle Initial	1c. Last Name	2a. First Name	2b. Middle Initial	2c. Last Name
1d. Business Name (use only if mailer is a company)			2d. Business Name (use only if addressee is a company)		
1e. Street Name (number, street, suite/apartment number)			2e. Street Name (number, street, suite/apartment number)		
1f. City	1g. State	1h. ZIP Code	2f. City	2g. State	2h. ZIP Code
1i. Telephone Number (include area code)			2i. Telephone Number (include area code)		

3. Payment Assignment— Alternate Payment Address			4. Description of Lost or Damaged Article(s)— Add Extra Sheets as Needed			
3a. Who Is to Receive Payment? (check one) ❑ Mailer ❑ Addressee			4a. Item No.	4b. Description of Article	4c. Value or Cost	4d. Purchase Date
			First			
3b. Street Name (if other than address above) (number, street, suite/apartment number)			Second			
			Third			
3c. City	3d. State	3e. ZIP Code	Fourth			

5. COD Amount to Be Remitted to Sender	6. Total Amount Claimed for All Articles

7. Certification and Signature

7a. Customer Submitting Claim: ❑ Mailer ❑ Addressee	7b. Signature of Customer Filing the Claim	7c. Date Signed (MM/DD/YYYY)

13. The payment is to be sent to the mailer in Houston, rather than in Dallas, the city listed in Box 1. How would the customer indicate this?
    A. Enter "Houston" in Box 1f
    B. Enter "Houston" in Box 2f
    C. Enter "Houston" in Box 3c
    D. Enter "Dallas" in Box 3c

14. Which of these would be a correct entry for Box 1i?
    A. "281-555-7983"
    B. "Houston"
    C. "225 Commercial Drive"
    D. A checkmark

15. Veronica Stark is filing this claim for her employer, Western Lighting Supply Company, which mailed the package. Where would Veronica Stark's name be entered?
    A. Box 1d
    B. Box 2a, Box 2b, and Box 2c
    C. Box 3a
    D. Box 7b

16. Which of these would be a correct entry for Box 6?
    A. "255 Commercial Drive"
    B. "$184.50"
    C. "halogen light fixtures"
    D. A signature

17. Where would you indicate the state of the addressee?
    A. Box 1g
    B. Box 2e
    C. Box 2g
    D. Box 3c

18. In which of these would a name be a correct entry?
    A. Box 1a
    B. Box 1d
    C. Box 2d
    D. All of the above

Practice Set 3 Answers

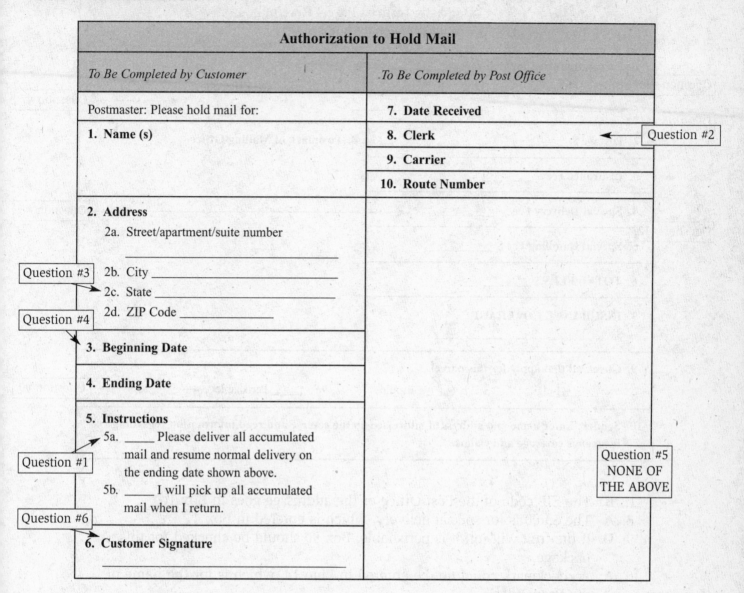

Authorization to Hold Mail

To Be Completed by Customer	To Be Completed by Post Office
Postmaster: Please hold mail for:	**7. Date Received**
1. Name (s)	**8. Clerk** ← Question #2
	9. Carrier
	10. Route Number
2. Address 2a. Street/apartment/suite number _____ Question #3 ► 2b. City _____ 2c. State _____ Question #4 ► 2d. ZIP Code _____	Question #5 NONE OF THE ABOVE
3. Beginning Date	
4. Ending Date	
5. Instructions Question #1 ► 5a. _____ Please deliver all accumulated mail and resume normal delivery on the ending date shown above. 5b. _____ I will pick up all accumulated mail when I return. Question #6 ►	
6. Customer Signature _____	

1. **C** Line 5a may be checked if the customer wishes the held accumulated mail to be delivered.
2. **A** Box 8 is for the clerk's name. The only name given is in answer A.
3. **D** Line 2c requires the name of a state.
4. **A** The beginning date for holding mail goes in Box 3.
5. **D** There is no space for the Post Office ZIP code, only for the customer's, so the answer is D, None of the above.
6. **A** The Post Office completes the boxes on the right of the form but would *not* complete Box 6, which is for the customer's signature.

Domestic Insured Parcel Receipt
(not for international mail)

1. Parcel Addressed for Delivery at

Question #10

1a. Post Office   1b. State   1c. ZIP Code   Question #7

_____   _____   _____

Question #11

2. Postage $ _____   **8. Postmark of Mailing Office**

3. Insurance Fee $ _____

4. Special Delivery Fee $ _____   Question #8

Question #12

5. Special Handling Fee $ _____

6. TOTAL FEES $ _____

7. INSURANCE COVERAGE

$ _____

9. Check all that apply for this parcel.

9a. _____ Fragile   9b. _____ Liquid   9c. _____ Perishable   Question #9

10. Sender: Enter name and address of addressee on the reverse and read information regarding insurance coverage and claims.

---

7. **B**   The ZIP code of the Post Office of the addressee goes in Box 1c.
8. **A**   The $3.00 is for special delivery, which is entered in Box 4.
9. **D**   If the fruit will rot, it is perishable. Box 9c should be checked for this package.
10. **A**   A checkmark could *not* be entered in Line 1a, which is for the name of the Post Office.
11. **B**   Postage is entered in Box 2.
12. **D**   If there is no insurance on the parcel, both Box 3 and Box 7 would be left blank.

DOMESTIC MAIL OR REGISTERED MAIL INQUIRY
To Be Completed by Customer

1. Mailer Information

1a. First Name	1b. Middle Initial	1c. Last Name

1d. Business Name
(use only if mailer is a company)

1e. Street Name
(number, street, suite/apartment number)

1f. City	1g. State	1h. ZIP Code

1i. Telephone Number (include area code)

2. Addressee Information

2a. First Name	2b. Middle Initial	2c. Last Name

2d. Business Name
(use only if addressee is a company)

2e. Street Name
(number, street, suite/apartment number)

2f. City	2g. State	2h. ZIP Code

2i. Telephone Number (include area code)

Question #14 → 1i
Question #17 → 2g

3. Payment Assignment—Alternate Payment Address

3a. Who Is to Receive Payment?
(check one)
❑ Mailer   ❑ Addressee

3b. Street Name (if other than address above)
(number, street, suite/apartment number)

3c. City	3d. State	3e. ZIP Code

Question #13 → 3c

4. Description of Lost or Damaged Article(s)—Add Extra Sheets as Needed

	4a. Item No.	4b. Description of Article	4c. Value or Cost	4d. Purchase Date
First				
Second				
Third				
Fourth				

5. COD Amount to Be Remitted to Sender
6. Total Amount Claimed for All Articles

Question #16 → 6

7. Certification and Signature

7a. Customer Submitting Claim: ❑ Mailer ❑ Addressee	7b. Signature of Customer Filing the Claim	7c. Date Signed (MM/DD/YYYY)

Question #15 → 7a
Question #18 ALL OF THE ABOVE

13. **C** If the address to which payment is to be sent is different from the initial address given, that information should be entered in Box 3. The city, in this case, Houston, should be entered in Box 3c.

14. **A** Box 1i is for a telephone number, including the area code.

15. **D** Veronica Stark's name could not appear in Box 1 or Box 2 because she was neither the initial mailer nor the addressee. But Box 7b is for the name (in the form of a signature) of the person filing the claim.

16. **B** Box 6 requires a dollar amount, the total amount claimed.

17. **C** The state of the addressee goes in Box 2g.

18. **D** A name could go in Box 1a (a first name), Box 1d (a business name), and Box 2d (also a business name). So the answer is D, All of the above.

Part C: Coding and Memory

WHAT TO EXPECT

The Coding and Memory part is divided into two sections: Section 1—Coding, and Section 2,Memory. The coding section is 6 minutes long and contains 36 questions. The memory section is 7 minutes long and contains 36 questions. This part tests your ability to use codes quickly and accurately. There is a penalty for guessing, so don't guess unless you can eliminate one or more of the choices. Don't guess blindly.

In Section 1—Coding, you are asked to identify the correct code to be assigned to an address.

In Section 2—Memory, you are asked to memorize codes to be assigned to a range of addresses.

- Expect the same **Coding Guide** to be used throughout both sections of Part C.
- Expect four delivery routes to be identified as A, B, C, and D.
- Expect the fourth route, Delivery Route D, to always be "All mail that doesn't fall in one of the address ranges listed above."
- Expect the first column of the **Coding Guide** to show the address range.
- Expect the second column of the **Coding Guide** to show a one-letter code for the delivery route that corresponds to the address ranges listed in that row.

CODING GUIDE

Address Range	Delivery Route
1–99 Bently Ct. 100–300 Summerville Dr. 15–25 S 35th Street	A
100–200 Bently Ct. 26–50 S 35th Street	B
2000–3200 Old Cayton Rd. 10–20 Rural Route 2 301–700 Summerville Dr.	C
All mail that doesn't fall in one of the address ranges listed above	D

WHAT YOU SHOULD KNOW

- You should know that in the sample above, Delivery Route A serves all address in each of the three ranges 1–99 Bently Ct., 100–300 Summerville Dr., and 15–25 S 35th Street.
- You should know that addresses run in order from the lowest listed to the highest listed.
- You should know that some of the street names appear twice in different delivery routes.

- You should know that if the street names appear twice, the address range will be different but the address range will be continuous: 1–99 Bently Ct. (Delivery Route A), 100–200 Bently Ct. (Delivery Route B).
- You should know that in the actual Coding section, you will complete a 2-minute sample unscored exercise and then a 1½-minute sample unscored exercise, followed by the actual scored test.
- You should know that in the actual Memory section, you will have a 3-minute study and memorization time, followed by a 1½-minute unscored practice, followed by a 5-minute study and memorization time, followed by the actual scored test.
- You should know that you should mark the answers to the sample unscored exercises on the sample answer grid.
- You should know that you should mark the actual scored test on the Answer Sheet.
- You should know that on Part C the question numbering will be continuous from 1 through 72 (Sections 1 and 2).

WHAT TO LOOK FOR

- Look for similarities and differences in the address range for Delivery Routes A, B, and C.

CODING GUIDE

Address Range	Delivery Route
1–99 Bently Ct. 100–300 Summerville Dr. 15–25 S 35th Street	A
100–200 Bently Ct. 26–50 S 35th Street	B
2000–3200 Old Cayton Rd. 10–20 Rural Route 2 301–700 Summerville Dr.	C
All mail that doesn't fall in one of the address ranges listed above	D

In the **Coding Guide** above, the similarities are that:

Bently Ct. is served by routes A and B.

S 35th Street is served by routes A and B.

Summerville Dr. is served by routes A and C.

Old Cayton Rd. and Rural Route 2 are served only by route C.

In the **Coding Guide** on page 63 the differences are that:

Bently Ct. is served by routes A and B, but the address ranges are different.

S 35th Street is served by routes A and B, but the address ranges are different.

Summerville Dr. is served by routes A and C, but the address ranges are different.

Note that although the address ranges are different, they are continuous for each.

- Look for unneeded information, that is, information you will *not* need to memorize.

WHAT YOU SHOULD DO

For the Coding Section

- Regardless of the technique you plan to use for the Memory section, for the Coding section you should quickly scan the information and look for repeated information (similarities) and differences (different number ranges) mentioned and listed earlier in What to Look For.
- Since you can refer back to the **Coding Guide** for this section, simply go ahead and start finding the delivery routes.
- You should work quickly and accurately because you have only 6 minutes to answer 36 questions.

Sample Guide

CODING GUIDE

Address Range	Delivery Route
1–99 Bently Ct. 100–300 Summerville Dr. 15–25 S 35th Street	A
100–200 Bently Ct. 26–50 S 35th Street	B
2000–3200 Old Cayton Rd. 10–20 Rural Route 2 301–700 Summerville Dr.	C
All mail that doesn't fall in one of the address ranges listed above	D

You might want to try a simple marking system where you mark similar items in the **Coding Guide**. See if this works for you.

Sample Guide with Possible Markings

CODING GUIDE

Address Range	Delivery Route
✗ 1–99 Bently Ct. → 100–300 Summerville Dr. ✓ 15–25 S 35th Street	A
✗ 100–200 Bently Ct. ✓ 26–50 S 35th Street	B
2000–3200 Old Cayton Rd. 10–20 Rural Route 2 → 301–700 Summerville Dr.	C
All mail that doesn't fall in one of the address ranges listed above	D

See if you can answer some questions using the Coding Guide above.

Sample Questions

	Address	Delivery Route
1.	14 Bently Ct.	(A) B C D
2.	35 Rural Route 2	A B (C)(D)
3.	310 Summerville Dr.	A B (C) D
4.	3200 Old Cayton Rd.	A B (C) D
5.	188 Bently Ct.	A (B) C D

In sample 1, 14 Bently Ct. is in Delivery Route A, in the range 1–99 Bently Ct.

In sample 2, 35 Rural Route 2 appears as though it might go in Delivery Route C, but on taking a closer look, we realize that the number 35 does not fall in the range 10–20 Rural Route 2. So the correct answer is Delivery Route D, all mail that doesn't fall in one of the address ranges listed above.

In sample 3, 310 Summerville Dr. is in Delivery Route C, in the range 301–700 Summerville Dr.

In sample 4, 3200 Old Cayton Rd. is in Delivery Route C, in the range 2000–3200 Old Cayton Rd.

In sample 5, 188 Bently Ct. is in Delivery Route B, in the range 100–200 Bently Ct.

Your sample answers should look like this.

1. ●	Ⓑ	Ⓒ	Ⓓ
2. Ⓐ	Ⓑ	Ⓒ	●
3. Ⓐ	Ⓑ	●	Ⓓ
4. Ⓐ	Ⓑ	●	Ⓓ
5. Ⓐ	●	Ⓒ	Ⓓ

For the Memory Section

- You should find a memorization technique that works for you and that you are comfortable with. Several techniques are commonly used for memorizing blocks of information, ranging from simple rote memory methods to associating, simplifying, reorganizing, visualizing, and so on. We will give you an overview of a few techniques that could be very helpful. Try these, as well as your own techniques, to see which one works best for you.
- Regardless of the memorization technique you use, memorize the street name completely. For example, memorize Bently Ct., as opposed to just Bently or Ben. This will save you having a problem with addresses such as Bently **St.** and Ben**der** Ct.
- Now, using the **Coding Guide** that we analyzed earlier, let's try out a few different memorization techniques.

CODING GUIDE

Address Range	Delivery Route
1–99 Bently Ct. 100–300 Summerville Dr. 15–25 S 35th Street	A
100–200 Bently Ct. 26–50 S 35th Street	B
2000–3200 Old Cayton Rd. 10–20 Rural Route 2 301–700 Summerville Dr.	C
All mail that doesn't fall in one of the address ranges listed above	D

Organize and Memorize

In this method you scan the information looking for similarities and differences (as shown earlier) and then mentally organize the address ranges and delivery routes as follows:

Put the street name first, the address range second, and the delivery route next, followed by the address range and the other delivery route (if the street is mentioned twice).

Street Name	Range	Delivery Route,	Range	Delivery Route
Bently Ct.	1–99	A,	100–200	B
Summerville Dr.	100–300	A,	301–700	C
S 35th Street	15–25	A,	26–50	B
Old Cayton Rd.	2000–3200	C		
Rural Route 2,	10–20	C		

Remember, you are organizing the information by putting the street name first, the address range second, and the delivery route next, followed by the address range and the other delivery route (if the street is mentioned twice).

Here is the block of information that you would memorize.

Bently Ct. 1–99 A, 100–200 B

Summerville Dr. 100–300 A, 301–700 C

S 35th Street 15–25 A, 26-50 B

Old Cayton Rd. 2000–3200 C

Rural Route 2, 10–20 C

Now silently repeat each of the lines. Pause at the comma (,).

Bently Ct. 1–99 A, 100–200 B
Bently Ct. 1–99 A, 100–200 B
Bently Ct. 1–99 A, 100–200 B
Bently Ct. 1–99 A, 100–200 B
Bently Ct. 1–99 A, 100–200 B
Bently Ct. 1–99 A, 100–200 B

Then go on to the next street, range, and delivery route.

> Summerville Dr. 100–300 A, 301–700 C
> Summerville Dr. 100–300 A, 301–700 C
> Summerville Dr. 100–300 A, 301–700 C
> Summerville Dr. 100–300 A, 301–700 C
> Summerville Dr. 100–300 A, 301–700 C
> Summerville Dr. 100–300 A, 301–700 C

and so on, through each of the address ranges and routes.

Silently repeating each of these should help you memorize them. The number of times you repeat each line is up to you.

Remember that if a street is given twice in the **Coding Guide**, the address number continues in order.

Organize, Simplify, and Memorize

Another method is to simplify the information to make it easier to memorize. Again, scan the information looking for similarities and differences (as shown earlier) and then mentally organize the address ranges and delivery routes as follows:

Address Range	Delivery Route
1–99 Bently Ct.	A
100–200 Bently Ct.	B

would be reorganized and simplified to

> Bently Ct. A B, 1–100–200

The street name is listed first and the two possible delivery routes second, followed by simplified address ranges: 1–99 is rounded to 1–100; then it is combined with the next range, 100–200 as 1–100–200.

Street Name	Delivery Route or Routes	Address Range or Ranges
Bently Ct.	A B,	1–100–200

If the question involves Bently Ct., you know immediately that the delivery route is probably either A or B. If the street address falls between 1 and 100 the route is A; if it falls between 100 and 200, the route is B.

If the street address falls out of either range given, then the answer is D. Because you have simplified the range, if the street address is 100 Bently Ct., you would guess A or B unless you remember that it is in the second range—choice B.

Address Range	Delivery Route
100–300 Summerville Dr.	A
301–700 Summerville Dr.	C

would be reorganized and simplified to

Summerville Dr. A C, 100–300–700

The street name is listed first and the two possible delivery routes second, followed by simplified address ranges: 100–300 and the second range, 301–700, which are simplified to 300–700. Then they are put in order as 100–300–700.

Street Name	Delivery Route or Routes	Address Range or Ranges
Summerville Dr.	A C,	100–300–700

If the question involves Summerville Dr., you know immediately that the delivery route is probably either A or C. If the street address falls between ①and 300, the route is A; if it falls between 300 and 700, the route is C.

If the street address falls out of either range given, then the answer is D. Because you have simplified the range, if the street address given is 300 Summerville Dr., you would guess A or C, unless you remember that it is in the first range—choice A.

Address Range	Delivery Route
15–25 S 35th Street	A
26–50 S 35th Street	B

would be reorganized and simplified to

S 35th Street A B, 15–25–50

The street name is listed first and the two possible delivery routes second, followed by simplified address ranges: 15–25 and the second range, 26–50, which have been simplified to 25–50. Then they are combined as 15–25–50.

Street Name	Delivery Route or Routes	Address Range or Ranges
S 35th Street	A B,	15–25–50

If the question involves S 35th Street, you know immediately that the delivery route is probably either A or B. If the street address falls between 15 and 25, the route is A; if it falls between 25 and 50, the route is B.

If the street address falls out of either range given, then the answer is D. Because you have simplified the range, if the street address given is 25 S 35th Street, you would guess A or B unless you remember that it is in the first range—choice A.

The last two address ranges given in this **Coding Guide** would be reorganized but memorized with exact numbers as follows:

Street Name	Delivery Route or Routes	Address Range or Ranges
Old Cayton Rd.	C	2000–3200

If the question involves Old Cayton Rd., you know immediately that the delivery route is probably C. If the street address falls between 2000 and 3200, the delivery route is C; if not, the delivery route is D.

Street Name	Delivery Route or Routes	Address Range or Ranges
Rural Route 2	C	10–20

If the question involves Rural Route 2, you know immediately that the delivery route is probably C. If the street address falls between 10 and 20, the route is C; if not, the delivery route is D.

In this method you are organizing the information by putting the street name first and the delivery route (or routes) next, followed by the address ranges, which have been simplified and put in order.

Here is the block of information that you would memorize using this technique.

Bently Ct. A B, 1–100–200

Summerville Dr. A C, 100–300–700

S 35th Street A B, 15–25–50

Old Cayton Rd. C, 2000–3200

Rural Route 2 C, 10–20

Now silently repeat each of the lines. Pause at the comma (,).

Bently Ct. A B, 1–100–200
Bently Ct. A B, 1–100–200
Bently Ct. A B, 1–100–200
Bently Ct. A B, 1–100–200
Bently Ct. A B, 1–100–200
Bently Ct. A B, 1–100–200

Then go on to the next street, range, and delivery route.

Summerville Dr. A C, 100–300–700
Summerville Dr. A C, 100–300–700
Summerville Dr. A C, 100–300–700
Summerville Dr. A C, 100–300–700
Summerville Dr. A C, 100–300–700
Summerville Dr. A C, 100–300–700

and so on, through each of the address ranges and routes.

Silently repeating each of these should help you memorize them. The number of times you repeat each line is up to you.

Again, remember that if a street is given twice in the **Coding Guide**, the address number continues in order.

Take a few minutes to memorize the previous Coding Guide using either of the techniques given, or your own technique, and see if you can answer the following questions.

	Address	Delivery Route			
6.	16 S 35th Street	A	B	C	D
7.	15 Rural Route 3	A	B	C	D
8.	44 Benson Ct.	A	B	C	D
9.	190 Summerville Dr.	A	B	C	D
10.	12 S 25th Street	A	B	C	D
11.	800 Summerville Dr.	A	B	C	D
12.	2700 Old Cayton Rd.	A	B	C	D
13.	103 Bently Ct.	A	B	C	D
14.	290 Summerville Dr.	A	B	C	D
15.	19 Rural Route 2	A	B	C	D

In sample 6, 16 S 35th Street is in Delivery Route A, in the range 15–25 S 35th Street.

In sample 7, 15 Rural Route 3, appears as though it might go in delivery route C, but remember that this lists Rural Route **3**, which is not one of the streets in the **Coding Guide**. So the correct answer is Delivery Route D—All mail that doesn't fall in one of the address ranges listed above.

In sample 8, 44 Benson Ct. is not one of the streets in the **Coding Guide**. So the correct answer is Delivery Route D—All mail that doesn't fall in one of the address ranges listed above. You should be careful; Benson Ct. could easily be mistaken for Bently Ct.

In sample 9, 190 Summerville Dr. is in Delivery Route A, in the range 100–300 Summerville Dr.

In sample 10, 12 S 25th Street appears as though it might go in Delivery Route A, but remember, there is no S 25th Street in the **Coding Guide**. So the correct answer is Delivery Route D—All mail that doesn't fall in one of the address ranges listed above.

In sample 11, 800 Summerville Dr. appears as though it might go in Delivery Route C, but remember that it is not in the address range 301–700 Summerville Dr. (which you memorized as Summerville Dr. A C, 100–300–700). So the correct answer is Delivery Route D—All mail that doesn't fall in one of the address ranges listed above.

In sample 12, 2700 Old Cayton Rd. is in Delivery Route C, in the range 2000–3200 Old Cayton Rd.

In sample 13, 103 Bently Ct. is in Delivery Route B, in the range 100–200 Bently Ct.

In sample 14, 290 Summerville Dr. is in Delivery Route A, in the range 100–200 Summerville Dr.

In sample 15, 19 Rural Route 2 is in Delivery Route C, in the range 10–20 Rural Route 2.

Your sample answers should look like this.

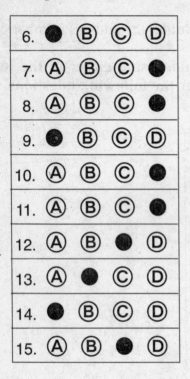

> Because the Memory section is the most difficult section for most people, as you practice, try a few different memory techniques to see which one works best for you. The key here is to find a technique that you are comfortable with and then practice, practice, practice.

PART C: CODING AND MEMORY PRACTICE SETS

SECTION 1: CODING

WARMING UP

Practice Set 1—10 questions

Refer to the first part of the Coding Guide shown below to answer the following 10 questions. For this practice exercise, take as much time as you need. Notice that in this practice exercise the answer will be either A or D. If the address is one in the range given, the answer will be A. If the address is **not** among those listed, the answer will be D.

CODING GUIDE PART 1

Address Range	Delivery Route
4881–5200 Merryweather Rd.	
990–1239 Two Pikes Parkway	A
8500–8899 Cormorant Blvd.	
All mail that doesn't fall in one of the address ranges listed above	D

	Address	Delivery Route
1.	998 Two Pikes Parkway	(A) D
2.	5985 Merryweather Rd.	A (D)
3.	8611 Cormorant Blvd.	(A) D
4.	1169 Two Pikes Parkway	(A) D
5.	11003 Two Pikes Parkway	A (D)
6.	9750 Cormorant Rd.	A (D)
7.	5022 Merryweather Rd.	(A) D
8.	1220 Twin Pikes Parkway	A (D)
9.	4971 Merryweather Rd.	(A) D
10.	8709 Cormorant Blvd.	(A) D

Practice Set 1 Answers

1. A	3. A	5. D	7. A	9. A
2. D	4. A	6. D	8. D	10. A

BUILDING SPEED

Practice Set 2—15 questions

Refer to the first two parts of the Coding Guide shown below to answer the following 15 questions. For this practice exercise, give yourself a time limit of three minutes. Notice that in this practice exercise the answer will be A, B, or D. If the address is one in the range given, the answer will be A or B. If the address is **not** among those listed, the answer will be D.

CODING GUIDE PARTS 1 AND 2

Address Range	Delivery Route
4881–5200 Merryweather Rd.	
990–1239 Two Pikes Parkway	A
8500–8899 Cormorant Blvd.	
5201–5900 Merryweather Rd.	
8900–9550 Cormorant Blvd.	B
All mail that doesn't fall in one of the address ranges listed above	D

Address	Delivery Route
1. 818 Two Pikes Parkway	A B Ⓓ
2. 5040 Merryweather Rd.	Ⓐ B D
3. 9887 Cormorant Blvd.	A B Ⓓ
4. 5833 Merryweather Rd.	A Ⓑ D
5. 1000 Two Pikes Parkway	Ⓐ B D
6. 9401 Cormorant Blvd.	A Ⓑ D
7. 999 Two Pikes Parkway	Ⓐ B D
8. 8703 Cormorant Blvd.	Ⓐ B D
9. 5623 Merryweather Rd.	A Ⓑ D
10. 5934 Merryweather Rd.	Ⓐ B Ⓓ
11. 8860 Cormordy Blvd.	A B Ⓓ
12. 591 Two Pikes Beltway	A B Ⓓ
13. 9449 Cormorant Blvd.	A Ⓑ D
14. 5047 Merryweather Rd.	Ⓐ B D
15. 8977 Cormorant Blvd.	A Ⓑ D

Practice Set 2 Answers

1. D	4. B	7. A	10. D	13. B
2. A	5. A	8. A	11. D	14. A
3. D	6. B	9. B	12. D	15. B

BUILDING ENDURANCE

Practice Set 3—20 questions

Refer to the complete Coding Guide, shown below to answer the following 20 questions. For this practice exercise, give yourself a time limit of four minutes. Notice that in this practice exercise the answer may be A, B, C, or D. If the address is one in the range given, the answer will be A, B, or C. If the address is **not** among those listed, the answer will be D.

COMPLETE CODING GUIDE

Address Range	Delivery Route
4881–5200 Merryweather Rd.	
990–1239 Two Pikes Parkway	A
8500–8899 Cormorant Blvd.	
5201–5900 Merryweather Rd.	
8900–9550 Cormorant Blvd.	B
52000–67000 County Rt. 80	
55–99 O'Reilly Place	C
1240–1649 Two Pikes Parkway	
All mail that doesn't fall in one of the address ranges listed above	D

	Address	Delivery Route
1.	77 O'Reilly Place	A B ⓒ D
2.	9051 Cormorant Blvd.	A Ⓑ C D
3.	63798 County Rt. 80	A B ⓒ D
4.	1003 Two Pikes Parkway	Ⓐ B C D
5.	46 O'Reilly Place	A B C Ⓓ
6.	1630 Two Pikes Parkway	A B ⓒ D
7.	6500 County Rt. 80	A B C Ⓓ
8.	1234 Two Pikes Parkway	Ⓐ B C D
9.	66 O'Reilly Place	A B ⓒ D
10.	9293 Cormorant Blvd.	A Ⓑ C D
11.	9549 Cormorant Blvd.	A Ⓑ C D
12.	1082 Two Pikes Parkway	Ⓐ B C D
13.	5193 Merryweather Rd.	Ⓐ B C D
14.	62649 County Road 80	A B C Ⓓ
15.	1573 Two Pikes Parkway	A B ⓒ D
16.	5128 Merrydale Rd.	A B C Ⓓ
17.	9373 Cormorant Blvd.	A Ⓑ C D
18.	1228 Two Pikes Parkway	Ⓐ B C D
19.	6788 Merryweather Rd.	A B C Ⓓ
20.	2767 Two Pikes Parkway	A B C Ⓓ

Practice Set 3 Answers

1. C	5. D	9. C	13. A	17. B
2. B	6. C	10. B	14. D	18. A
3. C	7. D	11. B	15. C	19. D
4. A	8. A	12. A	16. D	20. D

SECTION 2: MEMORY

WARMING UP

Practice Set 1—10 questions

Study the Coding Guide shown below for as long as you need to memorize the information. **Then answer the following 10 questions from memory without referring to this section of the Coding Guide.** For this practice exercise, take as much time as you need to answer the 10 questions.

CODING GUIDE

Address Range	Delivery Route
4881–5200 Merryweather Rd.	
990–1239 Two Pikes Parkway	A
8500–8899 Cormorant Blvd.	
5201–5900 Merryweather Rd.	
8900–9550 Cormorant Blvd.	B
52000–67000 County Rt. 80	
55–99 O'Reilly Place	C
1240–1649 Two Pikes Parkway	
All mail that doesn't fall in one of the address ranges listed above	D

	Address	Delivery Route
1.	1154 Two Pikes Parkway	(A) B C D
2.	5221 Merryweather Rd.	A (B) C D
3.	91 O'Reilly Place	A B (C) D
4.	8977 Cormorant St.	A (B) C D
5.	4908 Merryweather Rd.	(A) B C D
6.	61005 County Rt. 80	A B (C) D
7.	7657 Cormorant Blvd.	A B C (D)

78

Daly City Public Library – Westlake
dalycitylibrary.org
650.991.8071

Customer Name: CHEN, PEIYU

Items that you checked out

Title:
Barron's comprehensive postal exam,
473/473-C / Jerry Bobrow ; contributing
author and consultant, M
ID: 39043060022851
Due: Saturday, April 22, 2017

Total items: 1
Account balance: $0.00
4/1/2017 4:29 PM
Checked out: 2
Ready for pickup: 1

Daly City Public Library – Westlake
dailycitylibrary.org
1708 186 0511

Customer name: CHEN, PEIYU

Items that you checked out

Title
Barron's comprehensive posted exam
4737473-C / Jerry Borrow : continuing
author and continuing
ID: 39043088053825

Due: Saturday, April 22, 2017

Total items: 1
Account balance: $0.00
7/17/2017 4:39 PM
Checked out: 2
Ready for pickup: 1

Address	Delivery Route
8. 574 Two Peaks Parkway	A B C (D)
9. 8878 Cormorant Blvd.	(A) B C D
10. 1324 Two Pikes Parkway	A B (C) D

Practice Set 1 Answers

1. A	3. C	5. A	7. D	9. A
2. B	4. B	6. C	8. D	10. C

BUILDING SPEED

Practice Set 2—15 questions

Study the Coding Guide shown below. **Then answer the following 15 questions from memory without referring to these sections of the Coding Guide.** For this practice exercise, give yourself a time limit of four minutes.

CODING GUIDE

Address Range	Delivery Route
4881–5200 Merryweather Rd.	
990–1239 Two Pikes Parkway	A
8500–8899 Cormorant Blvd.	
5201–5900 Merryweather Rd.	
8900–9550 Cormorant Blvd.	B
52000–67000 County Rt. 80	
55–99 O'Reilly Place	C
1240–1649 Two Pikes Parkway	
All mail that doesn't fall in one of the address ranges listed above	D

Address	Delivery Route
1. 5898 Merryweather Rd.	A (B) C D
2. 9323 Cormorant Blvd.	A (B) C D
3. 1120 Two Pikes Parkway	(A) B C D
4. 5950 Merryweather Rd.	A B C (D)
5. 58 O'Reilly Place	A B (C) D
6. 9540 Cormorant Blvd.	A (B) C D
7. 5296 Merryweather Rd.	A (B) C D
8. 8000 Cormorant Ave.	A B C (D)
9. 52522 County Rt. 80	A B (C) D
10. 98 O'Reilly Place	A B (C) D
11. 9147 Cormorant Blvd.	A (B) C D
12. 1218 Two Pikes Parkway	(A) B C D
13. 950 Cormorant Blvd.	A B C (D)
14. 4896 Merryman Rd.	A B C (D)
15. 1097 Two Pikes Parkway	(A) B C D

Practice Set 2 Answers

1. B	4. D	7. B	10. C	13. D
2. B	5. C	8. A	11. B	14. D
3. A	6. B	9. C	12. A	15. A

BUILDING ENDURANCE

Practice Set 3—20 questions

Study the Coding Guide shown below. **Then answer the following 20 questions from memory without referring to the Coding Guide.** For this practice exercise, give yourself a time limit of four minutes.

CODING GUIDE

Address Range	Delivery Route
4881–5200 Merryweather Rd.	
990–1239 Two Pikes Parkway	A
8500–8899 Cormorant Blvd.	
5201–5900 Merryweather Rd.	
8900–9550 Cormorant Blvd.	B
52000–67000 County Rt. 80	
55–99 O'Reilly Place	C
1240–1649 Two Pikes Parkway	
All mail that doesn't fall in one of the address ranges listed above	D

	Address	Delivery Route
1.	9060 Cormorant Blvd.	A (B) C D
2.	5866 Merryweather Rd.	A (B) C D
3.	1155 Two Pikes Parkway	(A) B C D
4.	5800 Cormorant Blvd.	A B C (D)
5.	88 O'Reilly Place	A B (C) D
6.	1009 Two Pikes Parkway	(A) B C D
7.	35 O'Reilly Place	A B C (D)
8.	9090 Cormorant Blvd.	A (B) C D
9.	53700 County Rt. 80	A B (C) D
10.	5137 Merryweather Rd.	(A) B C D
11.	8902 Commoner Blvd.	A B C (D)
12.	1212 Two Pikes Parkway	(A) B C D
13.	8871 Cormorant Blvd.	(A) B C D
14.	83 O'Reilly Place	A B (C) D
15.	6160 Two Pikes Parkway	A B C (D)
16.	60 O'Reilly Plaza	A B C (D)
17.	58756 County Rt. 90	A B C (D)
18.	1324 Two Pikes Parkway	A B (C) D
19.	1160 Three Pikes Parkway	A B C (D)
20.	5711 Merryweather Rd.	A (B) C D

Practice Set 3 Answers

1. B	5. C	9. C	13. A	17. D
2. B	6. A	10. A	14. C	18. C
3. A	7. D	11. D	15. D	19. D
4. D	8. B	12. A	16. C	20. B

Part D: Personal Characteristics and Experience Inventory

WHAT TO EXPECT

The Personal Characteristics and Experience Inventory is 90 minutes long and contains 236 test items. That gives you about 20 to 25 seconds to complete each item. These questions assess personal characteristics, tendencies, or experiences related to performing effectively as an employee of the Postal Service.

- Expect Section 1 (Agree/Disagree) to have questions where the four choices are always:

  A. Strongly Agree
  B. Agree
  C. Disagree
  D. Strongly Disagree

- Expect Section 2 (Frequency) to have questions where the four choices are always:

  A. Very Often
  B. Often
  C. Sometimes
  D. Rarely

- Expect Section 3 (Experience) to have questions with four to nine answer choices. The choices will vary depending on the question.

WHAT YOU SHOULD KNOW

- You should know that in some questions there may appear to be more than one appropriate choice, but you can choose only one.
- You should know that you should choose the one that seems to fit the best.
- You should know that in some cases more than one response describes you or your experience, but you can choose only one.

WHAT TO LOOK FOR

- In Section 1, look for statements to respond to, rather than questions.

  Example:
  You like a job where you can work in a quiet setting.

  A. Strongly Agree
  B. Agree
  C. Disagree
  D. Strongly Disagree

83

- In Section 2, look for statements to respond to, rather than questions.

    Example:
    You plan things carefully before getting started.

    A. Very Often
    B. Often
    C. Sometimes
    D. Rarely

- In Section 3, look for questions that ask about your experience.

    Example:
    What type of work do you like the most?

    A. Work that requires constant interaction with customers
    B. Work that requires some interaction with customers
    C. Work that requires constant interaction with supervisors
    D. Work that needs to be done in groups
    E. Work that needs to be done at a slow, constant pace
    F. None of the above

You should note that in Section 3, some of the choices may be: not sure, none of the above, all of the above, and so on.

WHAT YOU SHOULD DO

- Read each question or statement carefully before marking an answer.
- Try to respond to items in terms of what you have done, felt, or believed in a work setting.
- Base your responses on experiences that are similar to work if you cannot relate them directly to work.
- Because there is no right or wrong answer, respond to each question honestly based on your experience.

Since there is no particular advantage to practicing your responses on these statements and questions, no practice exercises or tests are given here for them.

Part III

Six Full-Length Practice Examinations

HOW TO TAKE THE PRACTICE EXAMINATIONS

Now that you have slowly and carefully worked though the introductory chapters that focused on analyzing the question types, take the full-length practice tests in the following manner:

1. Find a quiet work space with good lighting and a clean, flat surface.
2. Note the time limit for the first section.
3. Set your alarm clock for that amount of time or short yourself a minute or two.
4. Use the appropriate answer sheet that you have removed from the book.
5. Take the test under timed test conditions (no breaks, no interruptions).
6. Stop when the time is up; then go to the next section, and repeat the above procedure.
7. At the conclusion of the test, review all your responses using the explanations of answers following the complete examination.

Note: The following tests are geared to the format of Postal Exam 473/473–C and have complete answers and explanations. The sample tests are equivalent to the actual test in question structure, number of questions, level of difficulty, and time allotments. The questions used are not taken directly from Postal Exam 473/473–C, as those questions are copyrighted and cannot be reproduced.

Now please turn to the next page, remove the answer sheets, and begin Sample Test 1.

PRACTICE EXAMINATION 1

ANSWER SHEET FOR PRACTICE EXAMINATION 1

PART A: ADDRESS CHECKING

1. Ⓐ Ⓑ Ⓒ Ⓓ   16. Ⓐ Ⓑ Ⓒ Ⓓ   31. Ⓐ Ⓑ Ⓒ Ⓓ   46. Ⓐ Ⓑ Ⓒ Ⓓ
2. Ⓐ Ⓑ Ⓒ Ⓓ   17. Ⓐ Ⓑ Ⓒ Ⓓ   32. Ⓐ Ⓑ Ⓒ Ⓓ   47. Ⓐ Ⓑ Ⓒ Ⓓ
3. Ⓐ Ⓑ Ⓒ Ⓓ   18. Ⓐ Ⓑ Ⓒ Ⓓ   33. Ⓐ Ⓑ Ⓒ Ⓓ   48. Ⓐ Ⓑ Ⓒ Ⓓ
4. Ⓐ Ⓑ Ⓒ Ⓓ   19. Ⓐ Ⓑ Ⓒ Ⓓ   34. Ⓐ Ⓑ Ⓒ Ⓓ   49. Ⓐ Ⓑ Ⓒ Ⓓ
5. Ⓐ Ⓑ Ⓒ Ⓓ   20. Ⓐ Ⓑ Ⓒ Ⓓ   35. Ⓐ Ⓑ Ⓒ Ⓓ   50. Ⓐ Ⓑ Ⓒ Ⓓ
6. Ⓐ Ⓑ Ⓒ Ⓓ   21. Ⓐ Ⓑ Ⓒ Ⓓ   36. Ⓐ Ⓑ Ⓒ Ⓓ   51. Ⓐ Ⓑ Ⓒ Ⓓ
7. Ⓐ Ⓑ Ⓒ Ⓓ   22. Ⓐ Ⓑ Ⓒ Ⓓ   37. Ⓐ Ⓑ Ⓒ Ⓓ   52. Ⓐ Ⓑ Ⓒ Ⓓ
8. Ⓐ Ⓑ Ⓒ Ⓓ   23. Ⓐ Ⓑ Ⓒ Ⓓ   38. Ⓐ Ⓑ Ⓒ Ⓓ   53. Ⓐ Ⓑ Ⓒ Ⓓ
9. Ⓐ Ⓑ Ⓒ Ⓓ   24. Ⓐ Ⓑ Ⓒ Ⓓ   39. Ⓐ Ⓑ Ⓒ Ⓓ   54. Ⓐ Ⓑ Ⓒ Ⓓ
10. Ⓐ Ⓑ Ⓒ Ⓓ   25. Ⓐ Ⓑ Ⓒ Ⓓ   40. Ⓐ Ⓑ Ⓒ Ⓓ   55. Ⓐ Ⓑ Ⓒ Ⓓ
11. Ⓐ Ⓑ Ⓒ Ⓓ   26. Ⓐ Ⓑ Ⓒ Ⓓ   41. Ⓐ Ⓑ Ⓒ Ⓓ   56. Ⓐ Ⓑ Ⓒ Ⓓ
12. Ⓐ Ⓑ Ⓒ Ⓓ   27. Ⓐ Ⓑ Ⓒ Ⓓ   42. Ⓐ Ⓑ Ⓒ Ⓓ   57. Ⓐ Ⓑ Ⓒ Ⓓ
13. Ⓐ Ⓑ Ⓒ Ⓓ   28. Ⓐ Ⓑ Ⓒ Ⓓ   43. Ⓐ Ⓑ Ⓒ Ⓓ   58. Ⓐ Ⓑ Ⓒ Ⓓ
14. Ⓐ Ⓑ Ⓒ Ⓓ   29. Ⓐ Ⓑ Ⓒ Ⓓ   44. Ⓐ Ⓑ Ⓒ Ⓓ   59. Ⓐ Ⓑ Ⓒ Ⓓ
15. Ⓐ Ⓑ Ⓒ Ⓓ   30. Ⓐ Ⓑ Ⓒ Ⓓ   45. Ⓐ Ⓑ Ⓒ Ⓓ   60. Ⓐ Ⓑ Ⓒ Ⓓ

PART B: FORMS COMPLETION

1. Ⓐ Ⓑ Ⓒ Ⓓ   9. Ⓐ Ⓑ Ⓒ Ⓓ   17. Ⓐ Ⓑ Ⓒ Ⓓ   25. Ⓐ Ⓑ Ⓒ Ⓓ
2. Ⓐ Ⓑ Ⓒ Ⓓ   10. Ⓐ Ⓑ Ⓒ Ⓓ   18. Ⓐ Ⓑ Ⓒ Ⓓ   26. Ⓐ Ⓑ Ⓒ Ⓓ
3. Ⓐ Ⓑ Ⓒ Ⓓ   11. Ⓐ Ⓑ Ⓒ Ⓓ   19. Ⓐ Ⓑ Ⓒ Ⓓ   27. Ⓐ Ⓑ Ⓒ Ⓓ
4. Ⓐ Ⓑ Ⓒ Ⓓ   12. Ⓐ Ⓑ Ⓒ Ⓓ   20. Ⓐ Ⓑ Ⓒ Ⓓ   28. Ⓐ Ⓑ Ⓒ Ⓓ
5. Ⓐ Ⓑ Ⓒ Ⓓ   13. Ⓐ Ⓑ Ⓒ Ⓓ   21. Ⓐ Ⓑ Ⓒ Ⓓ   29. Ⓐ Ⓑ Ⓒ Ⓓ
6. Ⓐ Ⓑ Ⓒ Ⓓ   14. Ⓐ Ⓑ Ⓒ Ⓓ   22. Ⓐ Ⓑ Ⓒ Ⓓ   30. Ⓐ Ⓑ Ⓒ Ⓓ
7. Ⓐ Ⓑ Ⓒ Ⓓ   15. Ⓐ Ⓑ Ⓒ Ⓓ   23. Ⓐ Ⓑ Ⓒ Ⓓ
8. Ⓐ Ⓑ Ⓒ Ⓓ   16. Ⓐ Ⓑ Ⓒ Ⓓ   24. Ⓐ Ⓑ Ⓒ Ⓓ

PART C: CODING AND MEMORY
SECTION 1—CODING

1. Ⓐ Ⓑ Ⓒ Ⓓ   10. Ⓐ Ⓑ Ⓒ Ⓓ   19. Ⓐ Ⓑ Ⓒ Ⓓ   28. Ⓐ Ⓑ Ⓒ Ⓓ
2. Ⓐ Ⓑ Ⓒ Ⓓ   11. Ⓐ Ⓑ Ⓒ Ⓓ   20. Ⓐ Ⓑ Ⓒ Ⓓ   29. Ⓐ Ⓑ Ⓒ Ⓓ
3. Ⓐ Ⓑ Ⓒ Ⓓ   12. Ⓐ Ⓑ Ⓒ Ⓓ   21. Ⓐ Ⓑ Ⓒ Ⓓ   30. Ⓐ Ⓑ Ⓒ Ⓓ
4. Ⓐ Ⓑ Ⓒ Ⓓ   13. Ⓐ Ⓑ Ⓒ Ⓓ   22. Ⓐ Ⓑ Ⓒ Ⓓ   31. Ⓐ Ⓑ Ⓒ Ⓓ
5. Ⓐ Ⓑ Ⓒ Ⓓ   14. Ⓐ Ⓑ Ⓒ Ⓓ   23. Ⓐ Ⓑ Ⓒ Ⓓ   32. Ⓐ Ⓑ Ⓒ Ⓓ
6. Ⓐ Ⓑ Ⓒ Ⓓ   15. Ⓐ Ⓑ Ⓒ Ⓓ   24. Ⓐ Ⓑ Ⓒ Ⓓ   33. Ⓐ Ⓑ Ⓒ Ⓓ
7. Ⓐ Ⓑ Ⓒ Ⓓ   16. Ⓐ Ⓑ Ⓒ Ⓓ   25. Ⓐ Ⓑ Ⓒ Ⓓ   34. Ⓐ Ⓑ Ⓒ Ⓓ
8. Ⓐ Ⓑ Ⓒ Ⓓ   17. Ⓐ Ⓑ Ⓒ Ⓓ   26. Ⓐ Ⓑ Ⓒ Ⓓ   35. Ⓐ Ⓑ Ⓒ Ⓓ
9. Ⓐ Ⓑ Ⓒ Ⓓ   18. Ⓐ Ⓑ Ⓒ Ⓓ   27. Ⓐ Ⓑ Ⓒ Ⓓ   36. Ⓐ Ⓑ Ⓒ Ⓓ

SECTION 2—MEMORY

37. Ⓐ Ⓑ Ⓒ Ⓓ   46. Ⓐ Ⓑ Ⓒ Ⓓ   55. Ⓐ Ⓑ Ⓒ Ⓓ   64. Ⓐ Ⓑ Ⓒ Ⓓ
38. Ⓐ Ⓑ Ⓒ Ⓓ   47. Ⓐ Ⓑ Ⓒ Ⓓ   56. Ⓐ Ⓑ Ⓒ Ⓓ   65. Ⓐ Ⓑ Ⓒ Ⓓ
39. Ⓐ Ⓑ Ⓒ Ⓓ   48. Ⓐ Ⓑ Ⓒ Ⓓ   57. Ⓐ Ⓑ Ⓒ Ⓓ   66. Ⓐ Ⓑ Ⓒ Ⓓ
40. Ⓐ Ⓑ Ⓒ Ⓓ   49. Ⓐ Ⓑ Ⓒ Ⓓ   58. Ⓐ Ⓑ Ⓒ Ⓓ   67. Ⓐ Ⓑ Ⓒ Ⓓ
41. Ⓐ Ⓑ Ⓒ Ⓓ   50. Ⓐ Ⓑ Ⓒ Ⓓ   59. Ⓐ Ⓑ Ⓒ Ⓓ   68. Ⓐ Ⓑ Ⓒ Ⓓ
42. Ⓐ Ⓑ Ⓒ Ⓓ   51. Ⓐ Ⓑ Ⓒ Ⓓ   60. Ⓐ Ⓑ Ⓒ Ⓓ   69. Ⓐ Ⓑ Ⓒ Ⓓ
43. Ⓐ Ⓑ Ⓒ Ⓓ   52. Ⓐ Ⓑ Ⓒ Ⓓ   61. Ⓐ Ⓑ Ⓒ Ⓓ   70. Ⓐ Ⓑ Ⓒ Ⓓ
44. Ⓐ Ⓑ Ⓒ Ⓓ   53. Ⓐ Ⓑ Ⓒ Ⓓ   62. Ⓐ Ⓑ Ⓒ Ⓓ   71. Ⓐ Ⓑ Ⓒ Ⓓ
45. Ⓐ Ⓑ Ⓒ Ⓓ   54. Ⓐ Ⓑ Ⓒ Ⓓ   63. Ⓐ Ⓑ Ⓒ Ⓓ   72. Ⓐ Ⓑ Ⓒ Ⓓ

PART D: PERSONAL CHARACTERISTICS AND EXPERIENCE INVENTORY

(236 Questions—not included here)

ADDRESS CHECKING SAMPLE QUESTIONS

Look at the row of information for sample question 1, which is labeled "S1" below. Carefully but quickly compare the **List to Be Checked** with the **Correct List**. Then decide if there are **No Errors** (select A), an error in the **Address Only** (select B), an error in the **ZIP Code Only** (select C), or an error in **Both** the address and the ZIP code (select D). Record your response to the sample questions in the **Sample Answer Grid** below. Complete the other three samples given, S2, S3, and S4, and record your responses on the **Sample Answer Grid**.

A. No Errors	B. Address Only	C. ZIP Code Only	D. Both

Correct List

	Address	ZIP Code
S1.	432 Rosewood Ct. Pasadena, CA	91106
S2.	1977 Hully Street Austin, TX	78734-1141
S3.	648 Central Dr. New York, NY	10034
S4.	9812 Pine Ave. Chicago, IL	60467-5113

List to Be Checked

Address	ZIP Code
432 Rosewood Ct. Pasedena, CA *B*	91106
1977 Holly Street Austin, TX *D*	78734-1114
648 Central Dr. New York, NY *C*	10054
9812 Pine Ave. Chicago, IL *A*	60467-5113

Sample Answer Grid

S1.	Ⓐ	Ⓑ	Ⓒ	Ⓓ
S2.	Ⓐ	Ⓑ	Ⓒ	Ⓓ
S3.	Ⓐ	Ⓑ	Ⓒ	Ⓓ
S4.	Ⓐ	Ⓑ	Ⓒ	Ⓓ

Completed Sample Answer Grid

S1.	Ⓐ	●	Ⓒ	Ⓓ
S2.	Ⓐ	Ⓑ	Ⓒ	●
S3.	Ⓐ	Ⓑ	●	Ⓓ
S4.	●	Ⓑ	Ⓒ	Ⓓ

In sample 1, the address in the **List to Be Checked** shows Pasedena, but the **Correct List** shows Pasadena. So there is an error in the address. Since the Zip codes are exactly the same, the correct answer is **B—Address Only**.

In sample 2, the address in the **List to Be Checked** shows Holly Street, but the **Correct List** shows Hully Street. So there is an error in the address. The **List to Be Checked** also shows an error in the ZIP code. The last four numbers are 1114, and they are 1141 in the **Correct List**. Because there is an error in the address and in the ZIP code, the correct answer is **D—Both**.

In sample 3, the addresses in the **List to Be Checked** and the **Correct List** are exactly the same, but there is an error in the ZIP code on the **List to Be Checked**. The **List to Be Checked** shows 10054, but the **Correct List** shows 10034. So there is an error in the ZIP code. The correct answer is **C—ZIP Code Only**.

In sample 4, the addresses in the **List to Be Checked** and the **Correct List** are exactly the same. The ZIP codes are also exactly the same. So the correct answer is **A—No Errors**.

Now turn to the next page and begin the address checking test.

PART A: ADDRESS CHECKING

For the following 60 items, compare the address in the **Correct List** with the address in the **List to Be Checked**. Determine if there are **No Errors** (answer A), an error in the **Address Only** (answer B), an error in the **ZIP Code Only** (answer C), or an error in **Both** (answer D). Mark your answers in the Address Checking section of the answer sheet. You have 11 minutes to complete this test.

A. No Errors	B. Address Only	C. ZIP Code Only	D. Both

	Correct List		List to Be Checked	
	Address	*ZIP Code*	*Address*	*ZIP Code*
1.	6085 Millcreek Ct. College Station, TX	77845	6805 Millcreek Ct. College Station, TX	77845
2.	16045 State Road 113 Madison, WI	53704-5767	16045 State Road 123 Madison, WI	53704-5767
3.	8222 Hidden Spring Lane Pittsburgh, PA	15238-6056	8222 Hidden Spring Lane Pittsburgh, PA	15238-6056
4.	796 Tipperary Rd. Manahawkin, NJ	08050	796 Tipperary Rd. Manahawkin, NJ	08850
5.	9045 Strickland Dr. Murfreesboro, TN	37127	9045 Strickland Dr. Murfreesboro, TN	37217
6.	7767 Meadowlands Way Greenville, SC	29615-0672	7767 Meadowlands Lane Greenville, SC	29615-0672
7.	P.O. Box 8243 Garden Grove, CA	92840	P.O. Box 8243 Garden Grove, CO	93840
8.	499 Newhall Street Hamden, CT	06517-8460	499 Newhill Street Hamden, CT	06516-8460
9.	7622 Business Park Cir. Saint Augustine, Florida	32095-1351	7622 Business Park Cir. Saint Augustine, Florida	32095-1351
10.	8877 Drawbridge Court Silver Spring, MD	20902-8139	8877 Drawbridge Court Silver Spring, MD	20902-8139
11.	5933 Corboy Road Hermitage, TN	37076	5933 Cowboy Road Hermitage, TN	30776

	Correct List		List to Be Checked	
	Address	*ZIP Code*	*Address*	*ZIP Code*
12.	1375 Aldoran Rd. Saginaw, MI	48603	1375 Aldoran Rd. Saginaw, MI	48693
13.	8335 Manzanita Hills Redding, CA	96001-5757	8335 Manzanita Hills Redding, CA	96001-5767
14.	3298 50th Ave. N Birmingham, Alabama	35207-2078	3298 50th Ave. N Birmington, Alabama	55207-2078
15.	6644 Ruth Hentz Ave. Panama City, FL	32405	6644 Ruth Hentz Ave. Panama City, FL	32450
16.	5073 Worchester Ave. Honolulu, HI	96818-4790	5073 Worchester Ct. Honolulu, HI	96818-4790
17.	2242 Meadowbridge Trl. Indianapolis, IN	46217	2242 Meadowbridge Trl. Indianapolis, IN	46217
18.	956 Jekyll Island Rd. Jessup, GA	31545-3457	956 Jekyll Island Rd. Jessup, MA	31545-3457
19.	9531 Torchiere Court Suwannee, FL	32692	9531 Torchiere Court Suwannee, FL	32692
20.	9698 Montague Place Florence, SC	29501-1514	9688 Montague Place Florence, SC	29501-1514
21.	3846 Calle Yaguez Villa Bornquen, PR	00725	3848 Calle Yaguez Villa Bornquen, PR	07725
22.	254 Oakcrest Dr. NW Salem, OR	97304-6455	254 Oakcrest Dr. NW Salem, OR	97304-6855
23.	8933 Denmont Ave. SW Marion, OH	44646-7560	8933 Denmont Ave. NW Marion, OH	44646-7560
24.	2080 N. Mannheim Road Melrose Park, IL	60164	2080 N. Mannheim Road Melrose Park, IL	80164
25.	9325 Creekview Avenue Trenton, NJ	08610-8532	9325 Creekside Avenue Trenton, NJ	06810-8532

	Correct List		**List to Be Checked**	
	Address	*ZIP Code*	*Address*	*ZIP Code*
26.	Rural Route 23 Centreville, VA	20120	Rural Route 23 Centerville, VA	20120
27.	8933 Phoenix St. Wilkes Barre, PA	18702-0607	8933 Phoenix St. Wilkes Barre, PA	18702-0667
28.	78 Emerson Rd. Apt. 4B Needham, MA	02492	78 Emerson Rd. Apt. 6B Needham, MA	02429
29.	5343 Upper Brandon Pl. Marietta, GA	30068-7876	5343 Upper Brandon Pl. Marietta, GA	30068-7876
30.	3490 E 16th Street Apopka, FL	32703-1736	3499 E 16th Street Apopka, FL	32703-1736
31.	9347 S Kalsman Avenue Compton, CA	90222	9347 S Kalsman Avenue Compton, CA	90322
32.	5711 S 123rd Street Omaha, NE	68137	5711 S 133rd Street Omaha, NE	86137
33.	7299 Rampart Chase Brightwood, VA	22715	7299 Rampart Chase Brightwood, VA	22715
34.	11311 E Tecumseh St. Tulsa, OK	74116-9080	11311 E Tecumseh St. Tulsa, OK	74116-3080
35.	6222 Persimmon Drive Killeen, Texas	76543-8732	6222 Persival Drive Killeen, Texas	76543-8732
36.	5090 S 118th Street Seattle, WA	98178-3669	5099 S 116th Street Seattle, WA	98718-3669
37.	5856 Marthaville Pike Smithfield, WV	26437-5211	5856 Marshville Pike Smithfield, WV	26437-5211
38.	3647 Edson Avenue Bronx, NY	10466-9229	3647 Edson Avenue Bronx, NY	19066-9229
39.	844 Nightingale Terr. Hope Mills, NC	28348	844 Nightingale Terr. Hope Mills, NM	28348
40.	5464 Church Hill Road Greeneville, TN	37743	5464 Church Hall Road Greeneville, TN	37743

	Correct List		**List to Be Checked**	
	Address	*ZIP Code*	*Address*	*ZIP Code*
41.	15422 Glencoe Ave. Cleveland, Ohio	44110-2233	15422 Glencoe Ave. Cleveland, Ohio	44110-2233
42.	9374 Fall Creek Run Chesapeake, VA	23322-5689	9374 Fall Creek Rd. Chesapeake, VA	23322-5699
43.	7310 Pinon Dr. Boulder, CO	80303-6365	7310 Pinion Dr. Boulder, CO	80303-6365
44.	4326 Remington St. Bridgeport, CT	06610-0787	4326 Remington St. Bridgeport, CT	06610-0787
45.	4387 Saginaw Road Mayersville, MS	39113-7591	4387 Saginaw Road Meyersville, MS	39133-7591
46.	2040 Serviceberry Court Louisville, KY	40241-7021	2040 Serviceberry Court Liston, KY	40361-7021
47.	P.O. Box 11223 Fort Wayne, IN	46856	P.O. Box 11323 Fort Wayne, IN	46856
48.	3445 Panamint Dr. Fountain Hills, AZ	85268	3445 Panamint Dr. Fountain Hills, AZ	85268
49.	5468 Owyhee Ln. Caldwell, ID	83605-7343	5468 Owyhee Ln. Caldwell, ID	83605-7334
50.	766 Markley Dr. Newark, DE	19713-1323	766 Markley Dr. Newark, DE	19713-1323
51.	13344 W 128th Terrace Shawnee Mission, KS	66213-3424	13344 W 128th Trace Shawnee Mission, KS	66213-3424
52.	8788 Rutledge Cir. Nadeau, MI	49863	8788 Rutledge Cir. Nadeau, ME	69863
53.	7845 NW Island Lake Rd. Duluth, MN	55803	7845 NW Island Lake Rd. Duluth, MN	55443
54.	9089 N Kristopher Bnd Saint Charles, MO	63303-5464	9089 N Cristopher Bnd Saint Charles, MO	63303-5464
55.	2458 Amber Oaks Ct. Dupree, SD	57623	2458 Amber Oaks Ct. Dupree, SD	75633

	Correct List		**List to Be Checked**	
	Address	*ZIP Code*	*Address*	*ZIP Code*
56.	1245 Parkside Center Blvd. Dallas, TX	75244-6756	1245 Parkside Center Blvd. Dallas, TX	75244-9756
57.	1020 N Heatherstone Drive Shreveport, LA	71129-8644	1020 N Featherstone Drive Shreveport, LA	71129-8644
58.	3247 W Fortification St. Falmouth, KY	41040	3247 W Fortification St. Falmouth, KY	41920
59.	58355 S. 14th Place Boise, ID	83702-1446	58355 S. 16th Place Boise, ID	83720-1446
60.	5472 Cranbrook Drive Kissimmee, FL	34758	5472 Cranbrook Drive Kissimmee, FL	34758

PART B: FORMS COMPLETION

Look at this sample form and answer the two questions below it. Mark your answers in the sample answer grid that follows the questions.

Sample Form

1. First Name	2. Middle Name	3. Last Name
4. Street Address		
5. City	6. State	7. ZIP Code

8. Fee
$ _____
	9. Date
	  9a. Day _____
	  9b. Month _____
	  9c. Year _____	

S1. Which of these would be a correct entry for Box 6?
   A. "2542 Oak Avenue"
   B. "November"
   C. "$6.80"
   D. "Nevada"

S2. Where should the middle name be entered on the form?
   A. Box 1
   B. Box 2
   C. Box 3
   D. Box 4

Sample Answer Grid				
S1.	Ⓐ	Ⓑ	Ⓒ	Ⓓ
S2.	Ⓐ	Ⓑ	Ⓒ	Ⓓ

Completed Sample Answer Grid				
S1.	Ⓐ	Ⓑ	Ⓒ	●
S2.	Ⓐ	●	Ⓒ	Ⓓ

On the form, Box 6 is labeled "State." So the correct answer for sample question 1 is "D. Nevada," which is the only state listed among the answers. Box 2 is labeled "Middle Name," so the correct answer for sample question 2 is "B. Box 2." The completed sample answer grid above shows these correct answers filled in.

Directions: Each of the following forms is followed by questions based on that form. Each part of the form is labeled with a number or a number and a letter. You will have 15 minutes to complete the 30 questions in this section.

Set 1: Forms Completion
Questions 1 through 6 are based on Form 1.

Form 1

CERTIFIED MAIL RECEIPT	
For Domestic Use Only	
No Insurance Coverage Provided	

1. Postage	$	
2. Certified Fee	$	
3. Return Receipt Fee (Signature of Receiver of Mail Required)	$	**7. Postmark Here**
4. Restricted Delivery Fee (Signature of Receiver of Mail Required)	$	
5. Total Postage and Fees	$	

6. Mail Sent To

6a. Name _____

6b. Street, Apt. No., or PO Box No. _____

6c. City, State, ZIP _____

1. Where would you enter the fee for restricted delivery?
   A. Box 1
   B. Box 3
   C. Box 4
   D. Line 6b

2. Which of these would be a correct entry for Box 7?
   A. "$3.50"
   B. A signature
   C. A postmark
   D. A checkmark

3. How would you indicate that a return receipt has been paid for?
   A. By entering the fee amount in Box 2
   B. By entering the fee amount in Box 3
   C. By entering a checkmark in Box 7
   D. By entering the name on Line 6a

4. Which of these would be a correct entry for Line 6c?
   A. "$2.70"
   B. A checkmark
   C. "Connie Marcus"
   D. "Lincoln, Nebraska 68516"

5. You could enter a dollar amount in each of the following boxes EXCEPT which one?
   A. Box 1
   B. Box 3
   C. Box 5
   D. Box 7

6. Where would you indicate that the postage charge is $1.20?
   A. Box 1
   B. Box 3
   C. Box 4
   D. Box 5

Set 2: Forms Completion

Questions 7 through 12 are based on Form 2.

Form 2

CERTIFICATE OF BULK MAILING

Mailer: Fill in this statement in ink. Affix meter stamp or uncanceled postage stamps covering fee in the block to the right.

1. Meter stamp or postage in payment of fee must be affixed here and canceled by postmarking, including date.

2. Fee for Certificate

	USE CURRENT RATE CHART
2a. Up to 1,000 pieces	
2b. For each additional 1,000 pieces or fraction	
2c. Duplicate copy of certificate	

3. Mailing Information

3a. Number of Identical Pieces	3b. Class of Mail	3c. Postage on Each	3d. Number of Pieces to the Pound	3e. Total Number of Pounds	3f. Total Postage Paid	3g. Fee Paid

4. Mailed For

5. Mailed By

Postmaster's Certificate

It is hereby certified that the above-described mailing has been received and the number of pieces and postage verified.

6. _____
(Signature of Postmaster or Designee)

7. Which of these would be a correct entry for Box 3a?
   A. A checkmark
   B. "$20.05"
   C. "Donald Delaney"
   D. "2,500"

8. Where would you enter a postmark?
   A. Box 1
   B. Box 2
   C. Box 3c
   D. Box 3g

9. How would you indicate that fewer than 1,000 pieces will be mailed?
   A. Circle Line 2b
   B. Affix a meter stamp in Box 2
   C. Enter the number of pieces in Box 3a
   D. Sign the form in Box 6

10. Which of these would be a correct entry for Box 3b?
    A. "$10.00"
    B. "30"
    C. "Star Corporation"
    D. "Third Class"

11. The postage on each piece of mail will be 18 cents. Where would you indicate this?
    A. Box 1
    B. Box 3a
    C. Box 3c
    D. Box 3f

12. Where would you indicate that the material is being mailed by Manuel DeSoto?
    A. Box 1
    B. Box 4
    C. Box 5
    D. Box 6

Form 3

STAMP VENDING MACHINE REIMBURSEMENT REQUEST

For Customer Use

1. **Customer Information:**

   1a. Name _____

   1b. Address _____

   _____

   _____

   1c. Daytime Phone Number (include area code) _____

2. **Loss Information:**

   2a. Amount of Loss $_____   2b. Date of Loss _____   2c. Time of Loss

   ❑ AM

   ❑ PM

3. **Machine Information:** Machine ID (6-digit number on front of vending machine) _____

4. **Occurrence Information:** What Happened? (circle all that apply)

4a. Did not receive product	4f. Money not returned
4b. Incorrect change given	4g. Currency lost
4c. Did not register/jammed	4h. Coin lost
4d. No change given	4i. Credit/debit lost
4e. No credit shown	4j. Other (enter in "Comments")

5. **Comments:** (optional)

For Postal Service Use

6. **Paid by**	7. **Date**

8. **Action Taken** (circle one)

   8a. Paid   8b. Not Paid

9. **Sales and Services Associate Signature** _____

13. Which boxes could be filled out by the customer?
    A. Box 1b and Box 1c
    B. Box 3 and Box 4
    C. Box 4 and Box 5
    D. All of the above

14. Where would you indicate that this reimbursement request was not paid?
    A. Line 2a
    B. Line 4f
    C. Box 5
    D. Line 8b

15. Which of these would be a correct entry for Line 2b?
    A. "7/14/06"
    B. "$1.00"
    C. A checkmark
    D. "John Markham"

16. Where would the machine ID number be entered?
    A. Box 2
    B. Box 3
    C. Box 5
    D. Box 8

17. When the customer, John Markham, attempted to buy stamps, the machine jammed and his dollar bill was lost. How would he indicate this?
    A. Circle Line 4b and Line 4c
    B. Circle Line 4c and Line 4e
    C. Circle Line 4c and Line 4g
    D. Circle Line 4g and Line 4j

18. The customer wishes to indicate that he spoke to a postal representative on the day of the occurrence. How would the customer indicate this?
    A. Add the information in Box 1
    B. Circle Line 4a
    C. Sign the form in Box 9
    D. Fill in this information in Box 5

Set 4: Forms Completion

Questions 19 through 24 are based on Form 4.

Form 4

EXPRESS MAIL			MAILING LABEL		
ORIGIN: **POSTAL SERVICE USE ONLY**			**DELIVERY:** **POSTAL SERVICE USE ONLY**		
1a. PO ZIP Code	1b. Day of Delivery ❏ Next ❏ 2nd	1c. Postage $	6a. Delivery Attempt Mo. ____ Day ____	6b. Time ❏ AM ❏ PM	6c. Employee Signature _____
2a. Date Accepted	2b. Scheduled Delivery Date	2c. Return Receipt Fee $	7a. Delivery Date Mo. ____ Day ____	7b. Time ❏ AM ❏ PM	7c. Employee Signature _____
3a. Time Accepted ❏ AM ❏ PM	3b. Scheduled Delivery Time ❏ Noon ❏ 3 PM	3c. COD Fee $ 3d. Insurance Fee $			
4a. Flat Rate ❏ OR Weight ___ lbs. ___ oz.	4b. Military Delivery Time ❏ 2nd Day ❏ 3rd Day	4c. Total Postage and Fees $			
5a. Acceptance Employee Initials _____					

CUSTOMER USE ONLY	

Payment by
  8a. ❏ Express Mail Account Number
    _____
	9a. ❏ Waiver of Signature

	9b. No Delivery ❏ Weekend ❏ Holiday
8b. ❏ Postal Service Account Number _____	9c. Customer Signature _____

10a. FROM: (Please Print)
    Phone (   ) _____
	10b. TO: (Please Print)
	    Phone ( ) _____

19. Which of these would be a correct entry
    for Box 9a?
    A. A checkmark
    B. A signature
    C. "125835"
    D. "July"

20. How could you indicate the scheduled
    delivery time for this mail?
    A. Enter the date in Box 2a
    B. Enter a checkmark in Box 3a
    C. Enter a checkmark in Box 3b
    D. Enter a checkmark in Box 4a

21. A time would be a correct entry for
    every box EXCEPT which one?
    A. Box 3a
    B. Box 4a
    C. Box 6b
    D. Box 7b

22. The mail is scheduled for delivery on
    the third day. Where would you indicate
    this?
    A. Box 1b
    B. Box 2b
    C. Box 4b
    D. Box 7a

23. Which boxes should contain
    checkmarks?
    A. Box 1a and Box 1b
    B. Box 3a and Box 3b
    C. Box 7a and Box 7b
    D. None of the above

24. Which of these would be a correct entry
    for Box 10a?
    A. "(555) 432-8693"
    B. "$9.90"
    C. A signature
    D. "9/9/06"

Questions 25 through 30 are based on Form 5.

Form 5

COD
Copy 1: Delivery Unit

Delivery Employee: Remove Copies 1 (Delivery Unit Copy) and 2 (Mailer's Copy) at Time of Delivery.

Collect the amount shown below if customer pays by CHECK made payable to the mailer.	Collect the amount shown below if customer pays in CASH (includes money order fee or fees).
1. Check Amount $	**2. Cash** Amount $

3a. ❑ Registered Mail	3b. ❑ Express Mail	3c. ❑ Form 3849-D Requested
4. Date of Mailing	**5. ❑ Remit COD Charges to Sender via Express Mail**	

6. From:	**7. To:**

8. Delivered By	**9. Date Delivered**	**10. Check Number**
11. Date Payment Sent to Mailer	**12. Date Form 3849-D Sent**	**13. Money Order Number(s)**

DO NOT allow the recipient to examine the contents before payment.
DO NOT deliver this article until payment is collected.
If payment is by check, enter check number above.
Have customer sign Form 3849.

25. The customer pays the carrier $85.60 in cash. Where would you indicate this?
    A. Box 1
    B. Box 2
    C. Box 5
    D. Box 11

26. Where would you indicate that Form 3849-D was sent?
    A. Box 3a
    B. Box 3c
    C. Box 10
    D. Box 12

27. Which of these would be a correct entry for Box 10?
    A. "5886"
    B. "10/11/06"
    C. "$85.60"
    D. "Cory Matlock"

28. Which box(es) should contain a date?
    A. Box 3c
    B. Box 4
    C. Box 4 and Box 8
    D. Box 9 and Box 13

29. How would you indicate that this COD has been sent by Express Mail?
    A. Enter an amount in Box 1
    B. Check Box 3b
    C. Check Box 5
    D. Enter a number in Box 12

30. Where would you indicate the date the mail was delivered?
    A. Box 9
    B. Box 10
    C. Box 11
    D. Box 12

PART C: CODING AND MEMORY

SECTION 1—CODING

Coding Exercise

Choose the correct delivery route, based on the Coding Guide, for each of the following 4 items and mark your answers on the answer sheet below. You have 2 minutes to complete this practice exercise. This exercise will not be scored.

CODING GUIDE

Address Range	Delivery Route
400–599 Apple Tree Lane	
31–70 Vernon Dr.	A
5100–5199 Old Hwy. 65 N	
600–700 Apple Tree Lane	
5200–5360 Old Hwy. 65 N	B
151–340 Summit Rd.	
9000–13000 W Village Cir.	C
71–200 Vernon Dr.	
All mail that doesn't fall in one of the address ranges listed above	D

	Address	Delivery Route
1.	69 Vernon Dr.	A B C D
2.	7500 W Village Cir.	A B C D
3.	157 Summit Rd.	A B C D
4.	505 Apple Tree Lane	A B C D

Sample Answer Grid				
1.	Ⓐ	Ⓑ	Ⓒ	Ⓓ
2.	Ⓐ	Ⓑ	Ⓒ	Ⓓ
3.	Ⓐ	Ⓑ	Ⓒ	Ⓓ
4.	Ⓐ	Ⓑ	Ⓒ	Ⓓ

Completed Sample Answer Grid				
1.	●	Ⓑ	Ⓒ	Ⓓ
2.	Ⓐ	Ⓑ	Ⓒ	●
3.	Ⓐ	Ⓑ	●	Ⓓ
4.	●	Ⓑ	Ⓒ	Ⓓ

CODING TEST

Choose the correct delivery route, based on the Coding Guide, for each of the following 36 items (items 1 through 36) and mark your answers in the Coding section of the Answer Sheet. You have 6 minutes to complete this test.

CODING GUIDE

Address Range	Delivery Route
400–599 Apple Tree Lane 31–70 Vernon Dr. 5100–5199 Old Hwy. 65 N	A
600–700 Apple Tree Lane 5200–5360 Old Hwy. 65 N	B
151–340 Summit Rd. 9000–13000 W Village Cir. 71–200 Vernon Dr.	C
All mail that doesn't fall in one of the address ranges listed above	D

	Address	Delivery Route
1.	5300 Old Hwy. 65 N	A B C D
2.	610 Apple Tree Lane	A B C D
3.	300 Vernon Dr.	A B C D
4.	5289 Hwy. 65 N	A B C D
5.	589 Apple Tree Lane	A B C D
6.	10000 W Village Cir.	A B C D
7.	5177 Old Hwy. 65 N	A B C D
8.	502 Vernon Dr.	A B C D
9.	5344 Old Hwy. 65 N	A B C D
10.	12999 W Village Cir.	A B C D

Address	Delivery Route
11. 310 Summit Rd.	A B (C) D
12. 644 Apple Tree Lane	A (B) C D
13. 4792 Old Hwy. 65 N	A B C (D)
14. 32 Vernon Dr.	(A) B C D
15. 175 Summit Rd.	A B (C) D
16. 9500 W Village Ct.	A B C (D)
17. 611 Apple Tree Lane	A (B) C D
18. 5302 Old Hwy. 75 N	A B C (D)
19. 623 Apple Tree Lane	A (B) C D
20. 5355 Old Hwy. 65 N	A (B) C D
21. 1170 W Village Cir.	A B (C) D
22. 592 Apple Tree Lane	(A) B C D
23. 58 Vernon Dr.	(A) B C D
24. 10408 W Village Cir.	A B (C) D
25. 146 Summit Rd.	A B C (D)
26. 165 Vernon Dr.	A B (C) D
27. 1076 W Village Cir.	A B C (D)
28. 5277 Old Hwy. 65 N	A (B) C D
29. 534 Apple Tree Lane	(A) B C D
30. 5353 Old Hwy. 65 N	A (B) C D
31. 828 Apple Tree Lane	A B C (D)
32. 653 Apple Tree Lane	A (B) C D
33. 372 Summit Dr.	A B C (D)
34. 10682 W Village Cir.	A B (C) D
35. 96 Vernon Dr.	A B (C) D
36. 5156 Old Hwy. 65 N	A B C (D)

SECTION 2—MEMORY

Memory Study Period 1

Use the time given to memorize the information in the following Coding Guide.

CODING GUIDE

Address Range	Delivery Route
400–599 Apple Tree Lane	
31–70 Vernon Dr.	A
5100–5199 Old Hwy. 65 N	
600–700 Apple Tree Lane	
5200–5360 Old Hwy. 65 N	B
151–340 Summit Rd.	
9000–13000 W Village Cir.	C
71–200 Vernon Dr.	
All mail that doesn't fall in one of the address ranges listed above	D

Memory Exercise

Choose the correct delivery route, based on your memory of the information in the Coding Guide, for each of the following 8 items and mark your answers on the answer sheet below. You have 90 seconds to complete this practice exercise. This exercise will not be scored.

Address	Delivery Route
1. 38 Vernon Dr.	A B C D
2. 5222 Old Hwy. 65 N	A B C D
3. 321 Summit Rd.	A B C D
4. 426 Apple Tree Lane	A B C D
5. 426 Summit Rd.	A B C D
6. 481 Apple Time Lane	A B C D
7. 5035 Old Hwy. 65 N	A B C D
8. 9802 W Village Cir.	A B C D

Sample Answer Grid				
1.	Ⓐ	Ⓑ	Ⓒ	Ⓓ
2.	Ⓐ	Ⓑ	Ⓒ	Ⓓ
3.	Ⓐ	Ⓑ	Ⓒ	Ⓓ
4.	Ⓐ	Ⓑ	Ⓒ	Ⓓ
5.	Ⓐ	Ⓑ	Ⓒ	Ⓓ
6.	Ⓐ	Ⓑ	Ⓒ	Ⓓ
7.	Ⓐ	Ⓑ	Ⓒ	Ⓓ
8.	Ⓐ	Ⓑ	Ⓒ	Ⓓ

Completed Sample Answer Grid				
1.	●	Ⓑ	Ⓒ	Ⓓ
2.	Ⓐ	●	Ⓒ	Ⓓ
3.	Ⓐ	Ⓑ	●	Ⓓ
4.	●	Ⓑ	Ⓒ	Ⓓ
5.	Ⓐ	Ⓑ	Ⓒ	●
6.	Ⓐ	Ⓑ	Ⓒ	●
7.	Ⓐ	Ⓑ	Ⓒ	●
8.	Ⓐ	Ⓑ	●	Ⓓ

Memory Study Period 2
Use the time given to memorize the information in the following Coding Guide.

CODING GUIDE

Address Range	Delivery Route
400–599 Apple Tree Lane	
31–70 Vernon Dr.	A
5100–5199 Old Hwy. 65 N	
600–700 Apple Tree Lane	
5200–5360 Old Hwy. 65 N	B
151–340 Summit Rd.	
9000–13000 W Village Cir.	C
71–200 Vernon Dr.	
All mail that doesn't fall in one of the address ranges listed above	D

MEMORY TEST
Choose the correct delivery route, based on your memory of the information in the Coding Guide, for each of the following 36 items (items 37 through 72) and mark your answers in the Memory section of the Answer Sheet. You have 7 minutes to complete this test.

	Address	Delivery Route
37.	194 Vernon Dr.	A B C D
38.	59 Vernon Dr.	A B C D
39.	11355 W Village Cir	A B C D
40.	630 Apple Tree Lane	A B C D
41.	402 Vernon Dr.	A B C D
42.	1266 N Village Cir.	A B C D
43.	690 Apple Tree Lane	A B C D
44.	520 Apple Tree Lane	A B C D
45.	5130 Old Hwy 65 N	A B C D

#131 04-11-2018 12:50PM
Item(s) checked out to LEUNG, YIM THONG.

TITLE: Barron's comprehensive postal exa
BARCODE: 39043066022851
DUE DATE: 05-02-18

DCPL Westlake - To Renew Items, Call
650-991-8071 www.dalycitylibrary.org

                    VB

Address	Delivery Route
46. 601 Apple Tree Lane	A B C D
47. 9264 W Village Cir.	A B C D
48. 145 Kernon Dr.	A B C D
49. 10386 W Village Cir.	A B C D
50. 626 Apple Tree Lane	A B C D
51. 5266 Old Hwy. 65 N	A B C D
52. 525 Apple Tree Dr.	A B C D
53. 5107 Old Hwy. 65 N	A B C D
54. 275 Summit Rd.	A B C D
55. 52 Vernon Dr.	A B C D
56. 6297 Apple Tree Lane	A B C D
57. 5243 Old Hwy. 65 N	A B C D
58. 5199 Old Hwy. 65 N	A B C D
59. 5399 Old Hwy. 65 N	A B C D
60. 170 Vernon Dr.	A B C D
61. 9342 W Village Cir.	A B C D
62. 5100 Old Hwy. 65 N	A B C D
63. 629 Apple Tree Lane	A B C D
64. 5899 Old Hwy. 65 N	A B C D
65. 120090 W Village Cir.	A B C D
66. 600 Apple Tree Lane	A B C D
67. 66 Vernon Dr.	A B C D
68. 179 Summit Rd.	A B C D
69. 11983 W Village Cir.	A B C D
70. 567 Apple Tree Lane	A B C D
71. 5359 Old Hwy. 65 N	A B C D
72. 14787 W Village Cir.	A B C D

PART D: PERSONAL CHARACTERISTICS AND EXPERIENCE INVENTORY

On the actual exam, the next part that you would take is Part D: Personal Characteristics and Experience Inventory. This part of the exam is 90 minutes long and has 236 items. Because there is no particular advantage to practicing your responses on these statements and questions, no tests are given here for them.

Scoring and Explanations for Practice Examination 1

ANSWER KEY

Part A: Address Checking

1. B	11. D	21. D	31. C	41. A	51. B
2. B	12. C	22. C	32. D	42. D	52. D
3. A	13. C	23. B	33. A	43. B	53. C
4. C	14. D	24. C	34. C	44. A	54. B
5. C	15. C	25. D	35. B	45. D	55. C
6. B	16. B	26. B	36. D	46. D	56. C
7. D	17. A	27. C	37. B	47. B	57. B
8. D	18. B	28. D	38. C	48. A	58. C
9. A	19. A	29. A	39. B	49. C	59. D
10. A	20. B	30. B	40. B	50. A	60. A

Part B: Forms Completion

1. C	6. A	11. C	16. B	21. B	26. D
2. C	7. D	12. C	17. C	22. C	27. A
3. B	8. A	13. D	18. D	23. B	28. B
4. D	9. C	14. D	19. A	24. A	29. B
5. D	10. D	15. A	20. C	25. B	30. A

Part C: Coding Test

1. B	7. A	13. D	19. B	25. D	31. D
2. B	8. D	14. A	20. B	26. C	32. B
3. D	9. B	15. C	21. C	27. D	33. D
4. D	10. C	16. D	22. A	28. B	34. C
5. A	11. C	17. B	23. A	29. A	35. C
6. C	12. B	18. D	24. C	30. B	36. A

Part C: Memory Test

37. C	43. B	49. C	55. A	61. C	67. A
38. A	44. A	50. B	56. D	62. A	68. C
39. C	45. A	51. B	57. B	63. B	69. C
40. B	46. B	52. D	58. A	64. D	70. A
41. D	47. C	53. A	59. D	65. D	71. B
42. D	48. D	54. C	60. C	66. B	72. D

SCORING

Part A: Address Checking

Enter the number you got right: _____

Enter the number you got wrong
(not including those left blank): _____

Divide the number wrong by 3
(or multiply by 1/3): _____

Subtract this answer from the number right: – _____

Raw Score _____

Part B: Forms Completion

Enter the number you got right
(no penalty for guessing): Raw Score _____

Part C: Coding and Memory

Enter the number you got right: _____

Enter the number you got wrong
(not including those left blank): _____

Divide the number wrong by 3
(or multiply by 1/3): _____

Subtract this answer from the number right: – _____

Raw Score _____

Part D: Personal Characteristics and Experience Inventory

Scoring system not given.

Explanations

PART A: ADDRESS CHECKING

		Correct List			List to Be Checked	
		Address	ZIP Code		Address	ZIP Code
1.	B	6085 Millcreek Ct. College Station, TX	77845		6805 Millcreek Ct. College Station, TX	77845 *B*
2.	B	16045 State Road 113 Madison, WI	53704-5767		16045 State Road 123 Madison, WI	53704-5767 *B*
3.	A	8222 Hidden Spring Lane Pittsburgh, PA	15238-6056		8222 Hidden Spring Lane Pittsburgh, PA	15238-6056 *A*
4.	C	796 Tipperary Rd. Manahawkin, NJ	08050		796 Tipperary Rd. Manahawkin, NJ	08850 *C*
5.	C	9045 Strickland Dr. Murfreesboro, TN	37127		9045 Strickland Dr. Murfreesboro, TN	37217 *C*
6.	B	7767 Meadowlands **Way** Greenville, SC	29615-0672		7767 Meadowlands **Lane** Greenville, SC	29615-0672 *B*
7.	D	P.O. Box 8243 Garden Grove, **CA**	92840		P.O. Box 8243 Garden Grove, **CO**	93840 *D*
8.	D	499 Newhall Street Hamden, CT	06517-8460		499 Newhill Street Hamden, CT	06516-8460 *D*
9.	A	7622 Business Park Cir. Saint Augustine, Florida	32095-1351		7622 Business Park Cir. Saint Augustine, Florida	32095-1351 *A*
10.	A	8877 Drawbridge Court Silver Spring, MD	20902-8139		8877 Drawbridge Court Silver Spring, MD	20902-8139 *A*
11.	D	5933 Corboy Road Hermitage, TN	37076		5933 Cowboy Road Hermitage, TN	30776 *D*
12.	C	1375 Aldoran Rd. Saginaw, MI	48603		1375 Aldoran Rd. Saginaw, MI	48693 *C*
13.	C	8335 Manzanita Hills Redding, CA	96001-5757		8335 Manzanita Hills Redding, CA	96001-5767 *C*
14.	D	3298 50th Ave. N Birming**ham**, Alabama	35207-2078		3298 50th Ave. N Birming**ton**, Alabama	55207-2078 *D*

		Correct List			List to Be Checked	
		Address	ZIP Code	Address		ZIP Code
15.	C	6644 Ruth Hentz Ave. Panama City, FL	32405	6644 Ruth Hentz Ave. Panama City, FL		32450 ✓
16.	B	5073 Worchester **Ave.** Honolulu, HI	96818-4790	5073 Worchester **Ct.** Honolulu, HI		96818-4790 *B*
17.	A	2242 Meadowbridge Trl. Indianapolis, IN	46217	2242 Meadowbridge Trl. Indianapolis, IN		46217 *A*
18.	B	956 Jekyll Island Rd. Jessup, **GA**	31545-3457	956 Jekyll Island Rd. Jessup, **MA**		31545-3457 *B*
19.	A	9531 Torchiere Court Suwannee, FL	32692	9531 Torchiere Court Suwannee, FL		32692 *A*
20.	B	9698 Montague Place Florence, SC	29501-1514	9688 Montague Place Florence, SC		29501-1514 *B*
21.	D	3846 Calle Yaguez Villa Bornquen, PR	00725	3848 Calle Yaguez Villa Bornquen, PR		07725 *D*
22.	C	254 Oakcrest Dr. NW Salem, OR	97304-6455	254 Oakcrest Dr. NW Salem, OR		97304-6855 *C*
23.	B	8933 Denmont Ave. **SW** Marion, OH	44646-7560	8933 Denmont Ave. **NW** Marion, OH		44646-7560 *B*
24.	C	2080 N. Mannheim Road Melrose Park, IL	60164	2080 N. Mannheim Road Melrose Park, IL		80164 *C*
25.	D	9325 Creek**view** Avenue Trenton, NJ	08610-8532	9325 Creek**side** Avenue Trenton, NJ		06810-8532 *D*
26.	B	Rural Route 23 Cent**re**ville, VA	20120	Rural Route 23 Cent**er**ville, VA		20120 *B*
27.	C	8933 Phoenix St. Wilkes Barre, PA	18702-0607	8933 Phoenix St. Wilkes Barre, PA		18702-0667 *C*
28.	D	78 Emerson Rd. Apt. **4**B Needham, MA	02492	78 Emerson Rd. Apt. **6**B Needham, MA		02429 *D*

		Correct List			List to Be Checked	
		Address	*ZIP Code*	*Address*		*ZIP Code*
29.	**A**	5343 Upper Brandon Pl. Marietta, GA	30068-7876	5343 Upper Brandon Pl. Marietta, GA	*A*	30068-7876
30.	**B**	349**0** E 16th Street Apopka, FL	32703-1736	349**9** E 16th Street Apopka, FL		32703-1736 *A*
31.	**C**	9347 S Kalsman Avenue Compton, CA	90**2**22	9347 S Kalsman Avenue Compton, CA		90**3**22 *C*
32.	**D**	5711 S 1**2**3rd Street Omaha, NE	**68**137	5711 S 1**3**3rd Street Omaha, NE		**86**137 *D*
33.	**A**	7299 Rampart Chase Brightwood, VA	22715	7299 Rampart Chase Brightwood, VA		22715 *A*
34.	**C**	11311 E Tecumseh St. Tulsa, OK	74116-**9**080	11311 E Tecumseh St. Tulsa, OK		74116-**3**080 *C*
35.	**B**	6222 Pers**immon** Drive Killeen, Texas	76543-8732	6222 Pers**ival** Drive Killeen, Texas	*B*	76543-8732
36.	**D**	50**90** S 11**8**th Street Seattle, WA	98**1**78-3669	50**99** S 11**6**th Street Seattle, WA	*D*	98**7**18-3669
37.	**B**	5856 **Martha**ville Pike Smithfield, WV	26437-5211	5856 **Marsh**ville Pike Smithfield, WV	*B*	26437-5211
38.	**C**	3647 Edson Avenue Bronx, NY	**10**466-9229	3647 Edson Avenue Bronx, NY	*C*	**19**066-9229
39.	**B**	844 Nightingale Terr. Hope Mills, **NC**	28348	844 Nightingale Terr. Hope Mills, **NM**		28348 *B*
40.	**B**	5464 Church H**i**ll Road Greeneville, TN	37743	5464 Church H**a**ll Road Greeneville, TN		37743 *B*
41.	**A**	15422 Glencoe Ave. Cleveland, Ohio	44110-2233	15422 Glencoe Ave. Cleveland, Ohio	*A*	44110-2233
42.	**D**	9374 Fall Creek **Run** Chesapeake, VA	23322-5689	9374 Fall Creek **Rd.** Chesapeake, VA	*D*	23322-5699

	Correct List		**List to Be Checked**	
	Address	ZIP Code	Address	ZIP Code

43. **B** 7310 Pin**on** Dr. 7310 Pi**nio**n Dr.
Boulder, CO   80303-6365   Boulder, CO   80303-6365 *L*

44. **A** 4326 Remington St. 4326 Remington St.
Bridgeport, CT   06610-0787   Bridgeport, CT   06610-0787 *A*

45. **D** 4387 Saginaw Road 4387 Saginaw Road
M**a**yersville, MS   391**1**3-7591   M**e**yersville, MS   391**3**3-7591 *D*

46. **D** 2040 Serviceberry Court 2040 Serviceberry Court
Louisville, KY   40**24**1-7021   **Liston,** KY   40**36**1-7021 *D*

47. **B** P.O. Box 11**2**23 P.O. Box 11**3**23
Fort Wayne, IN   46856   Fort Wayne, IN   46856 *B*

48. **A** 3445 Panamint Dr. 3445 Panamint Dr.
Fountain Hills, AZ   85268   Fountain Hills, AZ   85268 *A*

49. **C** 5468 Owyhee Ln. 5468 Owyhee Ln.
Caldwell, ID   83605-73**43**   Caldwell, ID   83605-73**34** *L*

50. **A** 766 Markley Dr. 766 Markley Dr.
Newark, DE   19713-1323   Newark, DE   19713-1323 *A*

51. **B** 13344 W 128th **Terrace** 13344 W 128th **Trace**
Shawnee Mission, KS   66213-3424   Shawnee Mission, KS   66213-3424 *B*

52. **D** 8788 Rutledge Cir. 8788 Rutledge Cir.
Nadeau, **MI**   **4**9863   Nadeau, **ME**   **6**9863 *B*

53. **C** 7845 NW Island Lake Rd. 7845 NW Island Lake Rd.
Duluth, MN   558**0**3   Duluth, MN   554**4**3 *L*

54. **B** 9089 N **K**ristopher Bnd 9089 N **C**ristopher Bnd
Saint Charles, MO   63303-5464   Saint Charles, MO   63303-5464 *B*

55. **C** 2458 Amber Oaks Ct. 2458 Amber Oaks Ct.
Dupree, SD   **5**7623   Dupree, SD   *A* **7**5633

56. **C** 1245 Parkside Center Blvd. 1245 Parkside Center Blvd.
Dallas, TX   75244-**6**756   Dallas, TX   75244-**9**756 *✓*

		Correct List		**List to Be Checked**	
		Address	*ZIP Code*	*Address*	*ZIP Code*
57.	**B**	1020 N Heatherstone Drive Shreveport, LA	71129-8644	1020 N Featherstone Drive Shreveport, LA	71129-8644 *B*
58.	**C**	3247 W Fortification St. Falmouth, KY	41040	3247 W Fortification St. Falmouth, KY	41920 *C*
59.	**D**	58355 S. 14th Place Boise, ID	83702-1446	58355 S. 16th Place Boise, ID	83720-1446 *D*
60.	**A**	5472 Cranbrook Drive Kissimmee, FL	34758	5472 Cranbrook Drive Kissimmee, FL	34758 *A*

PART B: FORMS COMPLETION

Set 1: Questions 1 through 6

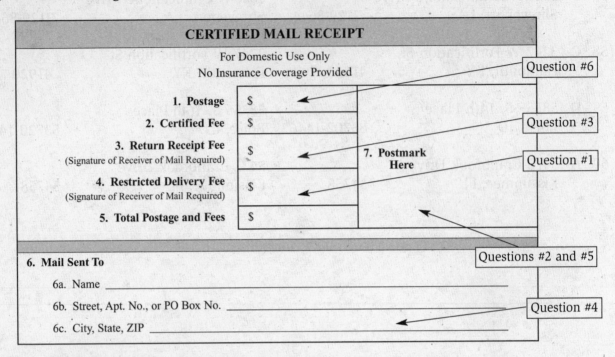

1. **C** Box 4 is labeled "Restricted Delivery Fee."
2. **C** A postmark should be placed in Box 7.
3. **B** A dollar amount indicating the amount paid for a return receipt would be entered in Box 3.
4. **D** Line 6c is for entry of the city, state, and ZIP code.
5. **D** Only Box 7 would *not* require a dollar amount (it requires a postmark).
6. **A** The postage amount is listed first in the form in Box 1.

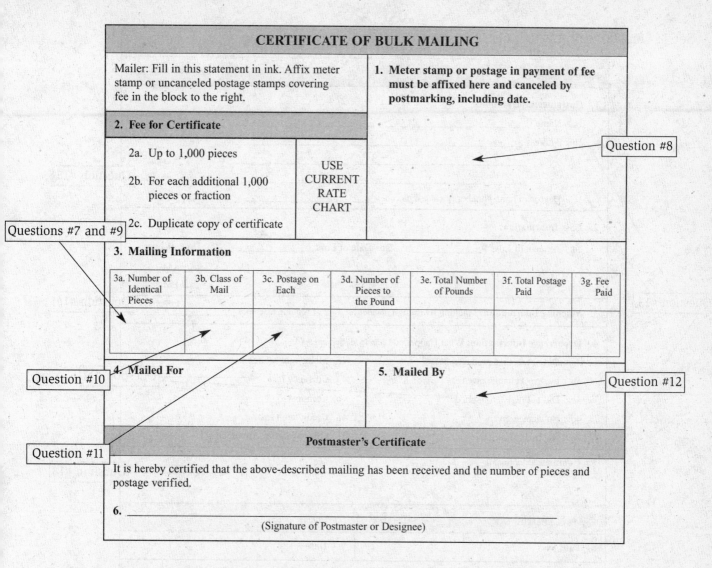

7. **D** Box 3a is labeled "Number of Identical Pieces." The only number listed in the answers is D, 2,500.

8. **A** A postmark will be placed in Box 1, which indicates that the meter stamp or postage will be "canceled by postmarking."

9. **C** Only in Box 3a can you list the number of pieces of mail. Although Line 2a says "Up to 1,000 pieces," there is no way to indicate the number of pieces there. Also notice that Line 2a is not among the answer choices.

10. **D** Box 3b requires the "Class of Mail."

11. **C** Box 3c is for entry of the postage on each piece of mail.

12. **C** The name of the person mailing the material should be entered in Box 5.

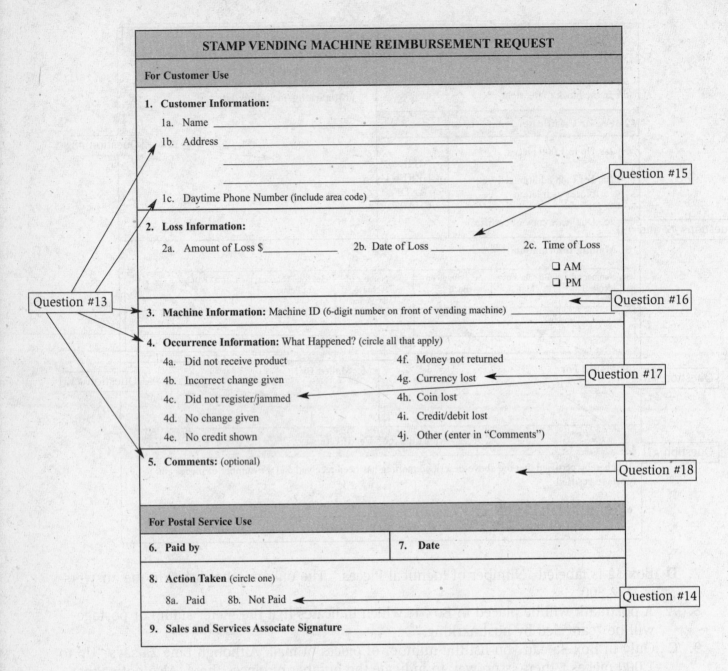

STAMP VENDING MACHINE REIMBURSEMENT REQUEST

For Customer Use

1. **Customer Information:**
   1a. Name _____
   1b. Address _____
   _____
   _____
   1c. Daytime Phone Number (include area code) _____

2. **Loss Information:**
   2a. Amount of Loss $_____ 2b. Date of Loss _____ 2c. Time of Loss
   ❏ AM
   ❏ PM

3. **Machine Information:** Machine ID (6-digit number on front of vending machine) _____

4. **Occurrence Information:** What Happened? (circle all that apply)
   4a. Did not receive product   4f. Money not returned
   4b. Incorrect change given   4g. Currency lost
   4c. Did not register/jammed   4h. Coin lost
   4d. No change given   4i. Credit/debit lost
   4e. No credit shown   4j. Other (enter in "Comments")

5. **Comments:** (optional)

For Postal Service Use

6. **Paid by**   7. **Date**

8. **Action Taken** (circle one)
   8a. Paid   8b. Not Paid

9. **Sales and Services Associate Signature** _____

Question #15
Question #13
Question #16
Question #17
Question #18
Question #14

13. **D** All the boxes listed are in the top part of the form, above the part labeled "For Postal Service Use," so all of them can be filled out by the customer.

14. **D** "Not Paid" would be circled on Line 8b.

15. **A** Line 2b requires a date. The only date among the answer choices is in answer A.

16. **B** The machine ID number should be entered in Box 3.

17. **C** The question lists two things that happened when the customer tried to buy stamps. The machine jammed, and he lost his dollar bill. Those two things are listed in Line 4c ("Did not register/jammed") and Line 4g ("Currency lost"), answer C.

18. **D** There are no boxes on the form that specifically mention talking to a postal representative. The only way the customer could indicate this fact is by entering the information in the "Comments" box, Box 5.

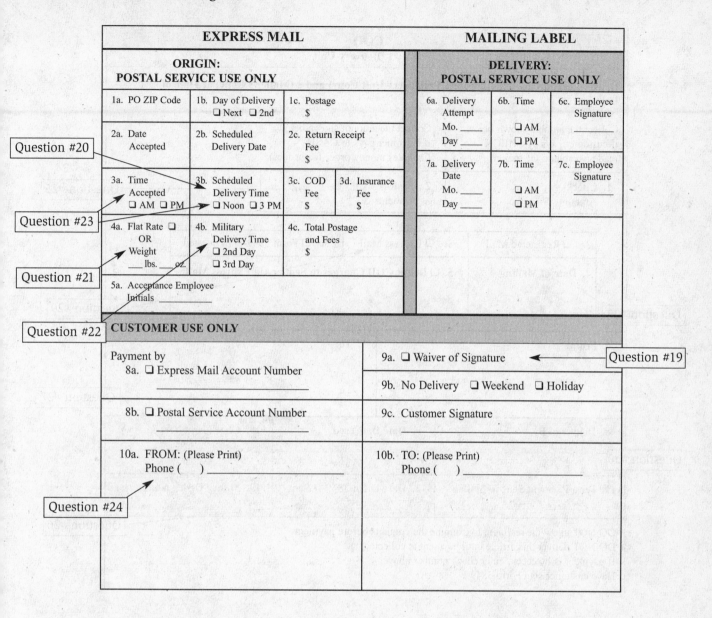

19. **A** The only thing that can be entered in Box 9a is a checkmark, indicating waiver of signature.

20. **C** By checking either "Noon" or "3 PM" in Box 3b, you can indicate the scheduled delivery time.

21. **B** In Box 4a, either "Flat Rate" should be checked or the weight of the mail should be entered. All the other boxes require that a time be entered. Remember, in this question, you're looking for the answer that does NOT require a time.

22. **C** The only box that gives the third day ("3rd Day") as a possible delivery time is Box 4b.

23. **B** The only pair of boxes listed in which *both* boxes require a checkmark is in answer B, Box 3a and Box 3b.

24. **A** Part of the information to be printed in Box 10a is a telephone number.

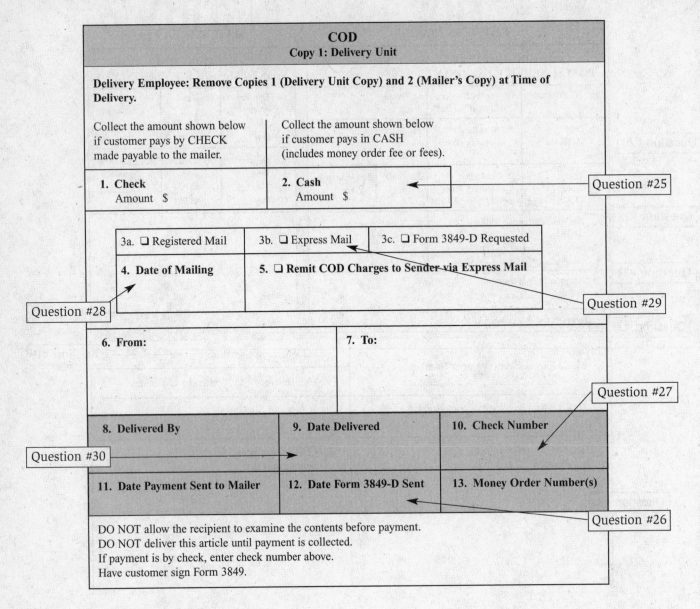

25. **B** A cash amount paid is shown in Box 2.
26. **D** Box 12 shows the date that Form 3849-D was sent. Notice that Box 3c mentions the form, but this space shows only that the form has been requested, not that it was sent.
27. **A** The check number is the information appropriate for Box 10. The only possible such number is given in choice A.
28. **B** Of the boxes listed, only in Box 4 and Box 9 would you enter a date, but Box 9 is paired with Box 13 in answer D, and no date should go in Box 13, so answer D can't be right.
29. **B** Only Box 3b mentions Express Mail.
30. **A** Box 9 is labeled "Date Delivered."

PRACTICE EXAMINATION 2

ANSWER SHEET FOR PRACTICE EXAMINATION 2

PART A: ADDRESS CHECKING

1. Ⓐ Ⓑ Ⓒ Ⓓ	16. Ⓐ Ⓑ Ⓒ Ⓓ	31. Ⓐ Ⓑ Ⓒ Ⓓ	46. Ⓐ Ⓑ Ⓒ Ⓓ
2. Ⓐ Ⓑ Ⓒ Ⓓ	17. Ⓐ Ⓑ Ⓒ Ⓓ	32. Ⓐ Ⓑ Ⓒ Ⓓ	47. Ⓐ Ⓑ Ⓒ Ⓓ
3. Ⓐ Ⓑ Ⓒ Ⓓ	18. Ⓐ Ⓑ Ⓒ Ⓓ	33. Ⓐ Ⓑ Ⓒ Ⓓ	48. Ⓐ Ⓑ Ⓒ Ⓓ
4. Ⓐ Ⓑ Ⓒ Ⓓ	19. Ⓐ Ⓑ Ⓒ Ⓓ	34. Ⓐ Ⓑ Ⓒ Ⓓ	49. Ⓐ Ⓑ Ⓒ Ⓓ
5. Ⓐ Ⓑ Ⓒ Ⓓ	20. Ⓐ Ⓑ Ⓒ Ⓓ	35. Ⓐ Ⓑ Ⓒ Ⓓ	50. Ⓐ Ⓑ Ⓒ Ⓓ
6. Ⓐ Ⓑ Ⓒ Ⓓ	21. Ⓐ Ⓑ Ⓒ Ⓓ	36. Ⓐ Ⓑ Ⓒ Ⓓ	51. Ⓐ Ⓑ Ⓒ Ⓓ
7. Ⓐ Ⓑ Ⓒ Ⓓ	22. Ⓐ Ⓑ Ⓒ Ⓓ	37. Ⓐ Ⓑ Ⓒ Ⓓ	52. Ⓐ Ⓑ Ⓒ Ⓓ
8. Ⓐ Ⓑ Ⓒ Ⓓ	23. Ⓐ Ⓑ Ⓒ Ⓓ	38. Ⓐ Ⓑ Ⓒ Ⓓ	53. Ⓐ Ⓑ Ⓒ Ⓓ
9. Ⓐ Ⓑ Ⓒ Ⓓ	24. Ⓐ Ⓑ Ⓒ Ⓓ	39. Ⓐ Ⓑ Ⓒ Ⓓ	54. Ⓐ Ⓑ Ⓒ Ⓓ
10. Ⓐ Ⓑ Ⓒ Ⓓ	25. Ⓐ Ⓑ Ⓒ Ⓓ	40. Ⓐ Ⓑ Ⓒ Ⓓ	55. Ⓐ Ⓑ Ⓒ Ⓓ
11. Ⓐ Ⓑ Ⓒ Ⓓ	26. Ⓐ Ⓑ Ⓒ Ⓓ	41. Ⓐ Ⓑ Ⓒ Ⓓ	56. Ⓐ Ⓑ Ⓒ Ⓓ
12. Ⓐ Ⓑ Ⓒ Ⓓ	27. Ⓐ Ⓑ Ⓒ Ⓓ	42. Ⓐ Ⓑ Ⓒ Ⓓ	57. Ⓐ Ⓑ Ⓒ Ⓓ
13. Ⓐ Ⓑ Ⓒ Ⓓ	28. Ⓐ Ⓑ Ⓒ Ⓓ	43. Ⓐ Ⓑ Ⓒ Ⓓ	58. Ⓐ Ⓑ Ⓒ Ⓓ
14. Ⓐ Ⓑ Ⓒ Ⓓ	29. Ⓐ Ⓑ Ⓒ Ⓓ	44. Ⓐ Ⓑ Ⓒ Ⓓ	59. Ⓐ Ⓑ Ⓒ Ⓓ
15. Ⓐ Ⓑ Ⓒ Ⓓ	30. Ⓐ Ⓑ Ⓒ Ⓓ	45. Ⓐ Ⓑ Ⓒ Ⓓ	60. Ⓐ Ⓑ Ⓒ Ⓓ

PART B: FORMS COMPLETION

1. Ⓐ Ⓑ Ⓒ Ⓓ	9. Ⓐ Ⓑ Ⓒ Ⓓ	17. Ⓐ Ⓑ Ⓒ Ⓓ	25. Ⓐ Ⓑ Ⓒ Ⓓ
2. Ⓐ Ⓑ Ⓒ Ⓓ	10. Ⓐ Ⓑ Ⓒ Ⓓ	18. Ⓐ Ⓑ Ⓒ Ⓓ	26. Ⓐ Ⓑ Ⓒ Ⓓ
3. Ⓐ Ⓑ Ⓒ Ⓓ	11. Ⓐ Ⓑ Ⓒ Ⓓ	19. Ⓐ Ⓑ Ⓒ Ⓓ	27. Ⓐ Ⓑ Ⓒ Ⓓ
4. Ⓐ Ⓑ Ⓒ Ⓓ	12. Ⓐ Ⓑ Ⓒ Ⓓ	20. Ⓐ Ⓑ Ⓒ Ⓓ	28. Ⓐ Ⓑ Ⓒ Ⓓ
5. Ⓐ Ⓑ Ⓒ Ⓓ	13. Ⓐ Ⓑ Ⓒ Ⓓ	21. Ⓐ Ⓑ Ⓒ Ⓓ	29. Ⓐ Ⓑ Ⓒ Ⓓ
6. Ⓐ Ⓑ Ⓒ Ⓓ	14. Ⓐ Ⓑ Ⓒ Ⓓ	22. Ⓐ Ⓑ Ⓒ Ⓓ	30. Ⓐ Ⓑ Ⓒ Ⓓ
7. Ⓐ Ⓑ Ⓒ Ⓓ	15. Ⓐ Ⓑ Ⓒ Ⓓ	23. Ⓐ Ⓑ Ⓒ Ⓓ	
8. Ⓐ Ⓑ Ⓒ Ⓓ	16. Ⓐ Ⓑ Ⓒ Ⓓ	24. Ⓐ Ⓑ Ⓒ Ⓓ	

PART C: CODING AND MEMORY
SECTION 1—CODING

1. Ⓐ Ⓑ Ⓒ Ⓓ   10. Ⓐ Ⓑ Ⓒ Ⓓ   19. Ⓐ Ⓑ Ⓒ Ⓓ   28. Ⓐ Ⓑ Ⓒ Ⓓ
2. Ⓐ Ⓑ Ⓒ Ⓓ   11. Ⓐ Ⓑ Ⓒ Ⓓ   20. Ⓐ Ⓑ Ⓒ Ⓓ   29. Ⓐ Ⓑ Ⓒ Ⓓ
3. Ⓐ Ⓑ Ⓒ Ⓓ   12. Ⓐ Ⓑ Ⓒ Ⓓ   21. Ⓐ Ⓑ Ⓒ Ⓓ   30. Ⓐ Ⓑ Ⓒ Ⓓ
4. Ⓐ Ⓑ Ⓒ Ⓓ   13. Ⓐ Ⓑ Ⓒ Ⓓ   22. Ⓐ Ⓑ Ⓒ Ⓓ   31. Ⓐ Ⓑ Ⓒ Ⓓ
5. Ⓐ Ⓑ Ⓒ Ⓓ   14. Ⓐ Ⓑ Ⓒ Ⓓ   23. Ⓐ Ⓑ Ⓒ Ⓓ   32. Ⓐ Ⓑ Ⓒ Ⓓ
6. Ⓐ Ⓑ Ⓒ Ⓓ   15. Ⓐ Ⓑ Ⓒ Ⓓ   24. Ⓐ Ⓑ Ⓒ Ⓓ   33. Ⓐ Ⓑ Ⓒ Ⓓ
7. Ⓐ Ⓑ Ⓒ Ⓓ   16. Ⓐ Ⓑ Ⓒ Ⓓ   25. Ⓐ Ⓑ Ⓒ Ⓓ   34. Ⓐ Ⓑ Ⓒ Ⓓ
8. Ⓐ Ⓑ Ⓒ Ⓓ   17. Ⓐ Ⓑ Ⓒ Ⓓ   26. Ⓐ Ⓑ Ⓒ Ⓓ   35. Ⓐ Ⓑ Ⓒ Ⓓ
9. Ⓐ Ⓑ Ⓒ Ⓓ   18. Ⓐ Ⓑ Ⓒ Ⓓ   27. Ⓐ Ⓑ Ⓒ Ⓓ   36. Ⓐ Ⓑ Ⓒ Ⓓ

SECTION 2—MEMORY

37. Ⓐ Ⓑ Ⓒ Ⓓ   46. Ⓐ Ⓑ Ⓒ Ⓓ   55. Ⓐ Ⓑ Ⓒ Ⓓ   64. Ⓐ Ⓑ Ⓒ Ⓓ
38. Ⓐ Ⓑ Ⓒ Ⓓ   47. Ⓐ Ⓑ Ⓒ Ⓓ   56. Ⓐ Ⓑ Ⓒ Ⓓ   65. Ⓐ Ⓑ Ⓒ Ⓓ
39. Ⓐ Ⓑ Ⓒ Ⓓ   48. Ⓐ Ⓑ Ⓒ Ⓓ   57. Ⓐ Ⓑ Ⓒ Ⓓ   66. Ⓐ Ⓑ Ⓒ Ⓓ
40. Ⓐ Ⓑ Ⓒ Ⓓ   49. Ⓐ Ⓑ Ⓒ Ⓓ   58. Ⓐ Ⓑ Ⓒ Ⓓ   67. Ⓐ Ⓑ Ⓒ Ⓓ
41. Ⓐ Ⓑ Ⓒ Ⓓ   50. Ⓐ Ⓑ Ⓒ Ⓓ   59. Ⓐ Ⓑ Ⓒ Ⓓ   68. Ⓐ Ⓑ Ⓒ Ⓓ
42. Ⓐ Ⓑ Ⓒ Ⓓ   51. Ⓐ Ⓑ Ⓒ Ⓓ   60. Ⓐ Ⓑ Ⓒ Ⓓ   69. Ⓐ Ⓑ Ⓒ Ⓓ
43. Ⓐ Ⓑ Ⓒ Ⓓ   52. Ⓐ Ⓑ Ⓒ Ⓓ   61. Ⓐ Ⓑ Ⓒ Ⓓ   70. Ⓐ Ⓑ Ⓒ Ⓓ
44. Ⓐ Ⓑ Ⓒ Ⓓ   53. Ⓐ Ⓑ Ⓒ Ⓓ   62. Ⓐ Ⓑ Ⓒ Ⓓ   71. Ⓐ Ⓑ Ⓒ Ⓓ
45. Ⓐ Ⓑ Ⓒ Ⓓ   54. Ⓐ Ⓑ Ⓒ Ⓓ   63. Ⓐ Ⓑ Ⓒ Ⓓ   72. Ⓐ Ⓑ Ⓒ Ⓓ

PART D: PERSONAL CHARACTERISTICS AND EXPERIENCE INVENTORY

(236 Questions—not included here)

ADDRESS CHECKING SAMPLE QUESTIONS

Look at the row of information for sample question 1, which is labeled "S1" below. Carefully but quickly compare the **List to Be Checked** with the **Correct List**. Then decide if there are **No Errors** (select A), an error in the **Address Only** (select B), an error in the **ZIP Code Only** (select C), or an error in **Both** the address and the ZIP code (select D). Record your response to the sample questions in the **Sample Answer Grid** below. Complete the other three samples given, S2, S3, and S4, and record your responses on the **Sample Answer Grid**.

A. No Errors	B. Address Only	C. ZIP Code Only	D. Both

Correct List

	Address	ZIP Code
S1.	432 Rosewood Ct. Pasadena, CA	91106
S2.	1977 Hully Street Austin, TX	78734-1141
S3.	648 Central Dr. New York, NY	10034
S4.	9812 Pine Ave. Chicago, IL	60467-5113

List to Be Checked

	Address	ZIP Code
S1.	432 Rosewood Ct. Pasedena, CA	91106
S2.	1977 Holly Street Austin, TX	78734-1114
S3.	648 Central Dr. New York, NY	10054
S4.	9812 Pine Ave. Chicago, IL	60467-5113

Sample Answer Grid

S1.	Ⓐ	Ⓑ	Ⓒ	Ⓓ
S2.	Ⓐ	Ⓑ	Ⓒ	Ⓓ
S3.	Ⓐ	Ⓑ	Ⓒ	Ⓓ
S4.	Ⓐ	Ⓑ	Ⓒ	Ⓓ

Completed Sample Answer Grid

S1.	Ⓐ	●	Ⓒ	Ⓓ
S2.	Ⓐ	Ⓑ	Ⓒ	●
S3.	Ⓐ	Ⓑ	●	Ⓓ
S4.	●	Ⓑ	Ⓒ	Ⓓ

In sample 1, the address in the **List to Be Checked** shows Pasedena, but the **Correct List** shows Pasadena. So there is an error in the address. Since the Zip codes are exactly the same, the correct answer is **B—Address Only**.

In sample 2, the address in the **List to Be Checked** shows Holly Street, but the **Correct List** shows Hully Street. So there is an error in the address. The **List to Be Checked** also shows an error in the ZIP code. The last four numbers are 1114, and they are 1141 in the **Correct List**. Because there is an error in the address and in the ZIP code, the correct answer is **D—Both**.

In sample 3, the addresses in the **List to Be Checked** and the **Correct List** are exactly the same, but there is an error in the ZIP code on the **List to Be Checked**. The **List to Be Checked** shows 10054, but the **Correct List** shows 10034. So there is an error in the ZIP code. The correct answer is **C—ZIP Code Only**.

In sample 4, the addresses in the **List to Be Checked** and the **Correct List** are exactly the same. The ZIP codes are also exactly the same. So the correct answer is **A—No Errors**.

Now turn to the next page and begin the address checking test.

PART A: ADDRESS CHECKING

For the following 60 items, compare the address in the **Correct List** with the address in the **List to Be Checked.** Determine if there are **No Errors** (answer A), an error in the **Address Only** (answer B), an error in the **ZIP Code Only** (answer C), or an error in **Both** (answer D). Mark your answers in the Address Checking section of the answer sheet. You have 11 minutes to complete this test.

A. No Errors	B. Address Only	C. ZIP Code Only	D. Both

	Correct List		List to Be Checked	
	Address	*ZIP Code*	*Address*	*ZIP Code*
1.	8046 Lynn Haven Dr. Westminster, MD	21157-6060	8046 Lynn Haven Dr. Westminster, MD	21157-6060
2.	1345 Redondo Court Bakersfield, CA	93309	1345 Redondo Court Bakersfield, CA	93039
3.	88859 4th Ward St. Somerset, KY	42501-9349	88859 4th Wand St. Somerset, KY	43501-9349
4.	94749 Fieldcrest Lane Ypsilanti, MI	48197-0066	9479 Fieldcrest Lane Ypsilanti, MI	48197-0066
5.	2302 East Granada Dr. Brick, New Jersey	08723-7238	2302 East Granada Dr. Brick, New Jersey	08733-7238
6.	1932 New Spring Branch Rd. SE Roanoke, VA	24014	1932 New Springs Branch Rd. SE Roanoke, VA	24014
7.	9907 Bluestem Drive Garland, TX	75044	9977 Bluestem Drive Garland, TX	75044
8.	9316 New Moon Pkwy. Columbus, OH	43223-4656	9316 New Moon Way Columbus, OH	43223-4665
9.	1193 Garway Common St. South Bend, Indiana	46614	1193 Garwood Common St. South Bend, Indiana	46814
10.	6866 S Cumberland St. Metairie, LA	70003-9050	6866 S Cumberland St. Metairie, LA	70003-9050
11.	1926 Danube Way Bolingbrook, IL	60490	1926 Danube Way Bolingbrook, IL	90490

130

	Correct List		**List to Be Checked**	
	Address	*ZIP Code*	*Address*	*ZIP Code*
12.	7757 Forest Hill Rd. SW Dalton, GA	30720-4678	7759 Forest Hill Rd. SW Dalton, GA	30720-4678
13.	588 E Pasadena Phoenix, AZ	85012-2434	588 N Pasadena Phoenix, AZ	85012-2434
14.	Post Office Box AF Los Altos, CA	94023	Post Office Box AF Los Altos, CA	94023
15.	4272 SW Kirklawn Ave. Topeka, KS	66609-6424	4272 SW Kirklawn Ave. Topela, KS	66609-6424
16.	883 Evangeline Dr. Apt. 7D Darlington, SC	29532	883 Evangeline Dr. Apt. 7D Darlington, SC	29523
17.	1515 W 24th St. Texarkana, TX	75501	1615 W 24th St. Texarkana, TX	75521
18.	83332 State Route 9 SE Snohomish, WA	98296	83332 Star Route 9 SE Snohomish, WA	98296
19.	1803 William Penn Hwy. Easton, PA	18045-8354	1803 William Penn Hwy. Easton, PA	18045-3854
20.	6844 Gray Sea Eagle Ave. Las Vegas, Nevada	89117-9282	6844 Gray Eagle Ave. Las Vegas, Nevada	89917-9282
21.	957 E 150 N Orem, Utah	84097	957 E 150 N Orem, Utah	84092
22.	3389 Briarmont St. Ferrisburg, VT	05456-3667	3389 Briarmont Ln. Ferrisburg, VT	95456-3667
23.	2478 Hidden Ponds Blvd. Brighton, MI	48114-7643	2478 Hidden Ponds Blvd. Brighton, MI	48114-7643
24.	5647 W Lincoln Street Oroville, CA	95966	5647 W Lincoln Street Oroville, CA	95966
25.	580 Hudekoper Pl. NW Washington, DC	20007-9687	580 Hudekoper Pl. SW Washington, DC	20007-9687
26.	75747 Rural Route 06 Calhoun, GA	30701	75747 Rural Route 06 Calhoun, GA	30071

	Correct List		List to Be Checked	
	Address	*ZIP Code*	*Address*	*ZIP Code*
27.	747 Sunset Beach Court Merritt Island, FL	32952	747 Sunrise Beach Court Merritt Island, FL	32952
28.	8575 Cynthia Ave. Poquonock, CT	06064-0077	8575 Cynthia Ave. Poquonock, CT	06064-0007
29.	7854 Canopy Cv. Alpharetta, GA	30022-5556	7854 Canopy Cv. Alphabetta, GA	30032-5556
30.	85635 N Fairmont Loop Coeur d'Alene, ID	83814-1402	85665 N Fairmont Loop Coeur d'Alene, ID	83814-1402
31.	1727 Galaxie Dr. Apt. 334 Fredericksburg, VA	22407-7077	1727 Galaxie Dr. Apt. 334 Fredericksburg, VA	22407-6777
32.	6647 22nd Ave. Kenosha, WI	53143	6647 22nd Ave. Kenosha, WI	53143
33.	3215 Yellowstone Dr. Cheyenne Wells, CO	80810	3215 Yellowstone Dr. Cheyenne, CO	80800
34.	7799 N Golf Course Dr. Crystal River, FL	34429-3399	7799 N Gulf Course Dr. Crystal River, FL	34429-3399
35.	9565 Getzelman Dr. Elgin, IL	60123	9565 Getzelman Dr. Elgin, IL	60123
36.	441 Woodlawn Terrace Ct. Ballwin, MO	63021-3689	441 Woodlawn Terrace Ct. Ballwin, MO	63021-5689
37.	3467 Homans Ave. San Leandro, CA	94577	3467 Homans Ave. San Leandro, CA	94687
38.	8585 Fieldstone Court Aurora, IL	60504-7012	8585 Fieldstone Court Aurora, IN	50504-7012
39.	80536 Pisgah Rd. Gadsden, AL	35904-7161	80536 Pisgah Rd. Gasden, AL	35904-7161
40.	15678 Bitterroot Road Helena, MT	59602-0504	15678 Bitterroot Road Helena, MT	59620-0504
41.	5767 Marquette St. Tupelo, MS	38801	5767 Marquette St. Tupelo, MS	38801

	Correct List			List to Be Checked	
	Address	*ZIP Code*		*Address*	*ZIP Code*
42.	4423 Grayson Dr. Four Corners, WY	82715		4423 Grayson St. Four Corners, WY	82715
43.	4270 Baytree Ct. Christoval, TX	76935-7254		4270 Baytree Ct. Christoval, TX	76935-7254
44.	2132 Sherwood Gardens Alexandria, NH	03222-3330		2132 Sherwood Gardens Alexandria, NH	63222-3330
45.	8188 S Fawnwood Ct. Broken Arrow, OK	74011		8818 S Fawnwood Ct. Broken Arrow, OK	74001
46.	9022 Anderson Chapel Rd. Johnson City, TN	37601-5376		9022 Anderson Chapel Rd. Johnson City, TN	36601-5376
47.	1590 Prestwick Lane Newport News, VA	23602		1590 Preston Lane Newport News, VA	23602
48.	2002 E Cottonwood Rd. Kearney, NE	68845		2002 S Cottonwood Rd. Kearney, NE	66645
49.	539 Warmouth St. Manokotak, AK	99628		539 Warmouth St. Manokotak, AK	99468
50.	6890 Gorham Close Clarksville, DE	19970-6098		6890 Gorham Close Clarksville, DE	19970-6098
51.	4564 Keaolele Pl Waialua, HI	96791-2534		4564 Keaolele Dr. Waialua, HI	96791-2534
52.	3305 36th St. SW Fargo, ND	58104-4652		3305 36th St. SW Fargo, SD	58104-4652
53.	6844 NW Queens Ave. Corvallis, OR	97330		6844 NW Queens Ave. Corvallis, OR	97330
54.	88335 Star Route 99 Peace Dale RI	02883-2020		88355 Star Route 99 Peace Dale, RI	08283-2020
55.	4211 Haughland Dr. Apt. BD Cypress, TX	77433		4211 Haughland Dr. Apt. BD Cypress, TX	74743

	Correct List		**List to Be Checked**	
	Address	*ZIP Code*	*Address*	*ZIP Code*
56.	89398 5 Finger Peaks Rd. Gillette, WY	82716	89398 5 Finger Lakes Rd. Gillette, WY	82716
57.	1800 N Bucknell St. Philadelphia, PA	19121-2350	1800 N Bucknell St. Philadelphia, PA	19121-2530
58.	6022 Pennsylvania Ave. Hampton, VA	23661-1010	6022 Pennsylvania Ave. Hampton, MA	33661-1010
59.	4547 Mountwood St. Houston, TX	77018-8144	4547 Mountwood St. Houston, TX	77018-8144
60.	5423 Carthage Lane Schaumburg, IL	60194	5423 Carhart Lane Schaumburg, IL	60194

PART B: FORMS COMPLETION

Look at this sample form and answer the two questions below it. Mark your answers in the sample answer grid that follows the questions.

Sample Form

1. First Name	2. Middle Name	3. Last Name
4. Street Address		
5. City	6. State	7. ZIP Code
8. Fee $ _____	9. Date 9a. Day _____ 9b. Month _____ 9c. Year _____	

S1. Which of these would be a correct entry for Box 6?
   A. "2542 Oak Avenue"
   B. "November"
   C. "$6.80"
   D. "Nevada" ✓

S2. Where should the middle name be entered on the form?
   A. Box 1
   B. Box 2 ✓
   C. Box 3
   D. Box 4

Sample Answer Grid				
S1.	Ⓐ	Ⓑ	Ⓒ	Ⓓ
S2.	Ⓐ	Ⓑ	Ⓒ	Ⓓ

Completed Sample Answer Grid				
S1.	Ⓐ	Ⓑ	Ⓒ	●
S2.	Ⓐ	●	Ⓒ	Ⓓ

On the form, Box 6 is labeled "State." So the correct answer for sample question 1 is "D. Nevada," which is the only state listed among the answers. Box 2 is labeled "Middle Name," so the correct answer for sample question 2 is "B. Box 2." The completed sample answer grid above shows these correct answers filled in.

Directions: Each of the following forms is followed by questions based on that form. Each part of the form is labeled with a number or a number and a letter. You will have 15 minutes to complete the 30 questions in this section

Set 1: Forms Completion
Questions 1 through 6 are based on Form 1.

Form 1

<table>
<tr><td colspan="3" align="center">**APPLICATION FOR POST OFFICE BOX OR CALLER SERVICE**</td></tr>
<tr><td colspan="2" align="center">Customer:
Complete Shaded Boxes</td><td align="center">Post Office:
Complete White Boxes</td></tr>
<tr><td colspan="2">1. **Names to Which Box Numbers Are Assigned**</td><td>2. **Box or Caller Numbers**</td></tr>
<tr><td colspan="2">3. **Name of Person Applying**
Title (if person represents organization)
Name of Organization (if different from item 1)</td><td>4. **Will This Box Be Used for**
❑ Personal Use
❑ Business Use
(optional)</td></tr>
<tr><td colspan="2">5. **Address (number, street, apt. no., city, state, ZIP code)**
When address changes, cross out address here and put new address on back.</td><td>6. **Email Address**
(optional)</td></tr>
<tr><td colspan="2">7a. Date Application Received   7b. Box Size   7c. ID and Physical Address Verified by *(initials)*</td><td>8. **Telephone Number**
(include area code)</td></tr>
<tr><td>9. Two types of identification required. One must contain a photograph of addressee(s). Social Security cards, credit cards, and birth certificates are not acceptable as identification. Write in identifying information. Subject to verification.</td><td>10. **Eligible for Carrier Delivery:**
❑ city
❑ rural
❑ HCR
❑ none</td><td>11. **Dates of Service**
_____ through _____</td></tr>
<tr><td>12. List names of minors or names of others receiving mail in box. Others must present two forms of valid ID. If applicant is a firm, name each member receiving mail. Each member must have verifiable ID on request.</td><td>13. **Service Assigned**
❑ Box
❑ Caller
❑ Reserve No.</td><td>14. **Signature of Applicant**
(same as item 3) I agree to comply with all rules regarding Post Office box or caller service.</td></tr>
</table>

1. In which box would "Carmen Delgado" be a correct entry?
   A. Box 1
   B. Box 2
   C. Box 5
   D. All of the above

2. Which box contains optional information?
   A. Box 2
   B. Box 4
   C. Box 8
   D. Box 13

3. How would you indicate the forms of ID presented by the customer?
   A. Enter the information in Box 2
   B. Enter the information in Box 7c
   C. Enter the information in Box 9
   D. Enter the information in Box 12

4. Where would you indicate that the customer is eligible for rural delivery?
   A. Box 4
   B. Box 5
   C. Box 10
   D. Box 12

5. Which of these would be a correct entry for Box 7a?
   A. A checkmark
   B. "Large"
   C. "johndoe@business.com"
   D. "2/2/06"

6. Which of these would be a correct entry for Box 2?
   A. "$10.98"
   B. "Interstate Industries"
   C. "789"
   D. The verifier's initials

Set 2: Forms Completion
Questions 7 through 12 are based on Form 2.

Form 2

Delivery Notice/Reminder/Receipt

1. Sorry we missed you.

   1a. Today's Date _____ 1b. Sender's Name _____

2. Delivery

   2a. _____ We will redeliver the item
   2b. _____ Please pick up the item at the Post Office.

3. Check type of item

   3a. _____ Letter
   3b. _____ Large envelope, magazine, catalog, etc.
   3c. _____ Parcel
   3d. _____ Restricted Delivery
   3e. _____ Perishable Item
   3f. _____ Other:

4. If delivery confirmation is required, check type of mail service.

   4a. _____ Express Mail
   4b. _____ Certified Mail
   4c. _____ Recorded Delivery
   4d. _____ Registered Mail
   4e. _____ Insured Mail
   4f. _____ Return Receipt
   4g. _____ Delivery Confirmation

5. If article requires payment check type(s) and note total payment amount.

   5a. Postage Due _____   5b. COD _____   5c. Customs Fee _____
   5d. Total Amount Due $ _____

6. Final Notice: Article will be returned to sender on this date: _____

7. The type of item to be delivered is perishable. Where would you indicate this?
   A. Line 1b
   B. Line 2b
   C. Line 3e
   D. Line 4c

8. Which of these would be a correct entry for Line 1b?
   A. "Sean Lewis"
   B. "$2.44"
   C. A circle
   D. A checkmark

9. A dollar amount would be a correct entry for every line EXCEPT which one?
   A. Line 3f
   B. Line 5a
   C. Line 5c
   D. Line 5d

10. Which of these would be a correct entry for Line 1a?
    A. A checkmark
    B. "$13.33"
    C. "1/8/07"
    D. "Mavis Brown"

11. The customer should pick up the mail at the Post Office. Where would you indicate this?
    A. Line 1a
    B. Line 2b
    C. Line 3e
    D. Line 4g

12. The article is scheduled to be returned to the sender. Where would you indicate the sender's name?
    A. Line 1b
    B. Line 3f
    C. Line 4d
    D. Line 6

Set 3: Forms Completion

Questions 13 through 18 are based on Form 3.

Form 3

<table>
<tr><td colspan="4" align="center">CUSTOMS DECLARATION</td></tr>
<tr>
<td rowspan="3">1. Sender's Name and Address</td>
<td colspan="3">2. Sender's Customs Reference (if any)</td>
</tr>
<tr>
<td colspan="3">3. Insured Number</td>
</tr>
<tr>
<td colspan="3">4. Insured Amount</td>
</tr>
<tr>
<td></td>
<td colspan="3">5. Sender's Instructions in Case of Nondelivery
5a. ❏ Treat as Abandoned
5b. ❏ Return to Sender (return charges at sender's expense)
5c. ❏ Redirect to address below:</td>
</tr>
<tr>
<td>6. Addressee's Name and Address</td>
<td colspan="3">7. Addressee's Telephone/Fax/Email (if known)</td>
</tr>
<tr>
<td rowspan="2">8a. Description of Contents</td>
<td rowspan="2">8b. Quantity</td>
<td>8c. Weight</td>
<td>8d. Value</td>
</tr>
<tr>
<td>8e. Total Weight</td>
<td>8f. Total Value</td>
</tr>
<tr>
<td colspan="4">9. Check One: 9a. ❏ Airmail/Priority   9b. ❏ Surface/Nonpriority</td>
</tr>
<tr>
<td colspan="4">10. Check One: 10a. ❏ Gift   10b. ❏ Documents   10c. ❏ Commercial Sample
                10d. ❏ Returned Goods   10e. ❏ Other</td>
</tr>
<tr>
<td colspan="4">11. Date and Sender's Signature</td>
</tr>
</table>

13. You could enter a checkmark in each of the following EXCEPT which one?
    A. Line 5a
    B. Line 5c
    C. Box 8c
    D. Line 10e

14. Which of these would be a correct and complete entry for Box 11?
    A. A signature
    B. "5/19/07" and a signature
    C. "5/19/07" and "2794 Oak Ave."
    D. None of the above

15. Which of these would be a correct entry for Box 7?
    A. "555-827-6928"
    B. "cooper@uptown.org"
    C. "555-827-6928" and "555-204-2850"
    D. All of the above

16. The item is being sent to Fred Walker. Where would his name be entered?
    A. Box 1
    B. Box 6
    C. Box 8a
    D. Box 11

17. Which of these would be a correct entry for Box 8e?
    A. "3 pounds 5 ounces"
    B. "$86.00"
    C. "580933"
    D. "Fred Walker"

18. The material is being returned to the sender. Where would you indicate this?
    A. Box 1
    B. Box 5
    C. Box 8a
    D. Box 10d

Set 4: Forms Completion
Questions 19 through 24 are based on Form 4.

Form 4

<table>
<tr><td colspan="2" align="center">**Authorization to Hold Mail**</td></tr>
<tr><td>*To Be Completed by Customer*</td><td>*To Be Completed by Post Office*</td></tr>
<tr><td>Postmaster: Please hold mail for:</td><td>7. **Date Received**</td></tr>
<tr><td rowspan="4">1. **Name (s)**</td><td>8. **Clerk**</td></tr>
<tr><td>9. **Carrier**</td></tr>
<tr><td>10. **Route Number**</td></tr>
<tr><td rowspan="8"></td></tr>
<tr><td>2. **Address**

  2a. Street/apartment/suite number

_____

  2b. City _____
  2c. State _____
  2d. ZIP Code _____</td></tr>
<tr><td>3. **Beginning Date**</td></tr>
<tr><td>4. **Ending Date**</td></tr>
<tr><td>5. **Instructions**
  5a. _____ Please deliver all accumulated mail and resume normal delivery on the ending date shown above.
  5b. _____ I will pick up all accumulated mail when I return.</td></tr>
<tr><td>6. **Customer Signature**

_____</td></tr>
</table>

19. Teresa Gregg wishes her accumulated mail to be delivered on August 10. How would she indicate this?
    A. Enter the information in Box 3
    B. Enter the information in Box 4
    C. Enter the information in Line 5b
    D. Enter the information in Box 7

20. Which of these would be a correct entry for Line 6?
    A. The carrier's name
    B. The customer's printed name
    C. The clerk's initials
    D. The customer's signature

21. How would the customer indicate that mail is to be held for two people at the customer's address?
    A. List both names in Box 1
    B. Put a checkmark on Line 5a
    C. Put a checkmark on Line 5b
    D. Enter the number "2" in Box 10

22. Where would the customer indicate that he or she will pick up mail upon return?
    A. Line 2a
    B. Box 4
    C. Line 5a
    D. Line 5b

23. The customer would complete each of the following EXCEPT which one?
    A. Line 2b
    B. Line 2d
    C. Box 6
    D. Box 7

24. A date could be entered in each of the following EXCEPT which one?
    A. Box 3
    B. Box 4
    C. Box 7
    D. Box 10

Set 5: Forms Completion

Questions 25 through 30 are based on Form 5.

Form 5

<table>
<tr><td colspan="2" align="center">**Domestic Insured Parcel Receipt**
(not for international mail)</td></tr>
<tr><td colspan="2">**1. Parcel Addressed for Delivery at**

1a. Post Office   1b. State   1c. ZIP Code
_____   _____   _____</td></tr>
<tr><td>**2. Postage** $ _____

3. Insurance Fee $ _____

4. Special Delivery Fee $ _____

5. Special Handling Fee $ _____

6. TOTAL FEES $ _____

7. INSURANCE COVERAGE
    $ _____</td><td>**8. Postmark of Mailing Office**</td></tr>
<tr><td colspan="2">**9. Check all that apply for this parcel.**

9a. _____ Fragile   9b. _____ Liquid   9c. _____ Perishable</td></tr>
<tr><td colspan="2">**10. Sender: Enter name and address of addressee on the reverse and read information regarding insurance coverage and claims.**</td></tr>
</table>

25. Which of these would be a correct entry for Box 8?
    A. "Newark, New Jersey"
    B. A postmark
    C. "$12.20"
    D. None of the above

26. Where would you indicate that the parcel is fragile?
    A. Line 1a
    B. Box 7
    C. Line 9a
    D. Line 9c

27. The Special Handling fee is $1.30. Where would this be written?
    A. Box 3
    B. Box 4
    C. Box 5
    D. Box 6

28. Which of these would be a correct entry for Line 1b?
    A. A checkmark
    B. "Mississippi"
    C. "Knoxville"
    D. "U.S.A."

29. Where should the name and address of the addressee be entered?
    A. Box 1
    B. Box 7
    C. Box 10
    D. None of the above

30. Total fees for this domestic insured parcel would be entered where?
    A. Box 2
    B. Box 6
    C. Box 7
    D. Box 10

PART C: CODING AND MEMORY

SECTION 1—CODING

Coding Exercise

Choose the correct delivery route, based on the Coding Guide, for each of the following 4 items and mark your answers on the answer sheet below. You have 2 minutes to complete this practice exercise. This exercise will not be scored.

CODING GUIDE

Address Range	Delivery Route
2450–5999 E 24th Street	
51000–63700 State Highway MM	A
24–39 Whispering Pines Rd. E	
6000–8999 E 24th Street	
40–79 Whispering Pines Rd. E	B
201–1700 Columbia Place	
150–499 Versailles Ave.	C
63701–98000 State Highway MM	
All mail that doesn't fall in one of the address ranges listed above	D

	Address	Delivery Route
1.	56400 E 24th Street	A B C D
2.	262 Columbia Place	A B C D
3.	55 Whispering Pines Rd. E	A B C D
4.	8204 E 24th St.	A B C D

Sample Answer Grid				
1.	Ⓐ	Ⓑ	Ⓒ	Ⓓ
2.	Ⓐ	Ⓑ	Ⓒ	Ⓓ
3.	Ⓐ	Ⓑ	Ⓒ	Ⓓ
4.	Ⓐ	Ⓑ	Ⓒ	Ⓓ

Completed Sample Answer Grid				
1.	Ⓐ	Ⓑ	Ⓒ	●
2.	Ⓐ	Ⓑ	●	Ⓓ
3.	Ⓐ	●	Ⓒ	Ⓓ
4.	Ⓐ	●	Ⓒ	Ⓓ

CODING TEST

Choose the correct delivery route, based on the Coding Guide, for each of the following 36 items (items 1 through 36) and mark your answers in the Coding section of the Answer Sheet. You have 6 minutes to complete this test.

CODING GUIDE

Address Range	Delivery Route
2450–5999 E 24th Street 51000–63700 State Highway MM 24–39 Whispering Pines Rd. E	A
6000–8999 E 24th Street 40–79 Whispering Pines Rd. E	B
201–1700 Columbia Place 150–499 Versailles Ave. 63701–98000 State Highway MM	C
All mail that doesn't fall in one of the address ranges listed above	D

	Address	Delivery Route
1.	59 Whispering Pines Rd. E	A B C D
2.	7459 E 24th Street	A B C D
3.	55036 State Highway MM	A B C D
4.	78097 E 24th Street	A B C D
5.	336 Versailles Ave.	A B C D
6.	27 Whispering Pines Rd. N	A B C D
7.	8604 E 24th Street	A B C D
8.	1520 Columbia Place	A B C D
9.	69309 State Highway MM	A B C D
10.	79 Whispering Pines Rd. E	A B C D

Address	Delivery Route
11. 7630 E 25th Street	A B C D
12. 160 Columbia Place	A B C D
13. 454 Versailles Ave.	A B C D
14. 75 Whispering Pines Rd. E	A B C D
15. 57990 State Highway MM	A B C D
16. 24 Whispering Pines Rd. E	A B C D
17. 6261 E 24th Street	A B C D
18. 806 Columbine Place	A B C D
19. 93257 State Highway MM	A B C D
20. 63699 State Highway MM	A B C D
21. 25 Whispering Pines Rd. E	A B C D
22. 6354 E 24th Street	A B C D
23. 43698 State Highway MM	A B C D
24. 7643 E 24th Street	A B C D
25. 51754 State Highway NN	A B C D
26. 329 Versailles Ave.	A B C D
27. 38 Whispering Pines Rd. E	A B C D
28. 561 Columbia Place	A B C D
29. 22 Whispering Pines Rd. E	A B C D
30. 7865 E 24th Street	A B C D
31. 55399 State Highway MM	A B C D
32. 76 Whispering Pines Ave. E	A B C D
33. 211 Versailles Ave.	A B C D
34. 5700 W. 24th Street	A B C D
35. 47 Whispering Pines Rd. E	A B C D
36. 62550 State Highway MM	A B C D

SECTION 2—MEMORY

Memory Study Period 1
Use the time given to memorize the information in the following Coding Guide.

CODING GUIDE

Address Range	Delivery Route
2450–5999 E 24th Street	
51000–63700 State Highway MM	A
24–39 Whispering Pines Rd. E	
6000–8999 E 24th Street	
40–79 Whispering Pines Rd. E	B
201–1700 Columbia Place	
150–499 Versailles Ave.	C
63701–98000 State Highway MM	
All mail that doesn't fall in one of the address ranges listed above	D

Memory Exercise

Choose the correct delivery route, based on your memory of the information in the Coding Guide, for each of the following 8 items and mark your answers on the answer sheet below. You have 90 seconds to complete this practice exercise. This exercise will not be scored.

Address	Delivery Route
1. 96245 State Highway MM	A B C D
2. 333 Versailles Ave.	A B C D
3. 7844 W 24th Street	A B C D
4. 59255 State Highway MM	A B C D
5. 599 Versailles Ave.	A B C D
6. 71 Whispering Pines Rd. E	A B C D
7. 8654 E 24th Street	A B C D
8. 2539 E 24th Street	A B C D

Sample Answer Grid				
1.	Ⓐ	Ⓑ	Ⓒ	Ⓓ
2.	Ⓐ	Ⓑ	Ⓒ	Ⓓ
3.	Ⓐ	Ⓑ	Ⓒ	Ⓓ
4.	Ⓐ	Ⓑ	Ⓒ	Ⓓ
5.	Ⓐ	Ⓑ	Ⓒ	Ⓓ
6.	Ⓐ	Ⓑ	Ⓒ	Ⓓ
7.	Ⓐ	Ⓑ	Ⓒ	Ⓓ
8.	Ⓐ	Ⓑ	Ⓒ	Ⓓ

Completed Sample Answer Grid				
1.	Ⓐ	Ⓑ	●	Ⓓ
2.	Ⓐ	Ⓑ	●	Ⓓ
3.	Ⓐ	Ⓑ	Ⓒ	●
4.	●	Ⓑ	Ⓒ	Ⓓ
5.	Ⓐ	Ⓑ	Ⓒ	●
6.	Ⓐ	●	Ⓒ	Ⓓ
7.	Ⓐ	●	Ⓒ	Ⓓ
8.	●	Ⓑ	Ⓒ	Ⓓ

Memory Study Period 2
Use the time given to memorize the information in the following Coding Guide.

CODING GUIDE

Address Range	Delivery Route
2450–5999 E 24th Street 51000–63700 State Highway MM 24–39 Whispering Pines Rd. E	A
6000–8999 E 24th Street 40–79 Whispering Pines Rd. E	B
201–1700 Columbia Place 150–499 Versailles Ave. 63701–98000 State Highway MM	C
All mail that doesn't fall in one of the address ranges listed above	D

MEMORY TEST
Choose the correct delivery route, based on your memory of the information in the Coding Guide, for each of the following 36 items (items 37 through 72) and mark your answers in the Memory section of the Answer Sheet. You have 7 minutes to complete this test.

	Address	Delivery Route
37.	51999 State Highway MM	A B C D
38.	69950 E 24th Street	A B C D
39.	60 Whispering Pines Rd. E	A B C D
40.	588 Versalle Ave.	A B C D
41.	79909 State Highway MM	A B C D
42.	639 Versailles Ave.	A B C D
43.	3247 E 24th Street	A B C D
44.	25 Whispering Pines Rd. E	A B C D
45.	408 Columbia Place	A B C D

Address	Delivery Route
46. 50888 State Highway MM	A B C D
47. 6673 E 24th Street	A B C D
48. 437 Versailles Ave.	A B C D
49. 66700 Star Highway MM	A B C D
50. 2500 E 24th Street	A B C D
51. 628750 State Highway MM	A B C D
52. 73 Whispering Pines Rd. E	A B C D
53. 5799 E 24th Street	A B C D
54. 120 Versailles Ave.	A B C D
55. 63987 State Road MM	A B C D
56. 608 Columbia Place	A B C D
57. 6431 E 24th Street	A B C D
58. 29 Whispering Pines Rd. E	A B C D
59. 5258 E 24th Street	A B C D
60. 1820 Columbia Place	A B C D
61. 382 Versailles Ave.	A B C D
62. 50 Whispering Pines Rd. E	A B C D
63. 72721 State Highway MM	A B C D
64. 8965 N 24th Street	A B C D
65. 52996 State Highway MM	A B C D
66. 6300 E 24th Street	A B C D
67. 424 Versailles Ave.	A B C D
68. 245 Columbia Place	A B C D
69. 5204 E 24th Street	A B C D
70. 69287 State Highway M	A B C D
71. 84 Whispering Pines Rd. E	A B C D
72. 6037 E 24th Street	A B C D

PART D: PERSONAL CHARACTERISTICS AND EXPERIENCE INVENTORY

On the actual exam, the next part that you would take is Part D: Personal Characteristics and Experience Inventory. This part of the exam is 90 minutes long and has 236 items. Because there is no particular advantage to practicing your responses on these statements and questions, no tests are given here for them.

Scoring and Explanations for Practice Examination 2

ANSWER KEY

Part A: Address Checking

1. A	11. C	21. C	31. C	41. A	51. B
2. C	12. B	22. D	32. A	42. B	52. B
3. D	13. B	23. A	33. D	43. A	53. A
4. B	14. A	24. A	34. B	44. C	54. D
5. C	15. B	25. B	35. A	45. D	55. C
6. B	16. C	26. C	36. C	46. C	56. B
7. B	17. D	27. B	37. C	47. B	57. C
8. D	18. B	28. C	38. D	48. D	58. D
9. D	19. C	29. D	39. B	49. C	59. A
10. A	20. D	30. B	40. C	50. A	60. B

Part B: Forms Completion

1. A	6. C	11. B	16. B	21. A	26. C
2. C	7. C	12. A	17. A	22. D	27. C
3. C	8. A	13. C	18. D	23. D	28. B
4. C	9. A	14. B	19. B	24. D	29. D
5. D	10. C	15. D	20. B	25. B	30. B

Part C: Coding Test

1. B	7. B	13. C	19. C	25. D	31. A
2. B	8. C	14. B	20. A	26. C	32. D
3. A	9. C	15. A	21. A	27. A	33. C
4. D	10. B	16. A	22. B	28. C	34. D
5. C	11. D	17. B	23. D	29. D	35. B
6. D	12. D	18. D	24. B	30. B	36. A

Part C: Memory Test

37. A	43. A	49. D	55. D	61. C	67. C
38. D	44. A	50. A	56. C	62. B	68. C
39. B	45. C	51. D	57. B	63. C	69. A
40. D	46. A	52. B	58. A	64. D	70. D
41. C	47. B	53. A	59. A	65. A	71. D
42. D	48. C	54. D	60. D	66. B	72. B

SCORING

Part A: Address Checking

Enter the number you got right: _____

Enter the number you got wrong
(not including those left blank): _____

Divide the number wrong by 3
(or multiply by 1/3): _____

Subtract this answer from the number right: – _____

Raw Score _____

Part B: Forms Completion

Enter the number you got right
(no penalty for guessing): Raw Score _____

Part C: Coding and Memory

Enter the number you got right: _____

Enter the number you got wrong
(not including those left blank): _____

Divide the number wrong by 3
(or multiply by 1/3): _____

Subtract this answer from the number right: – _____

Raw Score _____

Part D: Personal Characteristics and Experience Inventory

Scoring system not given.

Explanations

PART A: ADDRESS CHECKING

	Correct List		List to Be Checked	
	Address	*ZIP Code*	*Address*	*ZIP Code*
1. **A**	8046 Lynn Haven Dr. Westminster, MD	21157-6060	8046 Lynn Haven Dr. Westminster, MD	21157-6060
2. **C**	1345 Redondo Court Bakersfield, CA	93**3**09	1345 Redondo Court Bakersfield, CA	93**0**39
3. **D**	88859 4th Wa**r**d St. Somerset, KY	4**2**501-9349	88859 4th Wa**n**d St. Somerset, KY	4**3**501-9349
4. **B**	94**749** Fieldcrest Lane Ypsilanti, MI	48197-0066	9**479** Fieldcrest Lane Ypsilanti, MI	48197-0066
5. **C**	2302 East Granada Dr. Brick, New Jersey	087**2**3-7238	2302 East Granada Dr. Brick, New Jersey	087**3**3-7238
6. **B**	1932 New Sprin**g** Branch Rd. SE Roanoke, VA	24014	1932 New Spring**s** Branch Rd. SE Roanoke, VA	24014
7. **B**	9**907** Bluestem Drive Garland, TX	75044	9**977** Bluestem Drive Garland, TX	75044
8. **D**	9316 New Moon **Pkwy.** Columbus, OH	43223-46**56**	9316 New Moon **Way** Columbus, OH	43223-46**65**
9. **D**	1193 Gar**way** Common St. South Bend, Indiana	46**6**14	1193 Gar**wood** Common St. South Bend, Indiana	46**8**14
10. **A**	6866 S Cumberland St. Metairie, LA	70003-9050	6866 S Cumberland St. Metairie, LA	70003-9050
11. **C**	1926 Danube Way Bolingbrook, IL	**6**0490	1926 Danube Way Bolingbrook, IL	**9**0490
12. **B**	775**7** Forest Hill Rd. SW Dalton, GA	30720-4678	775**9** Forest Hill Rd. SW Dalton, GA	30720-4678
13. **B**	588 **E** Pasadena Phoenix, AZ	85012-2434	588 **N** Pasadena Phoenix, AZ	85012-2434
14. **A**	Post Office Box AF Los Altos, CA	94023	Post Office Box AF Los Altos, CA	94023

		Correct List		**List to Be Checked**	
		Address	ZIP Code	Address	ZIP Code

15. **B** 4272 SW Kirklawn Ave.
Topeka, KS   66609-6424
    4272 SW Kirklawn Ave.
Topela, KS   66609-6424

16. **C** 883 Evangeline Dr. Apt. 7D
Darlington, SC   29532
    883 Evangeline Dr. Apt. 7D
Darlington, SC   29523

17. **D** 1515 W 24th St.
Texarkana, TX   75501
    1615 W 24th St.
Texarkana, TX   75521

18. **B** 83332 **State** Route 9 SE
Snohomish, WA   98296
    83332 **Star** Route 9 SE
Snohomish, WA   98296

19. **C** 1803 William Penn Hwy.
Easton, PA   18045-**8354**
    1803 William Penn Hwy.
Easton, PA   18045-**3854**

20. **D** 6844 Gray **Sea** Eagle Ave.
Las Vegas, Nevada   89117-9282
    6844 Gray **E**agle Ave.
Las Vegas, Nevada   89917-9282

21. **C** 957 E 150 N
Orem, Utah   84097
    957 E 150 N
Orem, Utah   84092

22. **D** 3389 Briarmont **St.**
Ferrisburg, VT   **0**5456-3667
    3389 Briarmont **Ln.**
Ferrisburg, VT   **9**5456-3667

23. **A** 2478 Hidden Ponds Blvd.
Brighton, MI   48114-7643
    2478 Hidden Ponds Blvd.
Brighton, MI   48114-7643

24. **A** 5647 W Lincoln Street
Oroville, CA   95966
    5647 W Lincoln Street
Oroville, CA   95966

25. **B** 580 Hudekoper Pl. **NW**
Washington, DC   20007-9687
    580 Hudekoper Pl. **S**W
Washington, DC   20007-9687

26. **C** 75747 Rural Route 06
Calhoun, GA   30701
    75747 Rural Route 06
Calhoun, GA   30071

27. **B** 747 Sun**set** Beach Court
Merritt Island, FL   32952
    747 Sun**rise** Beach Court
Merritt Island, FL   32952

28. **C** 8575 Cynthia Ave.
Poquonock, CT   06064-0077
    8575 Cynthia Ave.
Poquonock, CT   06064-0007

	Correct List		List to Be Checked	
	Address	*ZIP Code*	*Address*	*ZIP Code*

29. **D** 7854 Canopy Cv.
Alpha**r**etta, GA   300**2**2-5556   7854 Canopy Cv.
Alpha**b**etta, GA   300**3**2-5556

30. **B** 856**3**5 N Fairmont Loop
Coeur d'Alene, ID   83814-1402   856**6**5 N Fairmont Loop
Coeur d'Alene, ID   83814-1402

31. **C** 1727 Galaxie Dr. Apt. 334
Fredericksburg, VA   22407-**7**077   1727 Galaxie Dr. Apt. 334
Fredericksburg, VA   22407-**6**777

32. **A** 6647 22nd Ave.
Kenosha, WI   53143   6647 22nd Ave.
Kenosha, WI   53143

33. **D** 3215 Yellowstone Dr.
Cheyenne **Wells,** CO   80810   3215 Yellowstone Dr.
Cheyenne**,** CO   8080**0**

34. **B** 7799 N G**o**lf Course Dr.
Crystal River, FL   34429-3399   7799 N G**u**lf Course Dr.
Crystal River, FL   34429-3399

35. **A** 9565 Getzelman Dr.
Elgin, IL   60123   9565 Getzelman Dr.
Elgin, IL   60123

36. **C** 441 Woodlawn Terrace Ct.
Ballwin, MO   63021-**3**689   441 Woodlawn Terrace Ct.
Ballwin, MO   63021-**5**689

37. **C** 3467 Homans Ave.
San Leandro, CA   94**5**77   3467 Homans Ave.
San Leandro, CA   94**6**87

38. **D** 8585 Fieldstone Court
Aurora, **IL**   **6**0504-7012   8585 Fieldstone Court
Aurora, **IN**   **5**0504-7012

39. **B** 80536 Pisgah Rd.
Ga**d**sden, AL   35904-7161   80536 Pisgah Rd.
Ga**s**den, AL   35904-7161

40. **C** 15678 Bitterroot Road
Helena, MT   596**02**-0504   15678 Bitterroot Road
Helena, MT   596**20**-0504

41. **A** 5767 Marquette St.
Tupelo, MS   38801   5767 Marquette St.
Tupelo, MS   38801

42. **B** 4423 Grayson **Dr.**
Four Corners, WY   82715   4423 Grayson **St.**
Four Corners, WY   82715

		Correct List			List to Be Checked	

		Address	ZIP Code	Address	ZIP Code
43.	A	4270 Baytree Ct. Christoval, TX	76935-7254	4270 Baytree Ct. Christoval, TX	76935-7254
44.	C	2132 Sherwood Gardens Alexandria, NH	03222-3330	2132 Sherwood Gardens Alexandria, NH	63222-3330
45.	D	8188 S Fawnwood Ct. Broken Arrow, OK	74011	8818 S Fawnwood Ct. Broken Arrow, OK	74001
46.	C	9022 Anderson Chapel Rd. Johnson City, TN	37601-5376	9022 Anderson Chapel Rd. Johnson City, TN	36601-5376
47.	B	1590 Prest**wick** Lane Newport News, VA	23602	1590 Prest**on** Lane Newport News, VA	23602
48.	D	2002 **E** Cottonwood Rd. Kearney, NE	68845	2002 **S** Cottonwood Rd. Kearney, NE	66645
49.	C	539 Warmouth St. Manokotak, AK	99628	539 Warmouth St. Manokotak, AK	99468
50.	A	6890 Gorham Close Clarksville, DE	19970-6098	6890 Gorham Close Clarksville, DE	19970-6098
51.	B	4564 Keaolele **Pl** Waialua, HI	96791-2534	4564 Keaolele **Dr.** Waialua, HI	96791-2534
52.	B	3305 36th St. SW Fargo, **ND**	58104-4652	3305 36th St. SW Fargo, **SD**	58104-4652
53.	A	6844 NW Queens Ave. Corvallis, OR	97330	6844 NW Queens Ave. Corvallis, OR	97330
54.	D	88335 Star Route 99 Peace Dale, RI	02883-2020	88355 Star Route 99 Peace Dale, RI	08283-2020
55.	C	4211 Haughland Dr. Apt. BD Cypress, TX	77433	4211 Haughland Dr. Apt. BD Cypress, TX	74743
56.	B	89398 5 Finger **Peaks** Rd. Gillette, WY	82716	89398 5 Finger **Lakes** Rd. Gillette, WY	82716

	Correct List		List to Be Checked	
	Address	*ZIP Code*	*Address*	*ZIP Code*
57. **C**	1800 N Bucknell St. Philadelphia, PA	19121-2**350**	1800 N Bucknell St. Philadelphia, PA	19121-2**530**
58. **D**	6022 Pennsylvania Ave. Hampton, **VA**	**2**3661-1010	6022 Pennsylvania Ave. Hampton, **MA**	**3**3661-1010
59. **A**	4547 Mountwood St. Houston, TX	77018-8144	4547 Mountwood St. Houston, TX	77018-8144
60. **B**	5423 **Carthage** Lane Schaumburg, IL	60194	5423 **Carhart** Lane Schaumburg, IL	60194

PART B: FORMS COMPLETION

Set 1: Questions 1 through 6

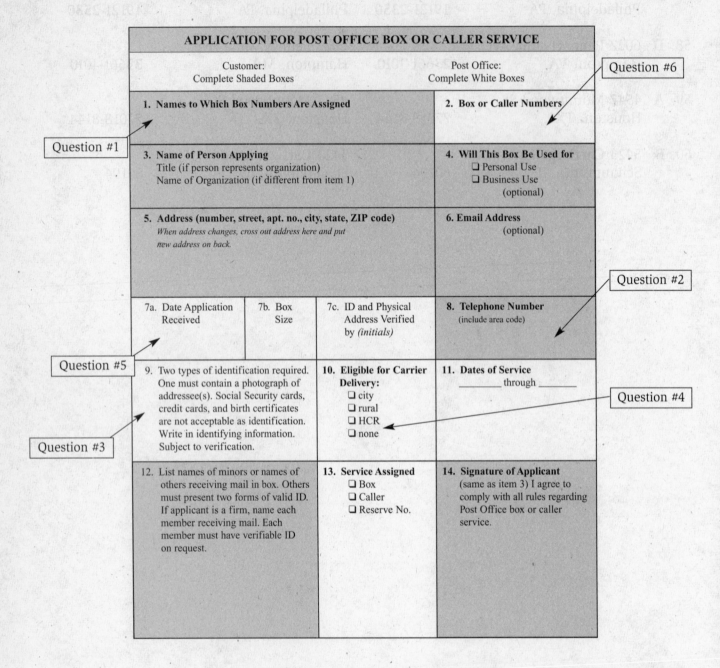

1. **A** Box 1 is labeled "Names to Which Box Numbers Are Assigned." A name is not appropriate in any of the other boxes listed.
2. **C** Two boxes on the form indicate that the information is optional (Box 6 and Box 8), but only Box 8 is one of the answer choices.
3. **C** The information concerning customer ID should be entered in Box 9.
4. **C** The types of delivery are listed in Box 10.
5. **D** Box 7a is labeled "Date Application Received." Only answer choice D lists a date.
6. **C** Either a box number or a caller number should be entered in Box 2. The only possible answer given is choice C.

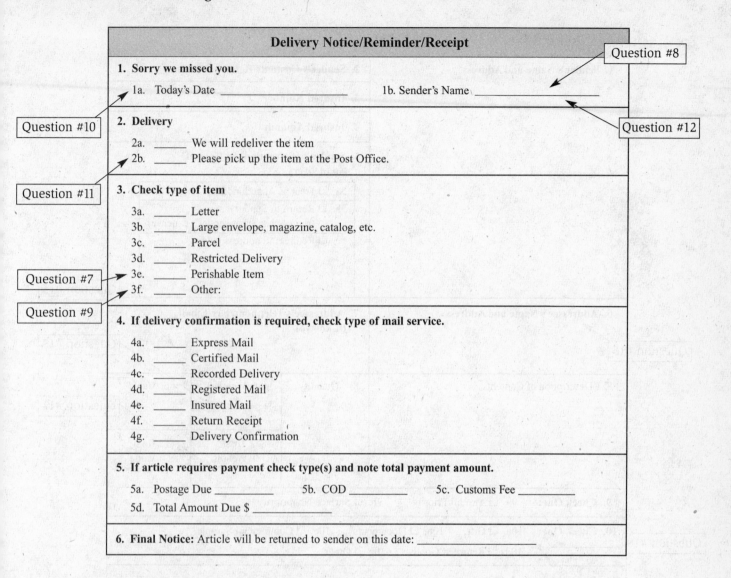

Delivery Notice/Reminder/Receipt

Question #8

1. **Sorry we missed you.**

   1a. Today's Date _____   1b. Sender's Name _____

Question #10

2. **Delivery**

   2a. _____ We will redeliver the item
   2b. _____ Please pick up the item at the Post Office.

Question #12

Question #11

3. **Check type of item**

   3a. _____ Letter
   3b. _____ Large envelope, magazine, catalog, etc.
   3c. _____ Parcel
   3d. _____ Restricted Delivery
   3e. _____ Perishable Item
   3f. _____ Other: _____

Question #7

Question #9

4. **If delivery confirmation is required, check type of mail service.**

   4a. _____ Express Mail
   4b. _____ Certified Mail
   4c. _____ Recorded Delivery
   4d. _____ Registered Mail
   4e. _____ Insured Mail
   4f. _____ Return Receipt
   4g. _____ Delivery Confirmation

5. **If article requires payment check type(s) and note total payment amount.**

   5a. Postage Due _____   5b. COD _____   5c. Customs Fee _____
   5d. Total Amount Due $ _____

6. **Final Notice:** Article will be returned to sender on this date: _____

7. **C** Line 3e indicates a perishable item.
8. **A** Line 1b requires a name, such as "Sean Lewis."
9. **A** A dollar amount would be a correct entry for Line 5a, Line 5c, and Line 5d, but *not* for Line 3f.
10. **C** Line 1a requires a date, such as the date given in choice C.
11. **B** Line 2b indicates that the customer should pick up the mail at the Post Office.
12. **A** The sender's name is listed on Line 1b. Be careful here. Line 6 is one of the choices, and although it mentions that the article will be returned to the sender, there is no place here for the sender's name.

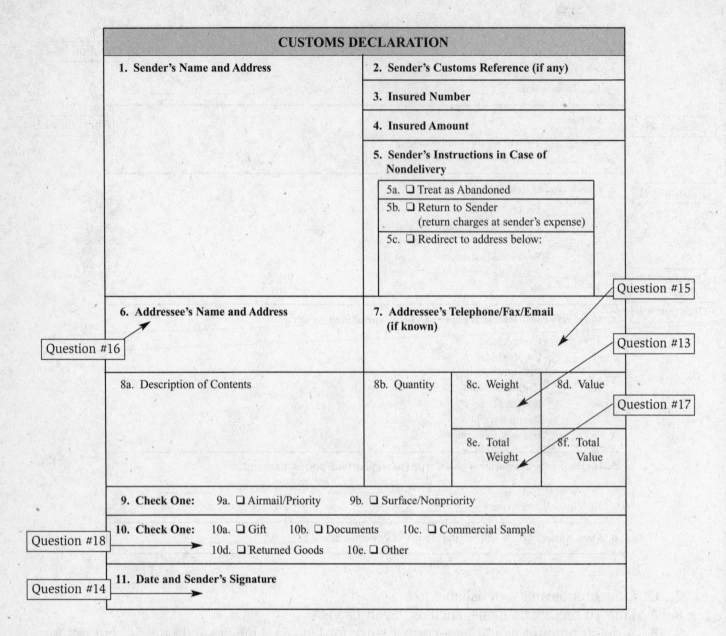

13. **C** The weight must be entered on line 8c, *not* a checkmark.
14. **B** Notice the words "correct" and "complete" in the question. Box 11 requires *both* a signature and a date. The only answer choice that gives both is choice B.
15. **D** Notice the words "if known" in Box 7. So any of these items (telephone, fax, email) can be listed but don't necessarily have to be listed. Answer choices A, B, and C all give possible items that could be listed in Box 7. So the best answer is D, All of the above.
16. **B** If the item is being sent to Fred Walker, he is the addressee. The addressee's name goes in Box 6.
17. **A** Box 8e requires a weight. The only weight given is in choice A.
18. **D** Box 10d is labeled "Returned Goods." When this item is checked, it indicates that the material is being returned. Box 5b mentions "Return to Sender," but this box shows only that the sender has requested this if necessary—not that the material actually is being returned.

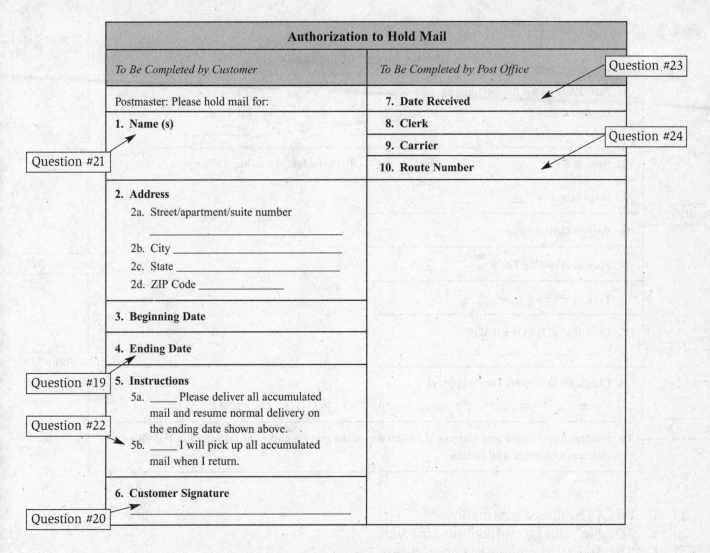

19. **B** The only answer choice that could work here is B, Box 4, because the question says that she must indicate the date. She could check Line 5a, saying she wanted the mail to be delivered, but she could not enter the date there.

20. **B** Line 6 requires a signature (*not* a printed name).

21. **A** Box 1 says "Name(s)," indicating that more than one person may be listed there.

22. **D** Checking Line 5b indicates that the customer will pick up the mail.

23. **D** All of the left side of the form is for the customer to complete. So Box 7 is the only box listed that is *not* completed by the customer.

24. **D** Of the boxes listed, only Box 10 does *not* require a date.

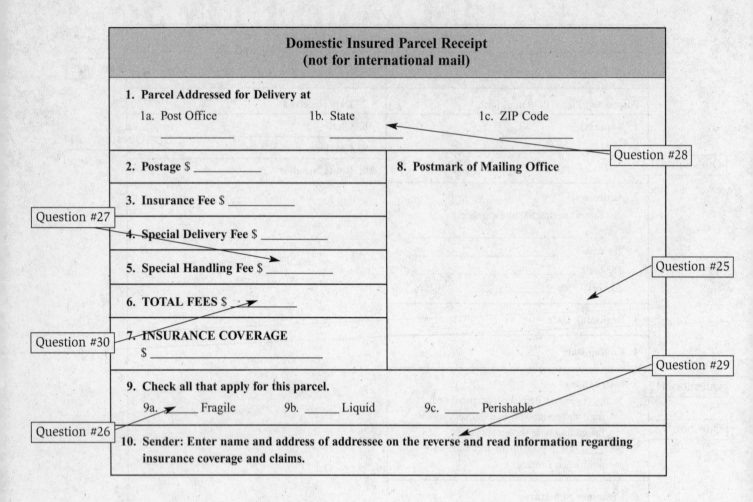

25. **B** Box 8 requires a postmark.
26. **C** "Fragile" can be checked on Line 9a.
27. **C** The Special Handling Fee goes in Box 5.
28. **B** Line 1b is labeled "State." The only state given is Mississippi, in answer choice B.
29. **D** The only place on the form that mentions the name and address of the addressee is Box 10. But that box says that the name and address should be entered on the *reverse* of the form, *not* in Box 10. So the correct answer here is D, None of the above.
30. **B** Total fees should be entered in Box 6.

PRACTICE EXAMINATION 3

ANSWER SHEET FOR PRACTICE EXAMINATION 3

PART A: ADDRESS CHECKING

1. Ⓐ Ⓑ Ⓒ Ⓓ   16. Ⓐ Ⓑ Ⓒ Ⓓ   31. Ⓐ Ⓑ Ⓒ Ⓓ   46. Ⓐ Ⓑ Ⓒ Ⓓ
2. Ⓐ Ⓑ Ⓒ Ⓓ   17. Ⓐ Ⓑ Ⓒ Ⓓ   32. Ⓐ Ⓑ Ⓒ Ⓓ   47. Ⓐ Ⓑ Ⓒ Ⓓ
3. Ⓐ Ⓑ Ⓒ Ⓓ   18. Ⓐ Ⓑ Ⓒ Ⓓ   33. Ⓐ Ⓑ Ⓒ Ⓓ   48. Ⓐ Ⓑ Ⓒ Ⓓ
4. Ⓐ Ⓑ Ⓒ Ⓓ   19. Ⓐ Ⓑ Ⓒ Ⓓ   34. Ⓐ Ⓑ Ⓒ Ⓓ   49. Ⓐ Ⓑ Ⓒ Ⓓ
5. Ⓐ Ⓑ Ⓒ Ⓓ   20. Ⓐ Ⓑ Ⓒ Ⓓ   35. Ⓐ Ⓑ Ⓒ Ⓓ   50. Ⓐ Ⓑ Ⓒ Ⓓ
6. Ⓐ Ⓑ Ⓒ Ⓓ   21. Ⓐ Ⓑ Ⓒ Ⓓ   36. Ⓐ Ⓑ Ⓒ Ⓓ   51. Ⓐ Ⓑ Ⓒ Ⓓ
7. Ⓐ Ⓑ Ⓒ Ⓓ   22. Ⓐ Ⓑ Ⓒ Ⓓ   37. Ⓐ Ⓑ Ⓒ Ⓓ   52. Ⓐ Ⓑ Ⓒ Ⓓ
8. Ⓐ Ⓑ Ⓒ Ⓓ   23. Ⓐ Ⓑ Ⓒ Ⓓ   38. Ⓐ Ⓑ Ⓒ Ⓓ   53. Ⓐ Ⓑ Ⓒ Ⓓ
9. Ⓐ Ⓑ Ⓒ Ⓓ   24. Ⓐ Ⓑ Ⓒ Ⓓ   39. Ⓐ Ⓑ Ⓒ Ⓓ   54. Ⓐ Ⓑ Ⓒ Ⓓ
10. Ⓐ Ⓑ Ⓒ Ⓓ   25. Ⓐ Ⓑ Ⓒ Ⓓ   40. Ⓐ Ⓑ Ⓒ Ⓓ   55. Ⓐ Ⓑ Ⓒ Ⓓ
11. Ⓐ Ⓑ Ⓒ Ⓓ   26. Ⓐ Ⓑ Ⓒ Ⓓ   41. Ⓐ Ⓑ Ⓒ Ⓓ   56. Ⓐ Ⓑ Ⓒ Ⓓ
12. Ⓐ Ⓑ Ⓒ Ⓓ   27. Ⓐ Ⓑ Ⓒ Ⓓ   42. Ⓐ Ⓑ Ⓒ Ⓓ   57. Ⓐ Ⓑ Ⓒ Ⓓ
13. Ⓐ Ⓑ Ⓒ Ⓓ   28. Ⓐ Ⓑ Ⓒ Ⓓ   43. Ⓐ Ⓑ Ⓒ Ⓓ   58. Ⓐ Ⓑ Ⓒ Ⓓ
14. Ⓐ Ⓑ Ⓒ Ⓓ   29. Ⓐ Ⓑ Ⓒ Ⓓ   44. Ⓐ Ⓑ Ⓒ Ⓓ   59. Ⓐ Ⓑ Ⓒ Ⓓ
15. Ⓐ Ⓑ Ⓒ Ⓓ   30. Ⓐ Ⓑ Ⓒ Ⓓ   45. Ⓐ Ⓑ Ⓒ Ⓓ   60. Ⓐ Ⓑ Ⓒ Ⓓ

PART B: FORMS COMPLETION

1. Ⓐ Ⓑ Ⓒ Ⓓ   9. Ⓐ Ⓑ Ⓒ Ⓓ   17. Ⓐ Ⓑ Ⓒ Ⓓ   25. Ⓐ Ⓑ Ⓒ Ⓓ
2. Ⓐ Ⓑ Ⓒ Ⓓ   10. Ⓐ Ⓑ Ⓒ Ⓓ   18. Ⓐ Ⓑ Ⓒ Ⓓ   26. Ⓐ Ⓑ Ⓒ Ⓓ
3. Ⓐ Ⓑ Ⓒ Ⓓ   11. Ⓐ Ⓑ Ⓒ Ⓓ   19. Ⓐ Ⓑ Ⓒ Ⓓ   27. Ⓐ Ⓑ Ⓒ Ⓓ
4. Ⓐ Ⓑ Ⓒ Ⓓ   12. Ⓐ Ⓑ Ⓒ Ⓓ   20. Ⓐ Ⓑ Ⓒ Ⓓ   28. Ⓐ Ⓑ Ⓒ Ⓓ
5. Ⓐ Ⓑ Ⓒ Ⓓ   13. Ⓐ Ⓑ Ⓒ Ⓓ   21. Ⓐ Ⓑ Ⓒ Ⓓ   29. Ⓐ Ⓑ Ⓒ Ⓓ
6. Ⓐ Ⓑ Ⓒ Ⓓ   14. Ⓐ Ⓑ Ⓒ Ⓓ   22. Ⓐ Ⓑ Ⓒ Ⓓ   30. Ⓐ Ⓑ Ⓒ Ⓓ
7. Ⓐ Ⓑ Ⓒ Ⓓ   15. Ⓐ Ⓑ Ⓒ Ⓓ   23. Ⓐ Ⓑ Ⓒ Ⓓ
8. Ⓐ Ⓑ Ⓒ Ⓓ   16. Ⓐ Ⓑ Ⓒ Ⓓ   24. Ⓐ Ⓑ Ⓒ Ⓓ

PART C: CODING AND MEMORY
SECTION 1—CODING

1. Ⓐ Ⓑ Ⓒ Ⓓ   10. Ⓐ Ⓑ Ⓒ Ⓓ   19. Ⓐ Ⓑ Ⓒ Ⓓ   28. Ⓐ Ⓑ Ⓒ Ⓓ
2. Ⓐ Ⓑ Ⓒ Ⓓ   11. Ⓐ Ⓑ Ⓒ Ⓓ   20. Ⓐ Ⓑ Ⓒ Ⓓ   29. Ⓐ Ⓑ Ⓒ Ⓓ
3. Ⓐ Ⓑ Ⓒ Ⓓ   12. Ⓐ Ⓑ Ⓒ Ⓓ   21. Ⓐ Ⓑ Ⓒ Ⓓ   30. Ⓐ Ⓑ Ⓒ Ⓓ
4. Ⓐ Ⓑ Ⓒ Ⓓ   13. Ⓐ Ⓑ Ⓒ Ⓓ   22. Ⓐ Ⓑ Ⓒ Ⓓ   31. Ⓐ Ⓑ Ⓒ Ⓓ
5. Ⓐ Ⓑ Ⓒ Ⓓ   14. Ⓐ Ⓑ Ⓒ Ⓓ   23. Ⓐ Ⓑ Ⓒ Ⓓ   32. Ⓐ Ⓑ Ⓒ Ⓓ
6. Ⓐ Ⓑ Ⓒ Ⓓ   15. Ⓐ Ⓑ Ⓒ Ⓓ   24. Ⓐ Ⓑ Ⓒ Ⓓ   33. Ⓐ Ⓑ Ⓒ Ⓓ
7. Ⓐ Ⓑ Ⓒ Ⓓ   16. Ⓐ Ⓑ Ⓒ Ⓓ   25. Ⓐ Ⓑ Ⓒ Ⓓ   34. Ⓐ Ⓑ Ⓒ Ⓓ
8. Ⓐ Ⓑ Ⓒ Ⓓ   17. Ⓐ Ⓑ Ⓒ Ⓓ   26. Ⓐ Ⓑ Ⓒ Ⓓ   35. Ⓐ Ⓑ Ⓒ Ⓓ
9. Ⓐ Ⓑ Ⓒ Ⓓ   18. Ⓐ Ⓑ Ⓒ Ⓓ   27. Ⓐ Ⓑ Ⓒ Ⓓ   36. Ⓐ Ⓑ Ⓒ Ⓓ

SECTION 2—MEMORY

37. Ⓐ Ⓑ Ⓒ Ⓓ   46. Ⓐ Ⓑ Ⓒ Ⓓ   55. Ⓐ Ⓑ Ⓒ Ⓓ   64. Ⓐ Ⓑ Ⓒ Ⓓ
38. Ⓐ Ⓑ Ⓒ Ⓓ   47. Ⓐ Ⓑ Ⓒ Ⓓ   56. Ⓐ Ⓑ Ⓒ Ⓓ   65. Ⓐ Ⓑ Ⓒ Ⓓ
39. Ⓐ Ⓑ Ⓒ Ⓓ   48. Ⓐ Ⓑ Ⓒ Ⓓ   57. Ⓐ Ⓑ Ⓒ Ⓓ   66. Ⓐ Ⓑ Ⓒ Ⓓ
40. Ⓐ Ⓑ Ⓒ Ⓓ   49. Ⓐ Ⓑ Ⓒ Ⓓ   58. Ⓐ Ⓑ Ⓒ Ⓓ   67. Ⓐ Ⓑ Ⓒ Ⓓ
41. Ⓐ Ⓑ Ⓒ Ⓓ   50. Ⓐ Ⓑ Ⓒ Ⓓ   59. Ⓐ Ⓑ Ⓒ Ⓓ   68. Ⓐ Ⓑ Ⓒ Ⓓ
42. Ⓐ Ⓑ Ⓒ Ⓓ   51. Ⓐ Ⓑ Ⓒ Ⓓ   60. Ⓐ Ⓑ Ⓒ Ⓓ   69. Ⓐ Ⓑ Ⓒ Ⓓ
43. Ⓐ Ⓑ Ⓒ Ⓓ   52. Ⓐ Ⓑ Ⓒ Ⓓ   61. Ⓐ Ⓑ Ⓒ Ⓓ   70. Ⓐ Ⓑ Ⓒ Ⓓ
44. Ⓐ Ⓑ Ⓒ Ⓓ   53. Ⓐ Ⓑ Ⓒ Ⓓ   62. Ⓐ Ⓑ Ⓒ Ⓓ   71. Ⓐ Ⓑ Ⓒ Ⓓ
45. Ⓐ Ⓑ Ⓒ Ⓓ   54. Ⓐ Ⓑ Ⓒ Ⓓ   63. Ⓐ Ⓑ Ⓒ Ⓓ   72. Ⓐ Ⓑ Ⓒ Ⓓ

PART D: PERSONAL CHARACTERISTICS AND EXPERIENCE INVENTORY

(236 Questions—not included here)

ADDRESS CHECKING SAMPLE QUESTIONS

Look at the row of information for sample question 1, which is labeled "S1" below. Carefully but quickly compare the **List to Be Checked** with the **Correct List**. Then decide if there are **No Errors** (select A), an error in the **Address Only** (select B), an error in the **ZIP Code Only** (select C), or an error in **Both** the address and the ZIP code (select D). Record your response to the sample questions in the **Sample Answer Grid** below. Complete the other three samples given, S2, S3, and S4, and record your responses on the **Sample Answer Grid**.

A. No Errors	B. Address Only	C. ZIP Code Only	D. Both

Correct List

	Address	ZIP Code
S1.	432 Rosewood Ct. Pasadena, CA	91106
S2.	1977 Hully Street Austin, TX	78734-1141
S3.	648 Central Dr. New York, NY	10034
S4.	9812 Pine Ave. Chicago, IL	60467-5113

List to Be Checked

	Address	ZIP Code
S1.	432 Rosewood Ct. Pasadena, CA	91106
S2.	1977 Holly Street Austin, TX	78734-1114
S3.	648 Central Dr. New York, NY	10054
S4.	9812 Pine Ave. Chicago, IL	60467-5113

Sample Answer Grid

S1.	Ⓐ	Ⓑ	Ⓒ	Ⓓ
S2.	Ⓐ	Ⓑ	Ⓒ	Ⓓ
S3.	Ⓐ	Ⓑ	Ⓒ	Ⓓ
S4.	Ⓐ	Ⓑ	Ⓒ	Ⓓ

Completed Sample Answer Grid

S1.	Ⓐ	●	Ⓒ	Ⓓ
S2.	Ⓐ	Ⓑ	Ⓒ	●
S3.	Ⓐ	Ⓑ	●	Ⓓ
S4.	●	Ⓑ	Ⓒ	Ⓓ

In sample 1, the address in the **List to Be Checked** shows Pasedena, but the **Correct List** shows Pasadena. So there is an error in the address. Since the Zip codes are exactly the same, the correct answer is **B—Address Only**.

In sample 2, the address in the **List to Be Checked** shows Holly Street, but the **Correct List** shows Hully Street. So there is an error in the address. The **List to Be Checked** also shows an error in the ZIP code. The last four numbers are 1114, and they are 1141 in the **Correct List**. Because there is an error in the address and in the ZIP code, the correct answer is **D—Both**.

In sample 3, the addresses in the **List to Be Checked** and the **Correct List** are exactly the same, but there is an error in the ZIP code on the **List to Be Checked**. The **List to Be Checked** shows 10054, but the **Correct List** shows 10034. So there is an error in the ZIP code. The correct answer is **C—ZIP Code Only**.

In sample 4, the addresses in the **List to Be Checked** and the **Correct List** are exactly the same. The ZIP codes are also exactly the same. So the correct answer is **A—No Errors**.

Now turn to the next page and begin the address checking test.

PART A: ADDRESS CHECKING

For the following 60 items, compare the address in the **Correct List** with the address in the **List to Be Checked**. Determine if there are **No Errors** (answer A), an error in the **Address Only** (answer B), an error in the **ZIP Code Only** (answer C), or an error in **Both** (answer D). Mark your answers in the Address Checking section of the answer sheet. You have 11 minutes to complete this test.

A. No Errors	B. Address Only	C. ZIP Code Only	D. Both

Correct List

	Address	ZIP Code
1.	2077 Greenway Court	
	Matthews, NC	28104-4511
2.	9033 S 69th Pl.	
	Springfield, Oregon	97478-9588
3.	1878 Comanche St.	
	Corpus Christi, TX	78408
4.	97221 Eau Claire Blvd.	
	Wausau, WI	54403-7221
5.	4744 Amberjack Bay E	
	Lake Havasu City, AZ	86406
6.	904 SW 189th Cir. Apt. 655	
	Dunnellon, FL	34432-1066
7.	9118 Chicopee Dr.	
	Medimont, ID	83842-6444
8.	P.O Box 835B	
	Monroe, MI	48161-8380
9.	9250 E Night Glow Way	
	Apache Junction, AZ	85219
10.	4686 Valencia St.	
	Pueblo, CO	81006
11.	3328 Chickasaw Ave.	
	Gillette, Wyoming	82718-7002

List to Be Checked

Address	ZIP Code
2077 Greenway Court	
Matthews, NC	28014-4511
9033 S 69th Pl.	
Springfield, Oregon	97478-9888
1878 Comanche St.	
Corpus Christi, TX	78408
97221 Eau Claire Blvd.	
Wausau, WI	64403-7221
4734 Amberjack Bay E	
Lake Havasu City, AZ	86406
904 SW 199th Cir. Apt. 655	
Dunnellon, FL	34423-1066
9118 Chincopee Dr.	
Medimont, ID	83842-6444
P.O Box 835B	
Monroe, MI	48161-6360
9250 E Night Glow Dr.	
Apache Junction, AZ	85219
4686 Valencia St.	
Pueblo, MO	81606
3328 Chickasaw Ave.	
Gillmore, Wyoming	82718-7002

170

	Correct List		List to Be Checked	
	Address	*ZIP Code*	*Address*	*ZIP Code*
12.	5042 SE Berghammer St. Portland, OR	97267-7905	5042 NE Berghammer St. Portland, OR	97267-7905
13.	7322 Dorrance St. Warwick, RI	02886-0920	7322 Dorrance St. Warwick, RI	02886-0920
14.	61701 Rural Route 40 Brooksville, FL	34601	6101 Rural Route 40 Brooksville, FL	34601
15.	6273 Lacroix Dr. Houma, LA	70364	6273 Lacroix Dr. Houma, LA	70363
16.	1131 6th Ave. SE Hagerstown, MD	21061-7124	1131 6th Ave. SE Hagersford, MD	21061-7124
17.	5537 Englewood Ave. Waterbury, CT	06705	6627 Englewood Ave. Waterbury, CT	96705
18.	4603 Catherine St. Vacaville, CA	95688	4603 Catherine St. Vacaville, CA	59688
19.	2271 Painted Valley Dr. Little Rock, AR	72212-3301	2271 Painted Valley Tr. Little Rock, AR	72212-3301
20.	4934 Baggett Rd. Meridian, MS	39301	4934 Baggett Rd. Meridian, MS	39331
21.	9232 Buena Suerta Dr. Hobbs, NM	88242-5584	9232 Bona Suerta Dr. Hobbs, NM	88242-5584
22.	1837 Sudbury Rd. Charlotte, NC	28205	1837 Sudbury Rd. Charlotte, NC	28250
23.	2062 3500 Road Shawnee, OK	74804-6047	2062 3550 Road Shawnee, OK	75404-6047
24.	2708 Collingswood Dr. Chesterfield, VA	23832-2270	2708 Collingswood Dr. Chesterfield, VA	23832-2270
25.	6087 San Joaquin St. Brownsville, TX	78521	2087 San Joaquin St. Brownsville, TX	78521

	Correct List		**List to Be Checked**	
	Address	ZIP Code	Address	ZIP Code
26.	3849 Parkridge Dr. Utica, MI	48315-8361	38849 Parkridge Dr. Utica, MI	48315-8361 *B*
27.	8033 S. Kirkland Ave. Chicago, IL	60652-1753	8033 S. Kirkland Ave. Chicago, IL	60652-1935 *C*
28.	41727 County Road 2665 Eureka Springs, AR	72631	41727 County Road 2665 Eureka Springs, AR	42631 *C*
29.	3472 Shakeley Lane Hillsburg, Indiana	46046	3472 Shakeley Lane Hillsburg, Indiana	46046 *A*
30.	8636 Forest Plains Ln. Salisbury, MD	21804-5820	8636 Forest Plains Ln. Salisburg, MD	X 21804-5800 *C*
31.	6143 Lucretia Ave. Minnetonka, MN	55345-1559	6413 Lucretia Ave. Minnetonka, MN	*B* 55345-1559
32.	93325 Highway 99 Madera, CA	93638	93325 Highway 99 Madera, CA	93638 *A*
33.	1020 Wendemere Court Jefferson City, MO	65109-9211	1020 Wendemere Court Jefferson City, MO	X 65109-9221 *C*
34.	6822 Blankenship Dr. Charleston, WV	25309-1646	6822 Blankenship Tr. Charleston, WV	*B* 25309-1646
35.	8725 S Wheeling St. Tuscarora, NV	89834	8725 S Wheeling St. Tuscarora, NV	89834 *A*
36.	2739 Saint Stanislaus St. Rochester, NY	14621	2739 Saint Stanislaus St. Rochester, NY	14621 *A*
37.	4022 Ave Calderon Carolina, PR	00985	6032 Ave Calderon Carolina, PR	09985 *D*
38.	4900 Pierpont Meadows Thetford Center, VT	05075	4900 Pierpont Meadows Medford Center, VT	05075 *B*
39.	5161 Guilford St. West Columbia, SC	29169-4806	5161 Guilford St. West Columbia, SC	29669-4806
				C

	Correct List		**List to Be Checked**	
	Address	*ZIP Code*	*Address*	*ZIP Code*
40.	37232 60th Ave. Saint Cloud, MN	56303-6333	37232 30th Ave. Saint Cloud, MN	56303-6423
41.	3967 Tampa Bay Drive Zephyrhills, FL	33543-2501	3967 Tampa Bay Drive Tampahills, FL	33543-2501
42.	4575 Hawthorne Ln. Greenwood, IN	46142	4577 Hawthorne Dr. Greenwood, IN	46124
43.	4683 Myrtle Street Ext. Norwalk, CT	06855	4683 Myrtle Street Ext. Norwalk, CT	68055
44.	4426 Fernando St. Newport Beach, CA	92661-5097	4426 Ferndale St. Newport Beach, CA	92661-5097
45.	1933 Highway 135 Pleasant Dale, Nebraska	68423	1933 Highway 135 Pleasant Dale, Nebraska	68323
46.	5414 N Commercial Street Manchester, NH	03101-7294	5414 N Commercial Street Manchester, NH	03101-7294
47.	2002 Haven Hill Rd. Lexington, NC	27292-0438	2002 Haven Hill Rd. Lexington, SC	22792-0438
48.	7335 Sullivan Garden Pkwy. Kingsport, TN	37660	7335 Sullivan Garden Pkwy. Kingsport, TN	37660
49.	9428 Stronghold Ct. Ashburn, VA	20147-5584	9428 Stronghold Ct. Ashbury, VA	20147-5584
50.	1204 Marvin Cutoff La Center, WA	98629	1204 Marvin Cutoff La Center, WA	98629
51.	2368 Glendora Ct. Sparks, NV	89436	2368 Glendora Ct. Sparks, NV	83636
52.	649 Casabella Cir. East Hartford, CT	06108-5410	649 Casabella Cir. East Hartford, CT	06008-5410
53.	3122 Declovina St. Santa Fe, NM	87505-1733	3122 Declovina St. Santa Fe, NM	87505-1773

Correct List

	Address	ZIP Code
54.	1201 Freight Rd. Mount Airy, GA	30563
55.	6728 Irvington Drive Buffalo, NY	14228-5420
56.	7742 Cleghorn St. Honolulu, HI	96815-6542
57.	9038 Elizabethtown Rd. Fayetteville, NC	28306
58.	3895 Tranquility Lane Ponderay, ID	83852-6031
59.	6510 Locust Ave. Montpelier, ND	58472-0686
60.	1820 Moffitt Place Altamont, IL	62411

List to Be Checked

Address	ZIP Code
1201 Fright Rd. Mount Airy, GA	30563
6828 Irvington Drive Buffalo, NY	14228-5420
7742 Clayton St. Honolulu, HI	96816-6542
9038 Elizabethtown Rd. Fayetteville, NC	28006
3895 Tranquility Lane Ponderay, ID	38852-6031
6510 Locust Ave. Montpelier, ND	58472-0686
1820 Moffitt Place Alvamont, IL	61411

PART B: FORMS COMPLETION

Look at this sample form and answer the two questions below it. Mark your answers in the sample answer grid that follows the questions.

Sample Form

1. First Name	2. Middle Name	3. Last Name
4. Street Address		
5. City	6. State	7. ZIP Code
8. Fee $ _____	9. Date 9a. Day _____ 9b. Month _____ 9c. Year _____	

S1. Which of these would be a correct entry for Box 6?
   A. "2542 Oak Avenue"
   B. "November"
   C. "$6.80"
   D. "Nevada"

S2. Where should the middle name be entered on the form?
   A. Box 1
   B. Box 2
   C. Box 3
   D. Box 4

Sample Answer Grid				
S1.	Ⓐ	Ⓑ	Ⓒ	Ⓓ
S2.	Ⓐ	Ⓑ	Ⓒ	Ⓓ

Completed Sample Answer Grid				
S1.	Ⓐ	Ⓑ	Ⓒ	●
S2.	Ⓐ	●	Ⓒ	Ⓓ

On the form, Box 6 is labeled "State." So the correct answer for sample question 1 is "D. Nevada," which is the only state listed among the answers. Box 2 is labeled "Middle Name," so the correct answer for sample question 2 is "B. Box 2." The completed sample answer grid above shows these correct answers filled in.

Directions: Each of the following forms is followed by questions based on that form. Each part of the form is labeled with a number or a number and a letter. You will have 15 minutes to complete the 30 questions in this section

Set 1: Forms Completion
Questions 1 through 6 are based on Form 1.

Form 1

<table>
<tr><td colspan="6" align="center">DOMESTIC MAIL OR REGISTERED MAIL INQUIRY
To Be Completed by Customer</td></tr>
<tr><td colspan="3">1. Mailer Information</td><td colspan="3">2. Addressee Information</td></tr>
<tr><td>1a. First Name</td><td>1b. Middle Initial</td><td>1c. Last Name</td><td>2a. First Name</td><td>2b. Middle Initial</td><td>2c. Last Name</td></tr>
<tr><td colspan="3">1d. Business Name
(use only if mailer is a company)</td><td colspan="3">2d. Business Name
(use only if addressee is a company)</td></tr>
<tr><td colspan="3">1e. Street Name
(number, street, suite/apartment number)</td><td colspan="3">2e. Street Name
(number, street, suite/apartment number)</td></tr>
<tr><td>1f. City</td><td>1g. State</td><td>1h. ZIP Code</td><td>2f. City</td><td>2g. State</td><td>2h. ZIP Code</td></tr>
<tr><td colspan="3">1i. Telephone Number (include area code)</td><td colspan="3">2i. Telephone Number (include area code)</td></tr>
</table>

<table>
<tr><td colspan="3">3. Payment Assignment—
Alternate Payment Address</td><td colspan="4">4. Description of Lost or Damaged Article(s)—
Add Extra Sheets as Needed</td></tr>
<tr><td colspan="3">3a. Who Is to Receive Payment?
(check one)
❑ Mailer   ❑ Addressee</td><td>4a. Item No.</td><td>4b. Description of Article</td><td>4c. Value or Cost</td><td>4d. Purchase Date</td></tr>
<tr><td colspan="3" rowspan="2">3b. Street Name (if other than address above)
(number, street, suite/apartment number)</td><td>First</td><td></td><td></td><td></td></tr>
<tr><td>Second</td><td></td><td></td><td></td></tr>
<tr><td>3c. City</td><td>3d. State</td><td>3e. ZIP Code</td><td>Third</td><td></td><td></td><td></td></tr>
<tr><td></td><td></td><td></td><td>Fourth</td><td></td><td></td><td></td></tr>
</table>

<table>
<tr><td colspan="2">5. COD Amount to Be Remitted to Sender</td><td>6. Total Amount Claimed for All Articles</td></tr>
<tr><td colspan="3">7. Certification and Signature</td></tr>
<tr><td>7a. Customer Submitting Claim:

❑ Mailer   ❑ Addressee</td><td>7b. Signature of Customer Filing the Claim</td><td>7c. Date Signed
(MM/DD/YYYY)</td></tr>
</table>

1. Where would the addressee's city be indicated?
   A. Box 1e
   B. Box 1f
   C. Box 2f
   D. Box 3c

2. You could enter a number in each of the following EXCEPT which one?
   A. Box 1c
   B. Box 1i
   C. Box 2h
   D. Box 4b

3. Which of these would be a correct entry for Box 7a?
   A. "Alabama"
   B. A checkmark
   C. "73545"
   D. "Mary Figuroa"

4. There is only one item that has been lost or damaged, with a value of $287. How would this value be noted?
   A. Write "$287" in Box 4c
   B. Write "$287" in Box 5
   C. Write "$574" in Box 6
   D. None of the above

5. Which of these would be a correct entry for Box 2b?
   A. "J"
   B. "Smith"
   C. "333-784-9874"
   D. A checkmark

6. The package was sent to Don Whipple. How would you indicate that Mr. Whipple should receive payment?
   A. Enter his name in Box 1
   B. Enter his name in Box 2
   C. Enter a checkmark in Box 3a
   D. Enter a checkmark in Box 7a

Set 2: Forms Completion

Questions 7 through 12 are based on Form 2.

Form 2

<table>
<tr><td colspan="3" align="center">**COD**
Copy 1: Delivery Unit</td></tr>
<tr><td colspan="3">**Delivery Employee: Remove Copies 1 (Delivery Unit Copy) and 2 (Mailer's Copy) at Time of Delivery.**</td></tr>
<tr><td colspan="2">Collect the amount shown below if customer pays by CHECK made payable to the mailer.</td><td>Collect the amount shown below if customer pays in CASH (includes money order fee or fees).</td></tr>
<tr><td colspan="2">**1. Check**
Amount $</td><td>**2. Cash**
Amount $</td></tr>
<tr><td>3a. ❑ Registered Mail</td><td>3b. ❑ Express Mail</td><td>3c. ❑ Form 3849-D Requested</td></tr>
<tr><td>**4. Date of Mailing**</td><td colspan="2">**5. ❑ Remit COD Charges to Sender via Express Mail**</td></tr>
<tr><td colspan="2">**6. From:**</td><td>**7. To:**</td></tr>
<tr><td>**8. Delivered By**</td><td>**9. Date Delivered**</td><td>**10. Check Number**</td></tr>
<tr><td>**11. Date Payment Sent to Mailer**</td><td>**12. Date Form 3849-D Sent**</td><td>**13. Money Order Number(s)**</td></tr>
<tr><td colspan="3">DO NOT allow the recipient to examine the contents before payment.
DO NOT deliver this article until payment is collected.
If payment is by check, enter check number above.
Have customer sign Form 3849.</td></tr>
</table>

7. Which of these would be a correct entry for Box 1?
   A. "2258209"
   B. "$58"
   C. "5/15/06"
   D. A checkmark

8. Where would the date the package was mailed be entered?
   A. Box 4
   B. Box 9
   C. Box 11
   D. Box 12

9. Which of these would be a correct entry for Box 5?
   A. "5/15/06"
   B. "$58"
   C. A checkmark
   D. "2258209"

10. The package is being sent to Harriet Washington. Where would the customer indicate this?
    A. Box 3a
    B. Box 5
    C. Box 6
    D. Box 7

11. Which of these would be a correct entry for Box 13?
    A. "5/15/06"
    B. "James Turner"
    C. A checkmark
    D. None of the above

12. Form 3849-D has been requested. Where would this be indicated?
    A. Box 3a
    B. Box 3c
    C. Box 8
    D. Box 12

Set 3: Forms Completion
Questions 13 through 18 are based on Form 3.

Form 3

CERTIFICATE OF BULK MAILING

Mailer: Fill in this statement in ink. Affix meter stamp or uncanceled postage stamps covering fee in the block to the right.

1. Meter stamp or postage in payment of fee must be affixed here and canceled by postmarking, including date.

2. Fee for Certificate

2a. Up to 1,000 pieces

2b. For each additional 1,000 pieces or fraction

2c. Duplicate copy of certificate

USE CURRENT RATE CHART

3. Mailing Information

3a. Number of Identical Pieces	3b. Class of Mail	3c. Postage on Each	3d. Number of Pieces to the Pound	3e. Total Number of Pounds	3f. Total Postage Paid	3g. Fee Paid

4. Mailed For

5. Mailed By

Postmaster's Certificate

It is hereby certified that the above-described mailing has been received and the number of pieces and postage verified.

6. _____

(Signature of Postmaster or Designee)

13. How would you indicate that the total bulk mailing weighs 75 pounds?
    A. Enter "75" in Box 1
    B. Enter "75" in Line 2a
    C. Enter "75" in Box 3d
    D. Enter "75" in Box 3e

14. Which of these would be a correct entry for Box 6?
    A. The signature of the Postmaster
    B. The initials of the Postmaster's designee
    C. The signature of the person named in Box 4
    D. The signature of the person named in Box 5

15. The fee for this Certificate of Bulk Mailing is $18.80. Where should you enter this fee?
    A. Box 1
    B. Line 2c
    C. Box 3g
    D. Box 6

16. Which of these would be a correct entry for Box 5?
    A. A checkmark
    B. "Kerry Walters"
    C. "$18.80"
    D. "25"

17. Kerry Walters is mailing the items for his company, Three Suns Electric Company. Where would you indicate the company name?
    A. Box 3b
    B. Box 4
    C. Box 5
    D. Box 6

18. Where would you find the correct amount of the fee for this certificate?
    A. Line 2a
    B. Line 2b
    C. Box 3c
    D. None of the above

Form 4

MAIL FORWARDING CHANGE OF ADDRESS ORDER		
1. Change of address for (check one) 1a. ❑ Individual 1b. ❑ Entire Family 1c. ❑ Business	**17. Official Use Only**	
	17a. Zone/Route ID Number	
2. Is this move temporary? (check one) 2a. ❑ Yes 2b. ❑ No	17b. Date Entered on Form 3982	
	17c. Clerk/Carrier Endorsement	
3. Start Date	**4. If the move is temporary, list date to discontinue forwarding.**	
5. Name 5a. Last Name	5b. First Name and Middle Initial	
6. If Business Move, Print Business Name		
PRINT OLD MAILING ADDRESS BELOW		
7. OLD Street Address or PO Box		
8. OLD City	**9. OLD State**	**10. OLD ZIP Code**
PRINT NEW MAILING ADDRESS BELOW		
11. NEW Street Address or PO Box		
12. NEW City	**13. NEW State**	**14. NEW ZIP Code**

15. Print and sign name:
   15a. Print: _____
   15b. Sign: _____
	16. Date Signed	

19. Which of these would be a correct entry for Box 3?
    A. "10/20/06"
    B. "Jane Foley"
    C. "65689-7900"
    D. "2269 Carwood Terrace"

20. Which of these would be a correct entry for Box 5a?
    A. A checkmark
    B. "A-One Auto Service"
    C. "Foley"
    D. "Jane J."

21. Where would you indicate that only the customer is moving?
    A. Line 1a
    B. Box 5
    C. Box 15a
    D. Box 16

22. The clerk accepting this form is Wally Peterson. Where would his name be entered?
    A. Box 5a
    B. Box 5b
    C. Box 15
    D. Box 17c

23. This customer is moving from Minnesota to Florida. Where would "Florida" be entered?
    A. Box 8
    B. Box 9
    C. Box 12
    D. Box 13

24. How would you indicate that the customer, Jane Foley, will be gone for a short time but will then return to her present address?
    A. Put a checkmark on Line 1a
    B. Put a checkmark on Line 1b
    C. Put a checkmark on Line 2a
    D. Put a checkmark on Line 2b

Form 5

STAMP VENDING MACHINE REIMBURSEMENT REQUEST

For Customer Use

1. Customer Information:

    1a. Name _____

    1b. Address _____

                   _____

                    _____

    1c. Daytime Phone Number (include area code) _____

2. Loss Information:

    2a. Amount of Loss $_____   2b. Date of Loss _____   2c. Time of Loss

                                                          ❑ AM

                                                          ❑ PM

3. Machine Information: Machine ID (6-digit number on front of vending machine) _____

4. Occurrence Information: What Happened? (circle all that apply)

4a. Did not receive product	4f. Money not returned
4b. Incorrect change given	4g. Currency lost
4c. Did not register/jammed	4h. Coin lost
4d. No change given	4i. Credit/debit lost
4e. No credit shown	4j. Other (enter in "Comments")

5. Comments: (optional)

For Postal Service Use

6. Paid by	7. Date

8. Action Taken (circle one)

    8a. Paid   8b. Not Paid

9. Sales and Services Associate Signature _____

25. Which of these would be a correct entry for Box 4?
   A. A checkmark
   B. A circle
   C. A dollar amount
   D. A date

26. Amos Tulley is the clerk who paid the customer. Where would Tulley's name be entered?
   A. Line 1a
   B. Box 5
   C. Box 6
   D. Box 8

27. The customer attempted to purchase these stamps at 7 o'clock in the evening. Where would the customer indicate this?
   A. Line 1c
   B. Line 2b
   C. Line 2c
   D. Line 4a

28. The customer's change was 40 cents but should have been 60 cents. How would the customer indicate this?
   A. Enter "60 cents" on Line 2a
   B. Enter "60 cents" on Line 2a and circle Line 4b
   C. Circle Line 4d
   D. Enter "20 cents" on Line 2a and circle Line 4b

29. Which of these would be a correct entry for Box 7?
   A. "3/26/06"
   B. "4550 Deer Run Court"
   C. "Canton, Ohio"
   D. "$1.20"

30. Where would the customer indicate his or her telephone number?
   A. Line 1b
   B. Line 1c
   C. Box 5
   D. Box 7

PART C: CODING AND MEMORY

SECTION 1—CODING

Coding Exercise

Choose the correct delivery route, based on the Coding Guide, for each of the following 4 items and mark your answers on the answer sheet below. You have 2 minutes to complete this practice exercise. This exercise will not be scored.

CODING GUIDE

Address Range	Delivery Route
25000–31999 County Road 5122 10–35 Hunters Cove	A
200–799 Ridgecroft Pkwy. 32000–44500 County Road 5122 36–60 Hunters Cove	B
7591–9700 Independence St. 650–1000 Clear Springs Lane 800–1200 Ridgecroft Pkwy.	C
All mail that doesn't fall in one of the address ranges listed above	D

	Address	Delivery Route
1.	849 Clear Springs Lane	A B C D
2.	9653 Independence St.	A B C D
3.	32 Hunters Cove	A B C D
4.	310 Ridgecroft Pkwy.	A B C D

Sample Answer Grid				
1.	Ⓐ	Ⓑ	Ⓒ	Ⓓ
2.	Ⓐ	Ⓑ	Ⓒ	Ⓓ
3.	Ⓐ	Ⓑ	Ⓒ	Ⓓ
4.	Ⓐ	Ⓑ	Ⓒ	Ⓓ

Completed Sample Answer Grid				
1.	Ⓐ	Ⓑ	●	Ⓓ
2.	Ⓐ	Ⓑ	●	Ⓓ
3.	●	Ⓑ	Ⓒ	Ⓓ
4.	Ⓐ	●	Ⓒ	Ⓓ

CODING TEST

Choose the correct delivery route, based on the Coding Guide, for each of the following 36 items (items 1 through 36) and mark your answers in the Coding section of the Answer Sheet. You have 6 minutes to complete this test.

CODING GUIDE

Address Range	Delivery Route
25000–31999 County Road 5122 10–35 Hunters Cove	A
200–799 Ridgecroft Pkwy. 32000–44500 County Road 5122 36–60 Hunters Cove	B
7591–9700 Independence St. 650–1000 Clear Springs Lane 800–1200 Ridgecroft Pkwy.	C
All mail that doesn't fall in one of the address ranges listed above	D

	Address	Delivery Route
1.	9800 Independence St.	A B C D ✓
2.	932 Clear Springs Lane	A B C ✓ D
3.	11 Hunters Cove	A ✓ B C D
4.	27799 County Road 5122	A ✓ B C D
5.	7595 Independence St.	A B C ✓ D
6.	328 Ridgecroft Pkwy.	A B ✓ C D
7.	800 Clear Springs Lane	A B C ✓ D
8.	659 Clear Springs Lane	A B C ✓ D
9.	70 Hunters Cove	A B C D ✓
10.	27445 County Road 5112	A ✓ B C D

188

Address	Delivery Route
11. 314 Ridgecroft Pkwy.	A **B** C D
12. 29907 County Road 5122	**A** B C D
13. 54 Hunters Cove	A **B** C D
14. 30000 County Road 5122	**A** B C D
15. 600 Clear Springs Road	A B **C** D
16. 7722 Independence St.	A B **C** D
17. 16 Harbor Cove	A B C **D**
18. 646 Ridgecroft Pkwy.	A **B** C D
19. 25787 County Road 5122	**A** B C D
20. 14 Hunters Cove	**A** B C D
21. 576 Ridgecroft Pkwy	A **B** C D
22. 966 Clear Springs Lane	A B **C** D
23. 34798 County Road 5122	A **B** C D
24. 75 Hunters Cove	A B C **D**
25. 758 Ridgecroft Pkwy.	A B **C** D
26. 29 Hunters Cove	**A** B C D
27. 30750 County Road 5122	**A** B C D
28. 97000 Independence St.	A B C **D**
29. 39778 County Road 5122	A **B** C D
30. 500 Ridgecroft Pkwy.	A **B** C D
31. 33101 County Road 5122	A **B** C D
32. 8119 Independence St.	A B **C** D
33. 361 Ridgeway Pkwy.	A B C **D**
34. 19 Hunters Cove	**A** B C D
35. 43913 County Road 5122	A **B** C D
36. 31000 County Road 5122	**A** B C D

SECTION 2—MEMORY

Memory Study Period 1
Use the time given to memorize the information in the following Coding Guide.

CODING GUIDE

Address Range	Delivery Route
25000–31999 County Road 5122	
10–35 Hunters Cove	A
200–799 Ridgecroft Pkwy.	
32000–44500 County Road 5122	B
36–60 Hunters Cove	
7591–9700 Independence St.	
650–1000 Clear Springs Lane	C
800–1200 Ridgecroft Pkwy.	
All mail that doesn't fall in one of the address ranges listed above	D

Memory Exercise

Choose the correct delivery route, based on your memory of the information in the Coding Guide, for each of the following 8 items and mark your answers on the answer sheet below. You have 90 seconds to complete this practice exercise. This exercise will not be scored.

Address	Delivery Route
1. 299 Ridgecroft Pkwy.	A B C D
2. 42 Hunters Cove	A B C D
3. 7990 Independence St.	A B C D
4. 990 Clear Springs Lane	A B C D
5. 31998 County Road 5122	A B C D
6. 9600 Independence Ave.	A B C D
7. 309 Ridgecroft Pkwy.	A B C D
8. 28878 County Road 5122	A B C D

Sample Answer Grid				
1.	Ⓐ	Ⓑ	Ⓒ	Ⓓ
2.	Ⓐ	Ⓑ	Ⓒ	Ⓓ
3.	Ⓐ	Ⓑ	Ⓒ	Ⓓ
4.	Ⓐ	Ⓑ	Ⓒ	Ⓓ
5.	Ⓐ	Ⓑ	Ⓒ	Ⓓ
6.	Ⓐ	Ⓑ	Ⓒ	Ⓓ
7.	Ⓐ	Ⓑ	Ⓒ	Ⓓ
8.	Ⓐ	Ⓑ	Ⓒ	Ⓓ

Completed Sample Answer Grid				
1.	Ⓐ	●	Ⓒ	Ⓓ
2.	Ⓐ	●	Ⓒ	Ⓓ
3.	Ⓐ	Ⓑ	●	Ⓓ
4.	Ⓐ	Ⓑ	●	Ⓓ
5.	●	Ⓑ	Ⓒ	Ⓓ
6.	Ⓐ	Ⓑ	Ⓒ	●
7.	Ⓐ	●	Ⓒ	Ⓓ
8.	●	Ⓑ	Ⓒ	Ⓓ

Memory Study Period 2

Use the time given to memorize the information in the following Coding Guide.

CODING GUIDE

Address Range	Delivery Route
25000–31999 County Road 5122 10–35 Hunters Cove	A
200–799 Ridgecroft Pkwy. 32000–44500 County Road 5122 36–60 Hunters Cove	B
7591–9700 Independence St. 650–1000 Clear Springs Lane 800–1200 Ridgecroft Pkwy.	C
All mail that doesn't fall in one of the address ranges listed above	D

MEMORY TEST

Choose the correct delivery route, based on your memory of the information in the Coding Guide, for each of the following 36 items (items 37 through 72) and mark your answers in the Memory section of the Answer Sheet. You have 7 minutes to complete this test.

	Address	Delivery Route
37.	1146 Ridgecroft Pkwy.	A B C D
38.	9696 Independence St.	A B C D
39.	33 Hunters Cove	A B C D
40.	27633 County Route 5122	A B C D
41.	478 Ridgecroft Pkwy.	A B C D
42.	23 Hunters Cove	A B C D
43.	3852 County Road 5122	A B C D
44.	952 Clear Springs Lane	A B C D
45.	51 Hunters Cove	A B C D

	Address	Delivery Route
46.	41767 County Road 5122	A B C D
47.	30008 County Road 5122	A B C D
48.	779 Clear Springs Lane	A B C D
49.	1099 Ridgecroft Beltway	A B C D
50.	6595 Independence St.	A B C D
51.	49 Hunters Cove	A B C D
52.	657 Ridgecroft Pkwy.	A B C D
53.	25607 County Road 5122	A B C D
54.	781 Clear Springs Lane	A B C D
55.	31214 County Road 5122	A B C D
56.	700 Ridgetree Pkwy.	A B C D
57.	890 Clear Springs Lane	A B C D
58.	55 Hunters Cove	A B C D
59.	25465 County Road 5122	A B C D
60.	31999 County Road 5122	A B C D
61.	404 Ridgecroft Pkwy	A B C D
62.	910 Clear Springs Lane	A B C D
63.	9599 Independence St.	A B C D
64.	45400 County Road 5122	A B C D
65.	32 Hunters Cove	A B C D
66.	600 Clear Springs Lane	A B C D
67.	700 Ridgecroft Pkwy.	A B C D
68.	8232 Independence St.	A B C D
69.	19 Hunters Cove	A B C D
70.	3999 County Road 5122	A B C D
71.	512 Ridgecroft Pkwy.	A B C D
72.	761 Clear Springs Lane	A B C D

PART D: PERSONAL CHARACTERISTICS AND EXPERIENCE INVENTORY

On the actual exam, the next part that you would take is Part D: Personal Characteristics and Experience Inventory. This part of the exam is 90 minutes long and has 236 items. Because there is no particular advantage to practicing your responses on these statements and questions, no tests are given here for them.

Scoring and Explanations for Practice Examination 3

ANSWER KEY

Part A: Address Checking

1. C	11. B	21. B	31. B	41. B	51. C
2. C	12. B	22. C	32. A	42. D	52. C
3. A	13. A	23. D	33. D	43. C	53. C
4. C	14. B	24. A	34. B	44. B	54. B
5. B	15. C	25. B	35. A	45. C	55. B
6. D	16. B	26. B	36. A	46. A	56. D
7. B	17. D	27. C	37. D	47. D	57. C
8. C	18. C	28. C	38. B	48. A	58. C
9. B	19. B	29. A	39. C	49. B	59. A
10. D	20. C	30. D	40. D	50. A	60. D

Part B: Forms Completion

1. C	6. C	11. D	16. B	21. A	26. C
2. D	7. B	12. B	17. B	22. D	27. C
3. B	8. A	13. D	18. D	23. D	28. D
4. A	9. C	14. A	19. A	24. C	29. A
5. A	10. D	15. C	20. C	25. B	30. B

Part C: Coding Test

1. D	7. C	13. B	19. A	25. B	31. B
2. C	8. C	14. A	20. A	26. A	32. C
3. A	9. D	15. D	21. B	27. A	33. D
4. A	10. D	16. C	22. C	28. D	34. A
5. C	11. B	17. D	23. B	29. B	35. B
6. B	12. A	18. B	24. D	30. B	36. A

Part C: Memory Test

37. C	43. D	49. D	55. A	61. B	67. B
38. C	44. C	50. D	56. D	62. C	68. C
39. A	45. B	51. B	57. C	63. C	69. A
40. D	46. B	52. B	58. B	64. D	70. D
41. B	47. A	53. A	59. A	65. A	71. B
42. A	48. C	54. C	60. A	66. D	72. C

SCORING

Part A: Address Checking

Enter the number you got right: _____

Enter the number you got wrong
(not including those left blank): _____

Divide the number wrong by 3
(or multiply by 1/3): _____

Subtract this answer from the number right: - _____

Raw Score _____

Part B: Forms Completion

Enter the number you got right
(no penalty for guessing): Raw Score _____

Part C: Coding and Memory

Enter the number you got right: _____

Enter the number you got wrong
(not including those left blank): _____

Divide the number wrong by 3
(or multiply by 1/3): _____

Subtract this answer from the number right: - _____

Raw Score _____

Part D: Personal Characteristics and Experience Inventory

Scoring system not given.

Explanations

PART A: ADDRESS CHECKING

	Correct List		List to Be Checked	
	Address	*ZIP Code*	*Address*	*ZIP Code*
1. **C**	2077 Greenway Court Matthews, NC	28**1**0**4**-4511	2077 Greenway Court Matthews, NC	28**01**4-4511
2. **C**	9033 S 69th Pl. Springfield, Oregon	97478-9**5**88	9033 S 69th Pl. Springfield, Oregon	97478-9**8**88
3. **A**	1878 Comanche St. Corpus Christi, TX	78408	1878 Comanche St. Corpus Christi, TX	78408
4. **C**	97221 Eau Claire Blvd. Wausau, WI	**5**4403-7221	97221 Eau Claire Blvd. Wausau, WI	**6**4403-7221
5. **B**	47**4**4 Amberjack Bay E Lake Havasu City, AZ	86406	47**3**4 Amberjack Bay E Lake Havasu City, AZ	86406
6. **D**	904 SW 1**8**9th Cir. Apt. 655 Dunnellon, FL	34**4**3**2**-1066	904 SW 1**9**9th Cir. Apt. 655 Dunnellon, FL	34**42**3-1066
7. **B**	9118 Ch**ic**opee Dr. Medimont, ID	83842-6444	9118 Ch**inc**opee Dr. Medimont, ID	83842-6444
8. **C**	P.O Box 835B Monroe, MI	48161-**8380**	P.O Box 835B Monroe, MI	48161-**6360**
9. **B**	9250 E Night Glow **Way** Apache Junction, AZ	85219	9250 E Night Glow **Dr.** Apache Junction, AZ	85219
10. **D**	4686 Valencia St. Pueblo, **CO**	81**0**06	4686 Valencia St. Pueblo, **MO**	81**6**06
11. **B**	3328 Chickasaw Ave. Gill**ette,** Wyoming	82718-7002	3328 Chickasaw Ave. Gill**more,** Wyoming	82718-7002
12. **B**	5042 **S**E Berghammer St. Portland, OR	97267-7905	5042 **N**E Berghammer St. Portland, OR	97267-7905
13. **A**	7322 Dorrance St. Warwick, RI	02886-0920	7322 Dorrance St. Warwick, RI	02886-0920
14. **B** 61**7**01 Rural Route 40 Brooksville, FL		34601	6101 Rural Route 40 Brooksville, FL	34601

		Correct List		**List to Be Checked**	
		Address	*ZIP Code*	*Address*	*ZIP Code*
15.	C	6273 Lacroix Dr. Houma, LA	70364	6273 Lacroix Dr. Houma, LA	70363
16.	B	1131 6th Ave. SE Hagers**town**, MD	21061-7124	1131 6th Ave. SE Hagers**ford**, MD	21061-7124
17.	D	**553**7 Englewood Ave. Waterbury, CT	06705	**662**7 Englewood Ave. Waterbury, CT	96705
18.	C	4603 Catherine St. Vacaville, CA	**95**688	4603 Catherine St. Vacaville, CA	**59**688
19.	B	2271 Painted Valley **Dr.** Little Rock, AR	72212-3301	2271 Painted Valley **Tr.** Little Rock, AR	72212-3301
20.	C	4934 Baggett Rd. Meridian, MS	39301	4934 Baggett Rd. Meridian, MS	39331
21.	B	9232 **Buena** Suerta Dr. Hobbs, NM	88242-5584	9232 **Bona** Suerta Dr. Hobbs, NM	88242-5584
22.	C	1837 Sudbury Rd. Charlotte, NC	28**205**	1837 Sudbury Rd. Charlotte, NC	28**250**
23.	D	2062 35**00** Road Shawnee, OK	**74**804-6047	2062 35**50** Road Shawnee, OK	**75**404-6047
24.	A	2708 Collingswood Dr. Chesterfield, VA	23832-2270	2708 Collingswood Dr. Chesterfield, VA	23832-2270
25.	B	**6**087 San Joaquin St. Brownsville, TX	78521	**2**087 San Joaquin St. Brownsville, TX	78521
26.	B	3**8**49 Parkridge Dr. Utica, MI	48315-8361	3**88**49 Parkridge Dr. Utica, MI	48315-8361
27.	C	8033 S. Kirkland Ave. Chicago, IL	60652-1**753**	8033 S. Kirkland Ave. Chicago, IL	60652-1**935**
28.	C	41727 County Road 2665 Eureka Springs, AR	**7**2631	41727 County Road 2665 Eureka Springs, AR	**4**2631

	Correct List		**List to Be Checked**	
	Address	ZIP Code	Address	ZIP Code
29. **A**	3472 Shakeley Lane Hillsburg, Indiana	46046	3472 Shakeley Lane Hillsburg, Indiana	46046
30. **D**	8636 Forest Plains Ln. Salis**bury,** MD	21804-58**20**	8636 Forest Plains Ln. Salis**burg,** MD	21804-58**00**
31. **B**	6**143** Lucretia Ave. Minnetonka, MN	55345-1559	6**413** Lucretia Ave. Minnetonka, MN	55345-1559
32. **A**	93325 Highway 99 Madera, CA	93638	93325 Highway 99 Madera, CA	93638
33. **D**	1020 Wend**em**ere Court Jefferson City, MO	65109-92**11**	1020 Wend**erm**ere Court Jefferson City, MO	65109-92**21**
34. **B**	6822 Blankenship **Dr.** Charleston, WV	25309-1646	6822 Blankenship **Tr.** Charleston, WV	25309-1646
35. **A**	8725 S Wheeling St. Tuscarora, NV	89834	8725 S Wheeling St. Tuscarora, NV	89834
36. **A**	2739 Saint Stanislaus St. Rochester, NY	14621	2739 Saint Stanislaus St. Rochester, NY	14621
37. **D**	**40**22 Ave Calderon Carolina, PR	**0**0985	**60**32 Ave Calderon Carolina, PR	**0**9985
38. **B**	4900 Pierpont Meadows **Thet**ford Center, VT	05075	4900 Pierpont Meadows **Med**ford Center, VT	05075
39. **C**	5161 Guilford St. West Columbia, SC	29**1**69-4806	5161 Guilford St. West Columbia, SC	29**6**69-4806
40. **D**	37232 **60**th Ave. Saint Cloud, MN	56303-6**333**	37232 **30**th Ave. Saint Cloud, MN	56303-6**423**
41. **B**	3967 Tampa Bay Drive **Zephyr**hills, FL	33543-2501	3967 Tampa Bay Drive **Tampa**hills, FL	33543-2501
42. **D**	457**5** Hawthorne **Ln.** Greenwood, IN	461**42**	457**7** Hawthorne **Dr.** Greenwood, IN	461**24**

		Correct List			List to Be Checked	

		Address	ZIP Code	Address	ZIP Code
43.	C	4683 Myrtle Street Ext. Norwalk, CT	**068**55	4683 Myrtle Street Ext. Norwalk, CT	**680**55
44.	B	4426 **Fernando** St. Newport Beach, CA	92661-5097	4426 **Ferndale** St. Newport Beach, CA	92661-5097
45.	C	1933 Highway 135 Pleasant Dale, Nebraska	68**4**23	1933 Highway 135 Pleasant Dale, Nebraska	68**3**23
46.	A	5414 N Commercial Street Manchester, NH	03101-7294	5414 N Commercial Street Manchester, NH	03101-7294
47.	D	2002 Haven Hill Rd. Lexington, **NC**	**27**292-0438	2002 Haven Hill Rd. Lexington, **SC**	**22**792-0438
48.	A	7335 Sullivan Garden Pkwy. Kingsport, TN	37660	7335 Sullivan Garden Pkwy. Kingsport, TN	37660
49.	B	9428 Stronghold Ct. Ash**burn,** VA	20147-5584	9428 Stronghold Ct. Ash**bury,** VA	20147-5584
50.	A	1204 Marvin Cutoff La Center, WA	98629	1204 Marvin Cutoff La Center, WA	98629
51.	C	2368 Glendora Ct. Sparks, NV	8**94**36	2368 Glendora Ct. Sparks, NV	8**36**36
52.	C	649 Casabella Cir. East Hartford, CT	06**1**08-5410	649 Casabella Cir. East Hartford, CT	06**0**08-5410
53.	C	3122 Declovina St. Santa Fe, NM	87505-1**733**	3122 Declovina St. Santa Fe, NM	87505-1**773**
54.	B	1201 F**rei**ght Rd. Mount Airy, GA	30563	1201 F**ri**ght Rd. Mount Airy, GA	30563
55.	B	6**7**28 Irvington Drive Buffalo, NY	14228-5420	6**8**28 Irvington Drive Buffalo, NY	14228-5420
56.	D	7742 **Cleghorn** St. Honolulu, HI	9681**5**-6542	7742 **Clayton** St. Honolulu, HI	9681**6**-6542

	Correct List		**List to Be Checked**	
	Address	*ZIP Code*	*Address*	*ZIP Code*
57. **C**	9038 Elizabethtown Rd. Fayetteville, NC	28306	9038 Elizabethtown Rd. Fayetteville, NC	28006
58. **C**	3895 Tranquility Lane Ponderay, ID	**83**852-6031	3895 Tranquility Lane Ponderay, ID	**38**852-6031
59. **A**	6510 Locust Ave. Montpelier, ND	58472-0686	6510 Locust Ave. Montpelier, ND	58472-0686
60. **D**	1820 Moffitt Place **Alta**mont, IL	62411	1820 Moffitt Place **Alva**mont, IL	61411

PART B: FORMS COMPLETION

Set 1: Questions 1 through 6

DOMESTIC MAIL OR REGISTERED MAIL INQUIRY
To Be Completed by Customer

1. Mailer Information			2. Addressee Information		
1a. First Name	1b. Middle Initial	1c. Last Name	2a. First Name	2b. Middle Initial	2c. Last Name
1d. Business Name (use only if mailer is a company)			2d. Business Name (use only if addressee is a company)		
1e. Street Name (number, street, suite/apartment number)			2e. Street Name (number, street, suite/apartment number)		
1f. City	1g. State	1h. ZIP Code	2f. City	2g. State	2h. ZIP Code
1i. Telephone Number (include area code)			2i. Telephone Number (include area code)		

Question #5 → (points to 2b/2c area)
Question #1 → (points to 2f/2i area)

3. Payment Assignment— Alternate Payment Address			4. Description of Lost or Damaged Article(s)— Add Extra Sheets as Needed			
3a. Who Is to Receive Payment? (check one) ❑ Mailer ❑ Addressee			4a. Item No.	4b. Description of Article	4c. Value or Cost	4d. Purchase Date
			First			
3b. Street Name (if other than address above) (number, street, suite/apartment number)			Second			
			Third			
3c. City	3d. State	3e. ZIP Code	Fourth			

Question #6 → (points to 3a checkboxes)
Question #4 → (points to 4b/4c area)
Question #2 → (points to 4b/4c area)

5. COD Amount to Be Remitted to Sender	6. Total Amount Claimed for All Articles

7. Certification and Signature		
7a. Customer Submitting Claim: ❑ Mailer ❑ Addressee	7b. Signature of Customer Filing the Claim	7c. Date Signed (MM/DD/YYYY)

Question #3 → (points to 7a checkboxes)

---

1. **C** Box 2f, under "Addressee Information," is for the city.
2. **D** Box 4b requires a description of the article, not a number. In the other three boxes, a number of some kind could be written—a street number, a telephone number, or a ZIP code.
3. **B** In Box 7a, you can put a checkmark for either "Mailer" or "Addressee."
4. **A** The value of a lost or damaged item should be entered in Box 4c.
5. **A** Box 2b is labeled "Middle Initial." The only single letter given in the answers is "J" in answer A.
6. **C** The fact that payment should be given to the addressee (Don Whipple) is noted in Box 3a, where you would check "Addressee."

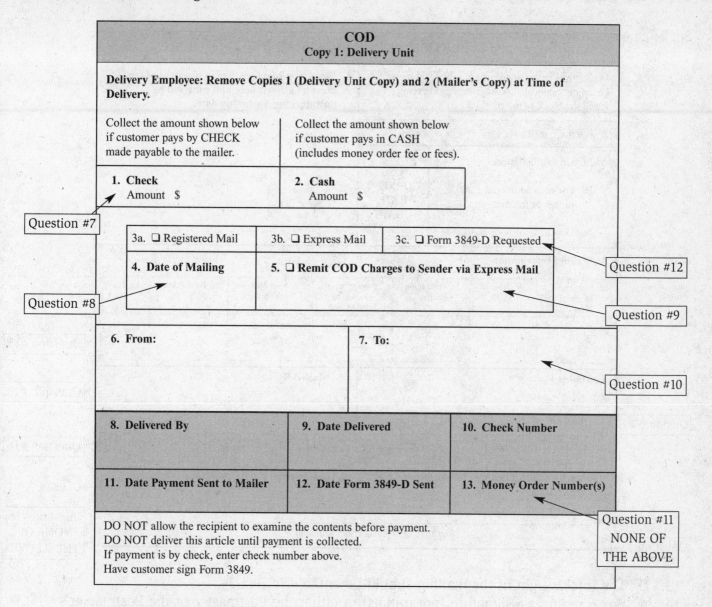

COD
Copy 1: Delivery Unit

Delivery Employee: Remove Copies 1 (Delivery Unit Copy) and 2 (Mailer's Copy) at Time of Delivery.

Collect the amount shown below if customer pays by CHECK made payable to the mailer.

Collect the amount shown below if customer pays in CASH (includes money order fee or fees).

1. **Check**
   Amount $

2. **Cash**
   Amount $

Question #7

3a. ❑ Registered Mail   3b. ❑ Express Mail   3c. ❑ Form 3849-D Requested

Question #12

4. **Date of Mailing**   5. ❑ **Remit COD Charges to Sender via Express Mail**

Question #8

Question #9

6. **From:**   7. **To:**

Question #10

8. **Delivered By**   9. **Date Delivered**   10. **Check Number**

11. **Date Payment Sent to Mailer**   12. **Date Form 3849-D Sent**   13. **Money Order Number(s)**

Question #11
NONE OF
THE ABOVE

DO NOT allow the recipient to examine the contents before payment.
DO NOT deliver this article until payment is collected.
If payment is by check, enter check number above.
Have customer sign Form 3849.

7. **B** Box 1 requires a dollar amount.
8. **A** The date the package was mailed goes in Box 4
9. **C** Box 5 requires a checkmark.
10. **D** Harriet Washington is the addressee, the person to whom the package is being sent. The customer would indicate that in Box 7.
11. **D** Box 13 is for a Money Order number. No such number is given in the answers, so the answer is D, None of the above.
12. **B** There is a box to be checked in Box 3c to indicate that this form has been requested.

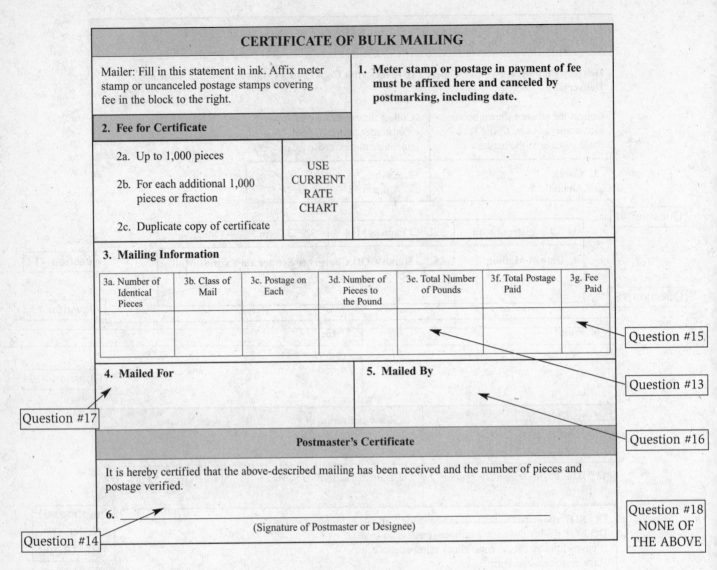

CERTIFICATE OF BULK MAILING

Mailer: Fill in this statement in ink. Affix meter stamp or uncanceled postage stamps covering fee in the block to the right.

1. Meter stamp or postage in payment of fee must be affixed here and canceled by postmarking, including date.

2. Fee for Certificate

2a. Up to 1,000 pieces

2b. For each additional 1,000 pieces or fraction

2c. Duplicate copy of certificate

USE CURRENT RATE CHART

3. Mailing Information

3a. Number of Identical Pieces	3b. Class of Mail	3c. Postage on Each	3d. Number of Pieces to the Pound	3e. Total Number of Pounds	3f. Total Postage Paid	3g. Fee Paid

Question #15

4. Mailed For

5. Mailed By

Question #13

Question #17

Question #16

Postmaster's Certificate

It is hereby certified that the above-described mailing has been received and the number of pieces and postage verified.

6. _____

(Signature of Postmaster or Designee)

Question #14

Question #18
NONE OF THE ABOVE

13. **D** The total weight of the mailing should be entered in Box 3e.
14. **A** Box 6 requires a signature (not initials) of either the Postmaster or the Postmaster's designee.
15. **C** The amount of the fee for the certificate should be entered in Box 3g.
16. **B** The name of the person mailing the items should go in Box 5.
17. **B** The company Kerry Walters is mailing the items *for* should go in Box 4, labeled "Mailed For."
18. **D** There is no place on this form to find the correct amount of the fee. Box 2 says "USE CURRENT RATE CHART," which is not shown on the form, so the answer here is D, None of the above.

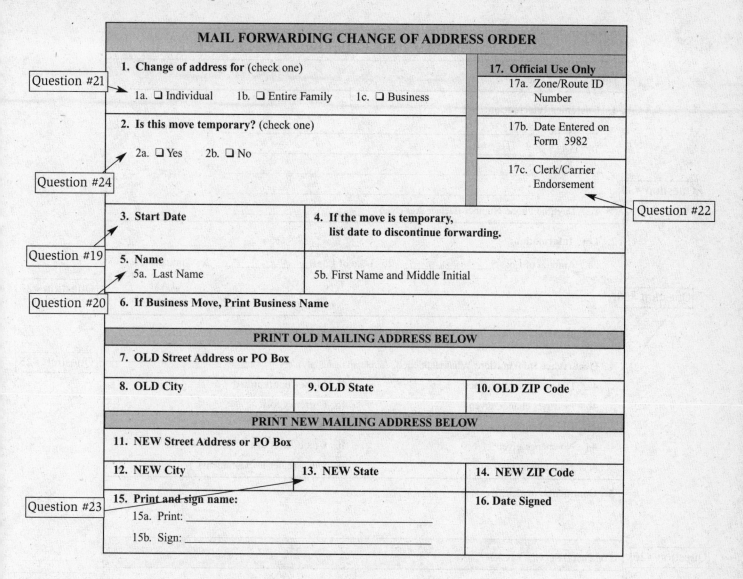

MAIL FORWARDING CHANGE OF ADDRESS ORDER

Question #21

1. Change of address for (check one)

1a. ❏ Individual   1b. ❏ Entire Family   1c. ❏ Business

2. Is this move temporary? (check one)

2a. ❏ Yes   2b. ❏ No

Question #24

17. Official Use Only

17a. Zone/Route ID Number

17b. Date Entered on Form 3982

17c. Clerk/Carrier Endorsement

Question #22

3. Start Date

4. If the move is temporary, list date to discontinue forwarding.

Question #19

5. Name
5a. Last Name

5b. First Name and Middle Initial

Question #20

6. If Business Move, Print Business Name

PRINT OLD MAILING ADDRESS BELOW

7. OLD Street Address or PO Box

8. OLD City   **9. OLD State**   **10. OLD ZIP Code**

PRINT NEW MAILING ADDRESS BELOW

11. NEW Street Address or PO Box

12. NEW City   **13. NEW State**   **14. NEW ZIP Code**

15. Print and sign name:
15a. Print: _____

15b. Sign: _____

Question #23

16. Date Signed

19. **A** The start date of the mail forwarding should be entered in Box 3.
20. **C** Box 5a requires the last name.
21. **A** Box 1 gives three possibilities for checkmarks, and if Line 1a is checked, it indicates that only this customer is moving (not an entire family, for example).
22. **D** The clerk's name would go in Box 17c.
23. **D** If the customer is moving to Florida, then "Florida" will be part of the new address and should be entered in Box 13.
24. **C** If Jane Foley's move will be temporary, that fact should be noted by checking Line 2a.

STAMP VENDING MACHINE REIMBURSEMENT REQUEST

For Customer Use

1. **Customer Information:**
   1a. Name _____
   1b. Address _____
   _____
   _____

   Question #30 →

   1c. Daytime Phone Number (include area code) _____

2. **Loss Information:**

   2a. Amount of Loss $_____   2b. Date of Loss _____   2c. Time of Loss

   Question #28 →   ❏ AM   ← **Question #27**
                                                                   ❏ PM

3. **Machine Information:** Machine ID (6-digit number on front of vending machine) _____

4. **Occurrence Information:** What Happened? (circle all that apply) ◄   **Question #25**

   4a. Did not receive product   4f. Money not returned
   4b. Incorrect change given   4g. Currency lost
   4c. Did not register/jammed   4h. Coin lost
   4d. No change given   4i. Credit/debit lost
   4e. No credit shown   4j. Other (enter in "Comments")

5. **Comments:** (optional)

Question #26 | **For Postal Service Use**

6. **Paid by**   7. **Date**   ◄   **Question #29**

8. **Action Taken** (circle one)
   8a. Paid   8b. Not Paid

9. **Sales and Services Associate Signature** _____

---

25. **B** Box 4 includes the instructions "circle all that apply."
26. **C** The name of the clerk who paid the customer goes in Box 6, which is labeled "Paid by."
27. **C** The time of the attempted purchase is noted on Line 2c.
28. **D** The customer got 40 cents back but should have received 60 cents, so the customer's loss is 20 cents. The amount of loss should be entered on Line 2a, and Line 4b, "Incorrect change given" should be circled.
29. **A** A date goes in Box 7 (the date the customer was paid).
30. **B** The customer's telephone number goes on Line 1c.

PRACTICE EXAMINATION 4

ANSWER SHEET FOR PRACTICE EXAMINATION 4

PART A: ADDRESS CHECKING

1. Ⓐ Ⓑ Ⓒ Ⓓ   16. Ⓐ Ⓑ Ⓒ Ⓓ   31. Ⓐ Ⓑ Ⓒ Ⓓ   46. Ⓐ Ⓑ Ⓒ Ⓓ
2. Ⓐ Ⓑ Ⓒ Ⓓ   17. Ⓐ Ⓑ Ⓒ Ⓓ   32. Ⓐ Ⓑ Ⓒ Ⓓ   47. Ⓐ Ⓑ Ⓒ Ⓓ
3. Ⓐ Ⓑ Ⓒ Ⓓ   18. Ⓐ Ⓑ Ⓒ Ⓓ   33. Ⓐ Ⓑ Ⓒ Ⓓ   48. Ⓐ Ⓑ Ⓒ Ⓓ
4. Ⓐ Ⓑ Ⓒ Ⓓ   19. Ⓐ Ⓑ Ⓒ Ⓓ   34. Ⓐ Ⓑ Ⓒ Ⓓ   49. Ⓐ Ⓑ Ⓒ Ⓓ
5. Ⓐ Ⓑ Ⓒ Ⓓ   20. Ⓐ Ⓑ Ⓒ Ⓓ   35. Ⓐ Ⓑ Ⓒ Ⓓ   50. Ⓐ Ⓑ Ⓒ Ⓓ
6. Ⓐ Ⓑ Ⓒ Ⓓ   21. Ⓐ Ⓑ Ⓒ Ⓓ   36. Ⓐ Ⓑ Ⓒ Ⓓ   51. Ⓐ Ⓑ Ⓒ Ⓓ
7. Ⓐ Ⓑ Ⓒ Ⓓ   22. Ⓐ Ⓑ Ⓒ Ⓓ   37. Ⓐ Ⓑ Ⓒ Ⓓ   52. Ⓐ Ⓑ Ⓒ Ⓓ
8. Ⓐ Ⓑ Ⓒ Ⓓ   23. Ⓐ Ⓑ Ⓒ Ⓓ   38. Ⓐ Ⓑ Ⓒ Ⓓ   53. Ⓐ Ⓑ Ⓒ Ⓓ
9. Ⓐ Ⓑ Ⓒ Ⓓ   24. Ⓐ Ⓑ Ⓒ Ⓓ   39. Ⓐ Ⓑ Ⓒ Ⓓ   54. Ⓐ Ⓑ Ⓒ Ⓓ
10. Ⓐ Ⓑ Ⓒ Ⓓ   25. Ⓐ Ⓑ Ⓒ Ⓓ   40. Ⓐ Ⓑ Ⓒ Ⓓ   55. Ⓐ Ⓑ Ⓒ Ⓓ
11. Ⓐ Ⓑ Ⓒ Ⓓ   26. Ⓐ Ⓑ Ⓒ Ⓓ   41. Ⓐ Ⓑ Ⓒ Ⓓ   56. Ⓐ Ⓑ Ⓒ Ⓓ
12. Ⓐ Ⓑ Ⓒ Ⓓ   27. Ⓐ Ⓑ Ⓒ Ⓓ   42. Ⓐ Ⓑ Ⓒ Ⓓ   57. Ⓐ Ⓑ Ⓒ Ⓓ
13. Ⓐ Ⓑ Ⓒ Ⓓ   28. Ⓐ Ⓑ Ⓒ Ⓓ   43. Ⓐ Ⓑ Ⓒ Ⓓ   58. Ⓐ Ⓑ Ⓒ Ⓓ
14. Ⓐ Ⓑ Ⓒ Ⓓ   29. Ⓐ Ⓑ Ⓒ Ⓓ   44. Ⓐ Ⓑ Ⓒ Ⓓ   59. Ⓐ Ⓑ Ⓒ Ⓓ
15. Ⓐ Ⓑ Ⓒ Ⓓ   30. Ⓐ Ⓑ Ⓒ Ⓓ   45. Ⓐ Ⓑ Ⓒ Ⓓ   60. Ⓐ Ⓑ Ⓒ Ⓓ

Remove answer sheet by cutting on dotted line

PART B: FORMS COMPLETION

1. Ⓐ Ⓑ Ⓒ Ⓓ   9. Ⓐ Ⓑ Ⓒ Ⓓ   17. Ⓐ Ⓑ Ⓒ Ⓓ   25. Ⓐ Ⓑ Ⓒ Ⓓ
2. Ⓐ Ⓑ Ⓒ Ⓓ   10. Ⓐ Ⓑ Ⓒ Ⓓ   18. Ⓐ Ⓑ Ⓒ Ⓓ   26. Ⓐ Ⓑ Ⓒ Ⓓ
3. Ⓐ Ⓑ Ⓒ Ⓓ   11. Ⓐ Ⓑ Ⓒ Ⓓ   19. Ⓐ Ⓑ Ⓒ Ⓓ   27. Ⓐ Ⓑ Ⓒ Ⓓ
4. Ⓐ Ⓑ Ⓒ Ⓓ   12. Ⓐ Ⓑ Ⓒ Ⓓ   20. Ⓐ Ⓑ Ⓒ Ⓓ   28. Ⓐ Ⓑ Ⓒ Ⓓ
5. Ⓐ Ⓑ Ⓒ Ⓓ   13. Ⓐ Ⓑ Ⓒ Ⓓ   21. Ⓐ Ⓑ Ⓒ Ⓓ   29. Ⓐ Ⓑ Ⓒ Ⓓ
6. Ⓐ Ⓑ Ⓒ Ⓓ   14. Ⓐ Ⓑ Ⓒ Ⓓ   22. Ⓐ Ⓑ Ⓒ Ⓓ   30. Ⓐ Ⓑ Ⓒ Ⓓ
7. Ⓐ Ⓑ Ⓒ Ⓓ   15. Ⓐ Ⓑ Ⓒ Ⓓ   23. Ⓐ Ⓑ Ⓒ Ⓓ
8. Ⓐ Ⓑ Ⓒ Ⓓ   16. Ⓐ Ⓑ Ⓒ Ⓓ   24. Ⓐ Ⓑ Ⓒ Ⓓ

PART C: CODING AND MEMORY
SECTION 1—CODING

1. Ⓐ Ⓑ Ⓒ Ⓓ	10. Ⓐ Ⓑ Ⓒ Ⓓ	19. Ⓐ Ⓑ Ⓒ Ⓓ	28. Ⓐ Ⓑ Ⓒ Ⓓ
2. Ⓐ Ⓑ Ⓒ Ⓓ	11. Ⓐ Ⓑ Ⓒ Ⓓ	20. Ⓐ Ⓑ Ⓒ Ⓓ	29. Ⓐ Ⓑ Ⓒ Ⓓ
3. Ⓐ Ⓑ Ⓒ Ⓓ	12. Ⓐ Ⓑ Ⓒ Ⓓ	21. Ⓐ Ⓑ Ⓒ Ⓓ	30. Ⓐ Ⓑ Ⓒ Ⓓ
4. Ⓐ Ⓑ Ⓒ Ⓓ	13. Ⓐ Ⓑ Ⓒ Ⓓ	22. Ⓐ Ⓑ Ⓒ Ⓓ	31. Ⓐ Ⓑ Ⓒ Ⓓ
5. Ⓐ Ⓑ Ⓒ Ⓓ	14. Ⓐ Ⓑ Ⓒ Ⓓ	23. Ⓐ Ⓑ Ⓒ Ⓓ	32. Ⓐ Ⓑ Ⓒ Ⓓ
6. Ⓐ Ⓑ Ⓒ Ⓓ	15. Ⓐ Ⓑ Ⓒ Ⓓ	24. Ⓐ Ⓑ Ⓒ Ⓓ	33. Ⓐ Ⓑ Ⓒ Ⓓ
7. Ⓐ Ⓑ Ⓒ Ⓓ	16. Ⓐ Ⓑ Ⓒ Ⓓ	25. Ⓐ Ⓑ Ⓒ Ⓓ	34. Ⓐ Ⓑ Ⓒ Ⓓ
8. Ⓐ Ⓑ Ⓒ Ⓓ	17. Ⓐ Ⓑ Ⓒ Ⓓ	26. Ⓐ Ⓑ Ⓒ Ⓓ	35. Ⓐ Ⓑ Ⓒ Ⓓ
9. Ⓐ Ⓑ Ⓒ Ⓓ	18. Ⓐ Ⓑ Ⓒ Ⓓ	27. Ⓐ Ⓑ Ⓒ Ⓓ	36. Ⓐ Ⓑ Ⓒ Ⓓ

SECTION 2—MEMORY

37. Ⓐ Ⓑ Ⓒ Ⓓ	46. Ⓐ Ⓑ Ⓒ Ⓓ	55. Ⓐ Ⓑ Ⓒ Ⓓ	64. Ⓐ Ⓑ Ⓒ Ⓓ
38. Ⓐ Ⓑ Ⓒ Ⓓ	47. Ⓐ Ⓑ Ⓒ Ⓓ	56. Ⓐ Ⓑ Ⓒ Ⓓ	65. Ⓐ Ⓑ Ⓒ Ⓓ
39. Ⓐ Ⓑ Ⓒ Ⓓ	48. Ⓐ Ⓑ Ⓒ Ⓓ	57. Ⓐ Ⓑ Ⓒ Ⓓ	66. Ⓐ Ⓑ Ⓒ Ⓓ
40. Ⓐ Ⓑ Ⓒ Ⓓ	49. Ⓐ Ⓑ Ⓒ Ⓓ	58. Ⓐ Ⓑ Ⓒ Ⓓ	67. Ⓐ Ⓑ Ⓒ Ⓓ
41. Ⓐ Ⓑ Ⓒ Ⓓ	50. Ⓐ Ⓑ Ⓒ Ⓓ	59. Ⓐ Ⓑ Ⓒ Ⓓ	68. Ⓐ Ⓑ Ⓒ Ⓓ
42. Ⓐ Ⓑ Ⓒ Ⓓ	51. Ⓐ Ⓑ Ⓒ Ⓓ	60. Ⓐ Ⓑ Ⓒ Ⓓ	69. Ⓐ Ⓑ Ⓒ Ⓓ
43. Ⓐ Ⓑ Ⓒ Ⓓ	52. Ⓐ Ⓑ Ⓒ Ⓓ	61. Ⓐ Ⓑ Ⓒ Ⓓ	70. Ⓐ Ⓑ Ⓒ Ⓓ
44. Ⓐ Ⓑ Ⓒ Ⓓ	53. Ⓐ Ⓑ Ⓒ Ⓓ	62. Ⓐ Ⓑ Ⓒ Ⓓ	71. Ⓐ Ⓑ Ⓒ Ⓓ
45. Ⓐ Ⓑ Ⓒ Ⓓ	54. Ⓐ Ⓑ Ⓒ Ⓓ	63. Ⓐ Ⓑ Ⓒ Ⓓ	72. Ⓐ Ⓑ Ⓒ Ⓓ

PART D: PERSONAL CHARACTERISTICS AND EXPERIENCE INVENTORY

(236 Questions—not included here)

ADDRESS CHECKING SAMPLE QUESTIONS

Look at the row of information for sample question 1, which is labeled "S1" below. Carefully but quickly compare the **List to Be Checked** with the **Correct List**. Then decide if there are **No Errors** (select A), an error in the **Address Only** (select B), an error in the **ZIP Code Only** (select C), or an error in **Both** the address and the ZIP code (select D). Record your response to the sample questions in the **Sample Answer Grid** below. Complete the other three samples given, S2, S3, and S4, and record your responses on the **Sample Answer Grid**.

A. No Errors	B. Address Only	C. ZIP Code Only	D. Both

Correct List

	Address	ZIP Code
S1.	432 Rosewood Ct. Pasadena, CA	91106
S2.	1977 Hully Street Austin, TX	78734-1141
S3.	648 Central Dr. New York, NY	10034
S4.	9812 Pine Ave. Chicago, IL	60467-5113

List to Be Checked

Address	ZIP Code
432 Rosewood Ct. Pasedena, CA	91106
1977 Holly Street Austin, TX	78734-1114
648 Central Dr. New York, NY	10054
9812 Pine Ave. Chicago, IL	60467-5113

Sample Answer Grid

S1.	Ⓐ	Ⓑ	Ⓒ	Ⓓ
S2.	Ⓐ	Ⓑ	Ⓒ	Ⓓ
S3.	Ⓐ	Ⓑ	Ⓒ	Ⓓ
S4.	Ⓐ	Ⓑ	Ⓒ	Ⓓ

Completed Sample Answer Grid

S1.	Ⓐ	●	Ⓒ	Ⓓ
S2.	Ⓐ	Ⓑ	Ⓒ	●
S3.	Ⓐ	Ⓑ	●	Ⓓ
S4.	●	Ⓑ	Ⓒ	Ⓓ

In sample 1, the address in the **List to Be Checked** shows Pasedena, but the **Correct List** shows Pasadena. So there is an error in the address. Since the Zip codes are exactly the same, the correct answer is **B—Address Only**.

In sample 2, the address in the **List to Be Checked** shows Holly Street, but the **Correct List** shows Hully Street. So there is an error in the address. The **List to Be Checked** also shows an error in the ZIP code. The last four numbers are 1114, and they are 1141 in the **Correct List**. Because there is an error in the address and in the ZIP code, the correct answer is **D—Both**.

In sample 3, the addresses in the **List to Be Checked** and the **Correct List** are exactly the same, but there is an error in the ZIP code on the **List to Be Checked**. The **List to Be Checked** shows 10054, but the **Correct List** shows 10034. So there is an error in the ZIP code. The correct answer is **C—ZIP Code Only**.

In sample 4, the addresses in the **List to Be Checked** and the **Correct List** are exactly the same. The ZIP codes are also exactly the same. So the correct answer is **A—No Errors**.

Now turn to the next page and begin the address checking test.

PART A: ADDRESS CHECKING

For the following 60 items, compare the address in the **Correct List** with the address in the **List to Be Checked.** Determine if there are **No Errors** (answer A), an error in the **Address Only** (answer B), an error in the **ZIP Code Only** (answer C), or an error in **Both** (answer D). Mark your answers in the Address Checking section of the answer sheet. You have 11 minutes to complete this test.

A. No Errors	B. Address Only	C. ZIP Code Only	D. Both

Correct List		**List to Be Checked**	
Address	*ZIP Code*	*Address*	*ZIP Code*
1. 4779 E Worcester Dr. Virginia Beach, VA	23455-5302	4779 E Worcester Dr. Virginia Beach, VA	23455-5302
2. 7487 Turtle Creek Dr. Warwick, RI	02889-7487	7487 Turtle Creek Dr. Warwick, RI	02889-4787
3. 140 Robinwood Cir. Anniston, Alabama	36207	140 Robinhood Cir. Anniston, Alabama	34207
4. 1938 Sherman Blvd. Pawleys Island, SC	29585-1938	1938 Sherman Blvd. Pawleys Island, SC	29585-2938
5. 70385 N 184th Ave. Surprise, AZ	85387	70385 N 184th Ter. Surprise, AZ	85387
6. 6280 Poplar Grove Road Johnson City, TN	37601	6280 Poplar Grove Road Johnson City, MN	77601
7. 8422 Section Line Trl. Hot Springs National Park, AR	71913	8242 Section Line Trl. Hot Springs National Park, AR	71913
8. 6862 Avatar Dr. Apt. 369 Grand Prairie, Texas	75052-0543	6862 Avatar Dr. Apt. 369 Grand Prairie, Texas	75052-0543
9. 2727 Ensenada Ave. Berkeley, CA	94707-6024	2727 Ensenada Ave. Berkeley, CA	96707-6024
10. Rural Route 2 South Burlington, VT	05403	Rural Route 2 South Burlington, VT	05430
11. 30330 S Mountain Brush Peak Littleton, CO	80126-9943	30330 S Mountain Brush Peak Littleton, CO	80126-9943

210

	Correct List		**List to Be Checked**	
	Address	*ZIP Code*	*Address*	*ZIP Code*

	Correct Address	Correct ZIP	Checked Address	Checked ZIP
12.	2834 Green Meadow Rd. Cookeville, TN	38506	2834 Green Meadow Rd. Cookesville, TN	38506
13.	4699 Calle Huescha Deland, FL	32724	4689 Calle Huescha Deland, FL	32224
14.	4322 Glamorgan Dr. Seneca, SC	29678	4322 Glamorgan Dr. Seneca, SC	29788
15.	8115 S Fairview Ave. Nampa, ID	83651-4483	8115 S Fairway Ave. Nampa, ID	83651-4483
16.	3840 Cat Rock Dr. Womelsdorf, PA	19567-1798	3840 Cat Rock Dr. Womelsdorf, PA	91567-1798
17.	5309 Audubon Way Warner Robins, GA	31088-5309	5309 Audubon Way Warner Robins, GA	31088-5309
18.	41606 Jameson Road Beaverton, CO	97005-4160	41606 Jameson Road Billingston, CO	97005-4160
19.	9222 W Swoope Ave. Winter Park, FL	32789	9222 W Swoope Ave. Winter Park, FL	32769
20.	P.O. Box 3731 Mansfield, Ohio	44907	P.O. Box 7331 Mansfield, Ohio	44907
21.	7144 Dairy View Lane Stamford, CT	06903-5181	7144 Dairy View Lane Stamford, CT	06903-5181
22.	9443 Cranberry Ridge Dr. SW Wilson, NC	27893	9443 Cranberry Ridge Dr. NW Wilson, NC	37893
23.	98237 Knight Road Ext. Framingham, MA	01701-8598	9837 Knight Road Ext. Framingham, MA	01791-8598
24.	5971 S Hommell St. Valley Stream, NY	11580-0876	5971 S Hommell Dr. Valley Stream, NY	11580-0876
25.	4020 County Route 67 Oakland, MI	49863	4020 County Route 67 Oakland, MI	44863

	Correct List		List to Be Checked	
	Address	*ZIP Code*	*Address*	*ZIP Code*
26.	6282 W Continental Dr. Gallup, NM	87301	6282 N Continental Dr. Gallup, NM	87301
27.	5199 120th Ave. NW Minneapolis, MN	55433-0063	5199 120th Ave. NW Minneapolis, MN	55433-0063
28.	6944 Allwood Rd. Apt. 11C Clifton, NJ	07014-2486	6944 Allwood Rd. Apt. 11D Clifton, NJ	07414-2486
29.	127 Ballantrae Ct. St. Louis, MO	63131	172 Ballantrae Ct. St. Louis, MO	63131
30.	5741 Theobald Dr. Reno, Nevada	89511-6915	5741 Theobald Dr. Reno, Nevada	89522-6915
31.	70521 Upper Millegan Rd. Great Falls, MT	59405-7052	70521 Upper Millegan Rd. Great Falls, MT	59045-7052
32.	8272 S 149th Cir. Omaha, NE	68138	8272 S 169th Cir. Omaha, NE	68138
33.	4883 Countryside Blvd. Leesburg, FL	34748	4883 Countryside Blvd. Leesburg, FL	34748
34.	3153 Upward Way Spartanburg, SC	29303-6959	3153 Upward Way Spartanburg, SC	29303-6959
35.	6114 Bunker Hill Road NE Washington, DC	20018	6114 Bunker Hill Road NE Washington, SC	20018
36.	3895 Paragon Pl. Pittsburgh, PA	15241-6765	3895 Paragon Pt. Pittsburgh, PA	05241-6765
37.	6463 Davenport St. Bridgeport, CT	06607-3629	6463 Davenport St. Bridgeport, CT	06667-3629
38.	6480 NW Sylvania Ct. Portland, OR	97229	6480 NW Sylvan Ct. Portland, OR	97229
39.	3223 Warrenton Blvd. Florissant, Colorado	80816	3223 Warrenton Blvd. Florissant, Colorado	80816

	Correct List		**List to Be Checked**	
	Address	*ZIP Code*	*Address*	*ZIP Code*
40.	2112 NE 129th St. Edmond, OK	73013-1541	2112 NE 129th St. Edward, OK	73013-1541
41.	4447 Summerfield Dr. Spring Valley, CA	91977-9191	4447 Summerville Dr. Spring Valley, CA	91997-9191
42.	6919 Lancaster Drive Hamilton, OH	45011-4421	6919 Lancaster Drive Hamilton, OH	45011-4241
43.	548 E Cobblestone Sq. Fayetteville, AR	72703	548 E Cobblestone Sq. Fayetteville, AR	72703
44.	4419 Devereaux Dr. Highlandville, IA	52149	4419 Devereaux Dr. Highlandville, IA	53249
45.	52320 Catalina St. Shawnee Mission, KS	66209-2250	25320 Catalina St. Shawnee Mission, KS	60209-2250
46.	7708 Ensleigh Lane Bowie, Maryland	20716-3919	7708 Ensleigh Lane Bowie, Maryland	20716-6919
47.	7442 Okeepa Road Casper, WY	82604-0224	7442 Okeepa Lane Casper, WY	82604-0224
48.	6357 Campo Del Sol Ave. Albuquerque, NM	87123	6357 Campo Del Sol Ave. Albuquerque, NM	97123
49.	2893 Black Cherry Rd. Hattiesburg, MS	39401	2893 Choke Cherry Rd. Hattiesburg, MS	39401
50.	3060 Santa Barbara Dr. Bismarck, ND	58504-2056	3060 Santa Barbara Dr. Bismarck, ND	58504-2056
51.	9275 W Silverleaf Ave. Springfield, MO	65807	9275 N Silverleaf Ave. Springfield, MO	65807
52.	2907 Nicholas Road Dayton, OH	45408-1699	2907 Nicholas Road Dayton, OH	45408-1690
53.	1482 Valleyfield St. Lexington, MA	02421	1482 Valefield St. Lexington, MA	02421

Correct List

	Address	ZIP Code
54.	475 Ervin Farm Rd. Mooresville, NC	28115-7392
55.	8164 Northcrest Xing E Clarkston, MI	48346-6544
56.	2702 Merrimac Rd. Poughkeepsie, NY	12603
57.	9483 W Interstate 20 Odessa, Texas	79761-3503
58.	7527 Newpoint Rd. Beaufort, SC	29902
59.	5128 Wadsworth St. Portland, ME	04103-0342
60.	1309 Bogman St. Providence, RI	02905

List to Be Checked

Address	ZIP Code
475 Erwin Farm Rd. Mooresville, NC	28225-7392
8164 Northcrest Xing E Clarkston, MI	48346-6454
2702 Merrimac Rd. Poughkeepsie, NY	12603
9583 W Interstate 20 Odessa, Texas	79761-3503
7527 Newpoint Rd. Beaufort, SC	20902
5128 Wadsworth St. Portland, ME	40103-0342
1309 Bogman Pl. Providence, RI	02095

PART B: FORMS COMPLETION

Look at this sample form and answer the two questions below it. Mark your answers in the sample answer grid that follows the questions.

Sample Form

1. First Name	2. Middle Name	3. Last Name
4. Street Address		
5. City	6. State	7. ZIP Code
8. Fee $ _____	9. Date 9a. Day _____ 9b. Month _____ 9c. Year _____	

S1. Which of these would be a correct entry for Box 6?
   A. "2542 Oak Avenue"
   B. "November"
   C. "$6.80"
   D. "Nevada"

S2. Where should the middle name be entered on the form?
   A. Box 1
   B. Box 2
   C. Box 3
   D. Box 4

Sample Answer Grid				
S1.	Ⓐ	Ⓑ	Ⓒ	Ⓓ
S2.	Ⓐ	Ⓑ	Ⓒ	Ⓓ

Completed Sample Answer Grid				
S1.	Ⓐ	Ⓑ	Ⓒ	●
S2.	Ⓐ	●	Ⓒ	Ⓓ

On the form, Box 6 is labeled "State." So the correct answer for sample question 1 is "D. Nevada," which is the only state listed among the answers. Box 2 is labeled "Middle Name," so the correct answer for sample question 2 is "B. Box 2." The completed sample answer grid above shows these correct answers filled in.

Directions: Each of the following forms is followed by questions based on that form. Each part of the form is labeled with a number or a number and a letter. You will have 15 minutes to complete the 30 questions in this section

Set 1: Forms Completion
Questions 1 through 6 are based on Form 1.

Form 1

APPLICATION FOR POST OFFICE BOX OR CALLER SERVICE	
Customer: Complete Shaded Boxes	Post Office: Complete White Boxes
1. Names to Which Box Numbers Are Assigned	**2. Box or Caller Numbers**
3. Name of Person Applying Title (if person represents organization) Name of Organization (if different from item 1)	**4. Will This Box Be Used for** ❏ Personal Use ❏ Business Use (optional)
5. Address (number, street, apt. no., city, state, ZIP code) *When address changes, cross out address here and put* *new address on back.*	**6. Email Address** (optional)
7a. Date Application Received — 7b. Box Size — 7c. ID and Physical Address Verified by *(initials)*	**8. Telephone Number** (include area code)
9. Two types of identification required. One must contain a photograph of addressee(s). Social Security cards, credit cards, and birth certificates are not acceptable as identification. Write in identifying information. Subject to verification. — **10. Eligible for Carrier Delivery:** ❏ city ❏ rural ❏ HCR ❏ none — **11. Dates of Service** _____ through _____
12. List names of minors or names of others receiving mail in box. Others must present two forms of valid ID. If applicant is a firm, name each member receiving mail. Each member must have verifiable ID on request. — **13. Service Assigned** ❏ Box ❏ Caller ❏ Reserve No. — **14. Signature of Applicant** (same as item 3) I agree to comply with all rules regarding Post Office box or caller service.

217

1. Which of these would be a correct entry for Box 11?
   A. "8/19/06" and "12/19/06"
   B. "December"
   C. Two checkmarks
   D. A signature

2. Box numbers are assigned to Harley Jones and Jennifer Conway, but the application is being made by True Right Siding Company. Where would you enter True Right Siding Company's name?
   A. Box 1
   B. Box 2
   C. Box 3
   D. Box 5

3. How would the customer indicate that the box will be used for personal use?
   A. Write "personal" in Box 1
   B. Enter a checkmark in Box 2
   C. Enter a checkmark in Box 4
   D. Enter a checkmark in Box 13

4. The customer is requesting a large size box. Where would the customer indicate this?
   A. Box 2
   B. Box 7b
   C. Box 7c
   D. Box 10

5. Which of these would be a correct entry for Box 7c?
   A. "6928 Red Oak Lane"
   B. "HO6398679"
   C. "James Connoly"
   D. "J. C."

6. Where would you indicate that caller service has been requested?
   A. Box 3
   B. Box 4
   C. Box 10
   D. Box 13

Set 2: Forms Completion

Questions 7 through 12 are based on Form 2.

Form 2

MAILING PERMIT APPLICATION AND CUSTOMER PROFILE

1. Two types of identification are required. One must contain a photograph of the addressee(s). Social Security cards, credit cards, and birth certificates are unacceptable as identification. The agent must write in identifying information. Subject to verification.

1a. Enter the first ID number.

1b. Enter the second ID number.

Application Information
(please print or type)

2. Individual or Company Name	3. Date
4. Applicant's Signature	5. Email Address

6. Address (Street and number, apartment or suite number, city, state, ZIP Code)

7. Other Names Under Which Company Does Business (if applicable)	8. How Can We Contact You? 8a. ❑ Phone 8b. ❑ Email 8c. ❑ Mail
9. Contact Person	10. Telephone (include area code)

For Postal Service Use
Check Type of Permit/Authorization Requested
(do not fill in shaded boxes)

	Permit Number	Date Issued	Date Fee Paid	Date Canceled	Sample Approved
11. ❑ **Permit Imprint Authorization** (fee applies) 11f. ❑ First-Class Mail 11g. ❑ Standard Mail 11h. ❑ Package Services 11i. ❑ Company Permit	11a.	11b.	11c.	11d.	11e.
12. ❑ **Precanceled Stamp or Government Precanceled Stamped Envelope Authorization** (no fee)	12a.	12b.	12c.	12d.	12e.
13. ❑ **Notification to Present Metered Mail in Bulk** (no fee)	13a.	13b.	13c.	13d.	13e.
13f. ❑ First-Class Mail 13g. ❑ Standard Mail 13h. ❑ Package Services	13i.	13j.	13k.	13l.	13m.
14. ❑ **Business Reply Mail (BRM) Authorization** (fee applies)	14a.	14b.	14c.	14d.	14e.
15. ❑ **Merchandise Return Service (MRS) Authorization** (fee applies)	15a.	15b.	15c.	15d.	15e.

15f. Type of Application ❑ Initial ❑ Reapplication	15g. Return Location ❑ Single ❑ Multiple	15h. Advance Deposit Account ❑ Each Location ❑ Centralized

7. The customer, Maria Torres, has presented a passport, a driver's license, and a birth certificate as identification. What should the postal agent do concerning this identification?
   A. Enter all three identification numbers in Box 1
   B. Enter the driver's license number and the passport number in Box 1
   C. Enter the driver's license number and the birth certificate number in Box 1
   D. Enter the passport number and the birth certificate number in Box 1

8. Where would the customer indicate that she should be contacted by mail?
   A. Box 5
   B. Box 6
   C. Box 8
   D. Box 9

9. The customer paid a fee for Business Reply Mail Authorization on February 10. Where would you enter this date?
   A. Box 3
   B. Box 11a
   C. Box 12c
   D. Box 14c

10. You could correctly fill in all of the following boxes EXCEPT which ones?
    A. Box 11a and Box 11c
    B. Box 12a and Box 12c
    C. Box 14a and Box 14c
    D. Box 15a and Box 15c

11. How would you indicate that the Permit Imprint Authorization is for Package Services?
    A. Put a checkmark in Box 11a
    B. Put a checkmark on Line 11h
    C. Put a checkmark on Line 13h
    D. Put a checkmark in Box 14

12. This is the customer's first application. Where would this be indicated?
    A. Box 3
    B. Box 12d
    C. Box 14d
    D. Box 15f

Set 3: Forms Completion

Questions 13 through 18 are based on Form 3.

Form 3

<table>
<tr><td colspan="2" align="center">**Domestic Insured Parcel Receipt**
(not for international mail)</td></tr>
<tr><td colspan="2">**1. Parcel Addressed for Delivery at**

1a. Post Office   1b. State   1c. ZIP Code
_____   _____   _____</td></tr>
<tr><td>**2. Postage $ _____**</td><td rowspan="5">**8. Postmark of Mailing Office**</td></tr>
<tr><td>**3. Insurance Fee $ _____**</td></tr>
<tr><td>**4. Special Delivery Fee $ _____**</td></tr>
<tr><td>**5. Special Handling Fee $ _____**</td></tr>
<tr><td>**6. TOTAL FEES $ _____**</td></tr>
<tr><td>**7. INSURANCE COVERAGE**
     $ _____</td><td></td></tr>
<tr><td colspan="2">**9. Check all that apply for this parcel.**

9a. _____ Fragile   9b. _____ Liquid   9c. _____ Perishable</td></tr>
<tr><td colspan="2">**10. Sender: Enter name and address of addressee on the reverse and read information regarding insurance coverage and claims.**</td></tr>
</table>

221

13. The Post Office from which the parcel is mailed is located in Smithville, North Carolina. Where would this information be shown?
    A. Line 1a
    B. Line 1b
    C. Line 1a and Line 1b
    D. Box 8

14. You could enter a dollar amount in each of the following EXCEPT which one?
    A. Box 1
    B. Box 2
    C. Box 4
    D. Box 6

15. How would you indicate that the parcel contains a glass bottle filled with a liquid?
    A. Write in the information in Box 1
    B. Put a checkmark on Lines 9a and 9b
    C. Put a checkmark on Line 9c
    D. Write in the information in Box 10

16. The customer pays an insurance fee of $1.20, a Special Delivery fee of $3.10, and a Special Handling fee of $2.30, for a total of $6.60. Where would you enter $6.60?
    A. Box 3
    B. Box 4
    C. Box 6
    D. Box 7

17. The package is to be shipped to Lisbon, Portugal. Where would you indicate this address?
    A. Box 1
    B. Box 8
    C. On the reverse of the form
    D. None of the above

18. The package is insured for $150. Where would you indicate this?
    A. Box 3
    B. Box 7
    C. Box 8
    D. Box 9

Set 4: Forms Completion

Questions 19 through 24 are based on Form 4.

Form 4

EXPRESS MAIL	MAILING LABEL

ORIGIN: POSTAL SERVICE USE ONLY			DELIVERY: POSTAL SERVICE USE ONLY		
1a. PO ZIP Code	1b. Day of Delivery ❏ Next ❏ 2nd	1c. Postage $	6a. Delivery Attempt Mo. _____ Day _____	6b. Time ❏ AM ❏ PM	6c. Employee Signature _____
2a. Date Accepted	2b. Scheduled Delivery Date	2c. Return Receipt Fee $	7a. Delivery Date Mo. _____ Day _____	7b. Time ❏ AM ❏ PM	7c. Employee Signature _____
3a. Time Accepted ❏ AM ❏ PM	3b. Scheduled Delivery Time ❏ Noon ❏ 3 PM	3c. COD Fee $ / 3d. Insurance Fee $			
4a. Flat Rate ❏ OR Weight ___ lbs. ___ oz.	4b. Military Delivery Time ❏ 2nd Day ❏ 3rd Day	4c. Total Postage and Fees $			
5a. Acceptance Employee Initials _____					

CUSTOMER USE ONLY	
Payment by 8a. ❏ Express Mail Account Number _____	9a. ❏ Waiver of Signature
	9b. No Delivery ❏ Weekend ❏ Holiday
8b. ❏ Postal Service Account Number _____	9c. Customer Signature _____
10a. FROM: (Please Print) Phone ( ) _____	10b. TO: (Please Print) Phone ( ) _____

19. How would you indicate that the carrier tried to deliver this package on July 14 but was unsuccessful?
   A. Write "July 14" in Box 2b
   B. Put a checkmark in Box 3a
   C. Put a checkmark in Box 4b
   D. Write "July 14" in Box 6a

20. The customer's Express Mail account number is 682947. Where would the customer enter this number?
   A. Box 4a
   B. Box 8a
   C. Box 8b
   D. Box 9c

21. A checkmark would be a correct entry for every box EXCEPT which one?
   A. Box 1a
   B. Box 1b
   C. Box 4b
   D. Box 9b

22. How would the customer indicate that he or she wants the mail to be delivered on the weekend?
   A. Put a checkmark in Box 3b
   B. Put a checkmark in Box 4b
   C. Put a checkmark in Box 9b
   D. None of the above

23. Which of these would be a correct entry for Box 7b?
   A. "10:00"
   B. "$10.00"
   C. "February 2"
   D. A signature

24. Where would you enter a COD fee of $2.00?
   A. Box 2c
   B. Box 3c
   C. Box 4a
   D. Box 4c

Set 5: Forms Completion

Questions 25 through 30 are based on Form 5.

Form 5

CUSTOMS DECLARATION	
1. Sender's Name and Address	**2. Sender's Customs Reference (if any)**
	3. Insured Number
	4. Insured Amount
	5. Sender's Instructions in Case of Nondelivery

5a. ❏ Treat as Abandoned

5b. ❏ Return to Sender
(return charges at sender's expense)

5c. ❏ Redirect to address below:

6. Addressee's Name and Address

7. Addressee's Telephone/Fax/Email (if known)

8a. Description of Contents	8b. Quantity	8c. Weight	8d. Value
		8e. Total Weight	8f. Total Value

9. Check One: 9a. ❏ Airmail/Priority   9b. ❏ Surface/Nonpriority

10. Check One: 10a. ❏ Gift   10b. ❏ Documents   10c. ❏ Commercial Sample
10d. ❏ Returned Goods   10e. ❏ Other

11. Date and Sender's Signature

25. The package contains 12 wristwatches. Where would you enter "12"?
    A. Box 3
    B. Box 8a
    C. Box 8b
    D. Box 10

26. Which of these would be a correct entry for Box 1?
    A. "Inez Samuels"
    B. "Wristwatches"
    C. "$340"
    D. "4/11/06"

27. If the package can't be delivered to the addressee, the sender wishes it to be sent to another person. Where would you indicate this?
    A. Box 1
    B. Box 5c
    C. Box 6
    D. Box 11

28. How would you indicate that this is not a priority mailing?
    A. Put a checkmark in Box 5b
    B. Put a checkmark on Line 9a
    C. Put a checkmark on Line 9b
    D. Put a checkmark in Box 10e

29. Which of these would be a correct entry for Box 3?
    A. "$58.75"
    B. "Sioux City, Iowa"
    C. "3/9/06"
    D. "583269"

30. You could enter a dollar amount for every box EXCEPT which one?
    A. Box 4
    B. Box 7
    C. Box 8d
    D. Box 8f

PART C: CODING AND MEMORY

SECTION 1—CODING

Coding Exercise

Choose the correct delivery route, based on the Coding Guide, for each of the following 4 items and mark your answers on the answer sheet below. You have 2 minutes to complete this practice exercise. This exercise will not be scored.

CODING GUIDE

Address Range	Delivery Route
1301–1500 State Hwy. 180	
370–839 Bennington Street	A
18000–22500 San Pedro Beltway	
1501–2100 State Hwy. 180	
22501–27000 San Pedro Beltway	B
200–799 Urbandale Bypass SW	
25–899 N Lockhart Rd.	C
840–1250 Bennington Street	
All mail that doesn't fall in one of the address ranges listed above	D

	Address	Delivery Route
1.	22699 San Pedro Beltway	A B C D
2.	632 N Lockhart Rd.	A B C D
3.	2004 State Hwy. 180	A B C D
4.	369 Bennington Street	A B C D

Sample Answer Grid				
1.	Ⓐ	Ⓑ	Ⓒ	Ⓓ
2.	Ⓐ	Ⓑ	Ⓒ	Ⓓ
3.	Ⓐ	Ⓑ	Ⓒ	Ⓓ
4.	Ⓐ	Ⓑ	Ⓒ	Ⓓ

Completed Sample Answer Grid				
1.	Ⓐ	●	Ⓒ	Ⓓ
2.	Ⓐ	Ⓑ	●	Ⓓ
3.	Ⓐ	●	Ⓒ	Ⓓ
4.	Ⓐ	Ⓑ	Ⓒ	●

CODING TEST

Choose the correct delivery route, based on the Coding Guide, for each of the following 36 items (items 1 through 36) and mark your answers in the Coding section of the Answer Sheet. You have 6 minutes to complete this test.

CODING GUIDE

Address Range	Delivery Route
1301–1500 State Hwy. 180	
370–839 Bennington Street	A
18000–22500 San Pedro Beltway	
1501–2100 State Hwy. 180	
22501–27000 San Pedro Beltway	B
200–799 Urbandale Bypass SW	
25–899 N Lockhart Rd.	C
840–1250 Bennington Street	
All mail that doesn't fall in one of the address ranges listed above	D

	Address	Delivery Route
1.	26343 San Pedro Beltway	A B C D
2.	775 Bennington Street	A B C D
3.	527 S Lockhart Rd.	A B C D
4.	1355 State Hwy. 180	A B C D
5.	369 Urbandale Bypass SW	A B C D
6.	23687 San Pedro Beltway	A B C D
7.	16008 State Hwy. 180	A B C D
8.	976 Bennington Street	A B C D
9.	597 N Lockhart Rd.	A B C D
10.	24898 San Pedro Beltway	A B C D

	Address	Delivery Route
11.	1453 State Hwy. 180	(A) B C D
12.	29668 San Pedro Beltway	A B C (D)
13.	1099 Bennington Street	A B (C) D
14.	18997 San Pedro Beltway	(A) B C D
15.	1908 State Hwy. 180	A (B) C D
16.	25411 San Pedro Beltway	A (B) C D
17.	700 Brockton Rd.	A B C (D)
18.	535 Urbandale Bypass SW	A B (C) D
19.	1660 State Hwy. 180	A (B) C D
20.	21667 San Pedro Beltway	(A) B C D
21.	381 Bennington Street	(A) B C D
22.	497 Urbandale Bypass SW	A B (C) D
23.	2040 State Hwy. 180	A (B) C D
24.	21805 San Pedro Highway	X (A) B C D
25.	15 N Lockhart Rd.	A B C (D)
26.	700 Urbandale Bypass SW	A B (C) D
27.	488 Bennington Street	(A) B C D
28.	2189 State Hwy 130	A B C (D)
29.	22777 San Pedro Beltway	A (B) C D
30.	331 N Lockhart Rd.	A B (C) D
31.	510 Bennington Street	(A) B C D
32.	26044 San Pedro Beltway	A (B) C D
33.	920 Bennington Street	A B (C) D
34.	1669 State Hwy. 180	A (B) C D
35.	20074 San Pedro Beltway	(A) B C (D)
36.	500 Warrendale Bypass SW	A B C (D)

SECTION 2—MEMORY

Memory Study Period 1
Use the time given to memorize the information in the following Coding Guide.

CODING GUIDE

Address Range	Delivery Route
1301–1500 State Hwy. 180	
370–839 Bennington Street	A
18000–22500 San Pedro Beltway	
1501–2100 State Hwy. 180	
22501–27000 San Pedro Beltway	B
200–799 Urbandale Bypass SW	
25–899 N Lockhart Rd.	C
840–1250 Bennington Street	
All mail that doesn't fall in one of the address ranges listed above	D

Memory Exercise

Choose the correct delivery route, based on your memory of the information in the Coding Guide, for each of the following 8 items and mark your answers on the answer sheet below. You have 90 seconds to complete this practice exercise. This exercise will not be scored.

	Address	Delivery Route
1.	1219 Bennington Street	A B C D
2.	202 N Lockhart Rd.	A B C D
3.	22230 San Pedro Beltway	A B C D
4.	291 Urbandale Bypass NW	A B C D
5.	25090 San Pedro Beltway	A B C D
6.	1443 State Hwy. 180	A B C D
7.	1099 State Hwy. 180	A B C D
8.	23654 San Pedro Beltway	A B C D

Sample Answer Grid		Completed Sample Answer Grid	
1.	Ⓐ Ⓑ Ⓒ Ⓓ	1.	Ⓐ Ⓑ ● Ⓓ
2.	Ⓐ Ⓑ Ⓒ Ⓓ	2.	Ⓐ Ⓑ ● Ⓓ
3.	Ⓐ Ⓑ Ⓒ Ⓓ	3.	● Ⓑ Ⓒ Ⓓ
4.	Ⓐ Ⓑ Ⓒ Ⓓ	4.	Ⓐ Ⓑ Ⓒ ●
5.	Ⓐ Ⓑ Ⓒ Ⓓ	5.	Ⓐ ● Ⓒ Ⓓ
6.	Ⓐ Ⓑ Ⓒ Ⓓ	6.	● Ⓑ Ⓒ Ⓓ
7.	Ⓐ Ⓑ Ⓒ Ⓓ	7.	Ⓐ Ⓑ Ⓒ ●
8.	Ⓐ Ⓑ Ⓒ Ⓓ	8.	Ⓐ ● Ⓒ Ⓓ

Memory Study Period 2
Use the time given to memorize the information in the following Coding Guide.

CODING GUIDE

Address Range	Delivery Route
1301–1500 State Hwy. 180 370–839 Bennington Street 18000–22500 San Pedro Beltway	A
1501–2100 State Hwy. 180 22501–27000 San Pedro Beltway	B
200–799 Urbandale Bypass SW 25–899 N Lockhart Rd. 840–1250 Bennington Street	C
All mail that doesn't fall in one of the address ranges listed above	D

MEMORY TEST
Choose the correct delivery route, based on your memory of the information in the Coding Guide, for each of the following 36 items (items 37 through 72) and mark your answers in the Memory section of the Answer Sheet. You have 7 minutes to complete this test.

	Address	Delivery Route
37.	1750 State Hwy. 180	A B C D
38.	771 Urbandale Bypass SW	A B C D
39.	818 Bennington Street	A B C D
40.	18465 San Pedro Beltway	A B C D
41.	1828 Bennington Street	A B C D
42.	57 N Lockhart Rd.	A B C D
43.	1601 State Hwy. 180	A B C D
44.	235560 San Pedro Beltway	A B C D
45.	1466 State Hwy. 180	A B C D

	Address	Delivery Route
46.	25812 San Pedro Beltway	A B C D
47.	199 N Lockhart Rd.	A B C D
48.	740 Urbandale Bypass SW	A B C D
49.	343 N Locksley Rd.	A B C D
50.	711 Bennington Street	A B C D
51.	1883 State Hwy. 180	A B C D
52.	971 Urbandale Bypass SW	A B C D
53.	255 N Lockhart Rd.	A B C D
54.	20462 San Pietro Beltway	A B C D
55.	830 Bennington Street	A B C D
56.	850 Bennington Street	A B C D
57.	22888 San Pedro Beltway	A B C D
58.	1851 State Hwy. 180	A B C D
59.	19999 San Pedro Beltway	A B C D
60.	1150 State Hwy. 180	A B C D
61.	604 N Lockhart Rd.	A B C D
62.	22491 San Pedro Beltway	A B C D
63.	1151 Bennington Street	A B C D
64.	998 N Lockhart Rd.	A B C D
65.	1860 State Hwy. 180	A B C D
66.	18225 San Pedro Beltway	A B C D
67.	949 Urbandale Bypass SW	A B C D
68.	1716 State Hwy. 180	A B C D
69.	990 Bennington Street	A B C D
70.	740 N Lockhart Rd.	A B C D
71.	799 Bennington Street	A B C D
72.	288 S Lockhart Rd.	A B C D

PART D: PERSONAL CHARACTERISTICS AND EXPERIENCE INVENTORY

On the actual exam, the next part that you would take is Part D: Personal Characteristics and Experience Inventory. This part of the exam is 90 minutes long and has 236 items. Because there is no particular advantage to practicing your responses on these statements and questions, no tests are given here for them.

Scoring and Explanations for Practice Examination 4

ANSWER KEY

Part A: Address Checking

1. A	11. A	21. A	31. C	41. D	51. B
2. C	12. B	22. D	32. B	42. C	52. C
3. D	13. D	23. D	33. A	43. A	53. B
4. C	14. C	24. B	34. A	44. C	54. D
5. B	15. B	25. C	35. B	45. D	55. C
6. D	16. C	26. B	36. D	46. C	56. A
7. B	17. A	27. A	37. C	47. B	57. B
8. A	18. B	28. D	38. B	48. C	58. C
9. C	19. C	29. B	39. A	49. B	59. C
10. C	20. B	30. C	40. B	50. A	60. D

Part B: Forms Completion

1. A	6. D	11. B	16. C	21. A	26. A
2. C	7. B	12. D	17. D	22. D	27. B
3. C	8. C	13. D	18. B	23. A	28. C
4. B	9. D	14. A	19. D	24. B	29. D
5. D	10. B	15. B	20. B	25. C	30. B

Part C: Coding Test

1. B	7. D	13. C	19. B	25. D	31. A
2. A	8. C	14. A	20. A	26. C	32. B
3. D	9. C	15. B	21. A	27. A	33. C
4. A	10. B	16. B	22. C	28. D	34. B
5. C	11. A	17. D	23. B	29. B	35. A
6. B	12. D	18. C	24. D	30. C	36. D

Part C: Memory Test

37. B	43. B	49. D	55. A	61. C	67. D
38. C	44. D	50. A	56. C	62. A	68. B
39. A	45. A	51. B	57. B	63. C	69. C
40. A	46. B	52. D	58. B	64. D	70. C
41. D	47. C	53. C	59. A	65. B	71. A
42. C	48. C	54. D	60. D	66. A	72. D

SCORING

Part A: Address Checking

Enter the number you got right: _____

Enter the number you got wrong
(not including those left blank): _____

Divide the number wrong by 3
(or multiply by 1/3): _____

Subtract this answer from the number right: − _____

Raw Score _____

Part B: Forms Completion

Enter the number you got right
(no penalty for guessing): Raw Score _____

Part C: Coding and Memory

Enter the number you got right: _____

Enter the number you got wrong
(not including those left blank): _____

Divide the number wrong by 3
(or multiply by 1/3): _____

Subtract this answer from the number right: − _____

Raw Score _____

Part D: Personal Characteristics and Experience Inventory

Scoring system not given.

Explanations

PART A: ADDRESS CHECKING

Correct List		List to Be Checked	
Address	*ZIP Code*	*Address*	*ZIP Code*
1. **A** 4779 E Worcester Dr. Virginia Beach, VA	23455-5302	4779 E Worcester Dr. Virginia Beach, VA	23455-5302
2. **C** 7487 Turtle Creek Dr. Warwick, RI	02889-**7487**	7487 Turtle Creek Dr. Warwick, RI	02889-**4787**
3. **D** 140 Robin**wood** Cir. Anniston, Alabama	3**6**207	140 Robin**hood** Cir. Anniston, Alabama	3**4**207
4. **C** 1938 Sherman Blvd. Pawleys Island, SC	29585-**1**938	1938 Sherman Blvd. Pawleys Island, SC	29585-**2**938
5. **B** 70385 N 184th **Ave.** Surprise, AZ	85387	70385 N 184th **Ter.** Surprise, AZ	85387
6. **D** 6280 Poplar Grove Road Johnson City, **TN**	**3**7601	6280 Poplar Grove Road Johnson City, **MN**	**7**7601
7. **B** 8**42**2 Section Line Trl. Hot Springs National Park, AR 71913		8**24**2 Section Line Trl. Hot Springs National Park, AR	71913
8. **A** 6862 Avatar Dr. Apt. 369 Grand Prairie, Texas	75052-0543	6862 Avatar Dr. Apt. 369 Grand Prairie, Texas	75052-0543
9. **C** 2727 Ensenada Ave. Berkeley, CA	**9**4707-6024	2727 Ensenada Ave. Berkeley, CA	**9**6707-6024
10. **C** Rural Route 2 South Burlington, VT	0540**3**	Rural Route 2 South Burlington, VT	0543**0**
11. **A** 30330 S Mountain Brush Peak Littleton, CO	80126-9943	30330 S Mountain Brush Peak Littleton, CO	80126-9943
12. **B** 2834 Green Meadow Rd. Cook**ev**ille, TN	38506	2834 Green Meadow Rd. Cook**es**ville, TN	38506
13. **D** 46**99** Calle Huescha Deland, FL	32**7**24	46**89** Calle Huescha Deland, FL	32**2**24
14. **C** 4322 Glamorgan Dr. Seneca, SC	296**78**	4322 Glamorgan Dr. Seneca, SC	297**88**

	Correct List		List to Be Checked	
	Address	*ZIP Code*	*Address*	*ZIP Code*
15. **B**	8115 S Fair**view** Ave. Nampa, ID	83651-4483	8115 S Fair**way** Ave. Nampa, ID	83651-4483
16. **C**	3840 Cat Rock Dr. Womelsdorf, PA	**19**567-1798	3840 Cat Rock Dr. Womelsdorf, PA	**91**567-1798
17. **A**	5309 Audubon Way Warner Robins, GA	31088-5309	5309 Audubon Way Warner Robins, GA	31088-5309
18. **B**	41606 Jameson Road **Beaver**ton, CO	97005-4160	41606 Jameson Road **Billings**ton, CO	97005-4160
19. **C**	9222 W Swoope Ave. Winter Park, FL	3278**9**	9222 W Swoope Ave. Winter Park, FL	3276**9**
20. **B**	P.O. Box **37**31 Mansfield, Ohio	44907	P.O. Box **73**31 Mansfield, Ohio	44907
21. **A**	7144 Dairy View Lane Stamford, CT	06903-5181	7144 Dairy View Lane Stamford, CT	06903-5181
22. **D**	9443 Cranberry Ridge Dr. **SW** Wilson, NC	**2**7893	9443 Cranberry Ridge Dr. **NW** Wilson, NC	**3**7893
23. **D**	98**237** Knight Road Ext. Framingham, MA	017**0**1-8598	9**837** Knight Road Ext. Framingham, MA	017**9**1-8598
24. **B**	5971 S Hommell **St.** Valley Stream, NY	11580-0876	5971 S Hommell **Dr.** Valley Stream, NY	11580-0876
25. **C**	4020 County Route 67 Oakland, MI	**49**863	4020 County Route 67 Oakland, MI	**44**863
26. **B**	6282 **W** Continental Dr. Gallup, NM	87301	6282 **N** Continental Dr. Gallup, NM	87301
27. **A**	5199 120th Ave. NW Minneapolis, MN	55433-0063	5199 120th Ave. NW Minneapolis, MN	55433-0063
28. **D**	6944 Allwood Rd. Apt. 11**C** Clifton, NJ	0**7**014-2486	6944 Allwood Rd. Apt. 11**D** Clifton, NJ	0**7**414-2486

		Correct List		List to Be Checked	
		Address	ZIP Code	Address	ZIP Code
29.	B	127 Ballantrae Ct. St. Louis, MO	63131	172 Ballantrae Ct. St. Louis, MO	63131
30.	C	5741 Theobald Dr. Reno, Nevada	89511-6915	5741 Theobald Dr. Reno, Nevada	89522-6915
31.	C	70521 Upper Millegan Rd. Great Falls, MT	59405-7052	70521 Upper Millegan Rd. Great Falls, MT	59045-7052
32.	B	8272 S 149th Cir. Omaha, NE	68138	8272 S 169th Cir. Omaha, NE	68138
33.	A	4883 Countryside Blvd. Leesburg, FL	34748	4883 Countryside Blvd. Leesburg, FL	34748
34.	A	3153 Upward Way Spartanburg, SC	29303-6959	3153 Upward Way Spartanburg, SC	29303-6959
35.	B	6114 Bunker Hill Road NE Washington, DC	20018	6114 Bunker Hill Road NE Washington, SC	20018
36.	D	3895 Paragon Pl. Pittsburgh, PA	15241-6765	3895 Paragon Pt. Pittsburgh, PA	05241-6765
37.	C	6463 Davenport St. Bridgeport, CT	06607-3629	6463 Davenport St. Bridgeport, CT	06667-3629
38.	B	6480 NW Sylvania Ct. Portland, OR	97229	6480 NW Sylvan Ct. Portland, OR	97229
39.	A	3223 Warrenton Blvd. Florissant, Colorado	80816	3223 Warrenton Blvd. Florissant, Colorado	80816
40.	B	2112 NE 129th St. Edmond, OK	73013-1541	2112 NE 129th St. Edward, OK	73013-1541
41.	D	4447 Summerfield Dr. Spring Valley, CA	91977-9191	4447 Summerville Dr. Spring Valley, CA	91997-9191
42.	C	6919 Lancaster Drive Hamilton, OH	45011-4421	6919 Lancaster Drive Hamilton, OH	45011-4241

	Correct List			List to Be Checked	
	Address	*ZIP Code*		*Address*	*ZIP Code*
43. **A**	548 E Cobblestone Sq. Fayetteville, AR	72703		548 E Cobblestone Sq. Fayetteville, AR	72703
44. **C**	4419 Devereaux Dr. Highlandville, IA	5**2**149		4419 Devereaux Dr. Highlandville, IA	5**3**249
45. **D**	**52**320 Catalina St. Shawnee Mission, KS	66209-2250		**25**320 Catalina St. Shawnee Mission, KS	60209-2250
46. **C**	7708 Ensleigh Lane Bowie, Maryland	20716-**3**919		7708 Ensleigh Lane Bowie, Maryland	20716-**6**919
47. **B**	7442 Okeepa **Road** Casper, WY	82604-0224		7442 Okeepa **Lane** Casper, WY	82604-0224
48. **C**	6357 Campo Del Sol Ave. Albuquerque, NM	**8**7123		6357 Campo Del Sol Ave. Albuquerque, NM	**9**7123
49. **B**	2893 **Black** Cherry Rd. Hattiesburg, MS	39401		2893 **Choke** Cherry Rd. Hattiesburg, MS	39401
50. **A**	3060 Santa Barbara Dr. Bismarck, ND	58504-2056		3060 Santa Barbara Dr. Bismarck, ND	58504-2056
51. **B**	9275 **W** Silverleaf Ave. Springfield, MO	65807		9275 **N** Silverleaf Ave. Springfield, MO	65807
52. **C**	2907 Nicholas Road Dayton, OH	45408-169**9**		2907 Nicholas Road Dayton, OH	45408-169**0**
53. **B**	1482 **Valley**field St. Lexington, MA	02421		1482 **Vale**field St. Lexington, MA	02421
54. **D**	475 Er**v**in Farm Rd. Mooresville, NC	28**1**15-7392		475 Er**w**in Farm Rd. Mooresville, NC	28**2**25-7392
55. **C**	8164 Northcrest Xing E Clarkston, MI	48346-6**544**		8164 Northcrest Xing E Clarkston, MI	48346-6**454**
56. **A**	2702 Merrimac Rd. Poughkeepsie, NY	12603		2702 Merrimac Rd. Poughkeepsie, NY	12603

	Correct List		**List to Be Checked**	
	Address	*ZIP Code*	*Address*	*ZIP Code*
57. **B**	9483 W Interstate 20 Odessa, Texas	79761-3503	9583 W Interstate 20 Odessa, Texas	79761-3503
58. **C**	7527 Newpoint Rd. Beaufort, SC	29902	7527 Newpoint Rd. Beaufort, SC	20902
59. **C**	5128 Wadsworth St. Portland, ME	04103-0342	5128 Wadsworth St. Portland, ME	40103-0342
60. **D**	1309 Bogman **St.** Providence, RI	02905	1309 Bogman **Pl.** Providence, RI	02095

PART B: FORMS COMPLETION

Set 1: Questions 1 through 6

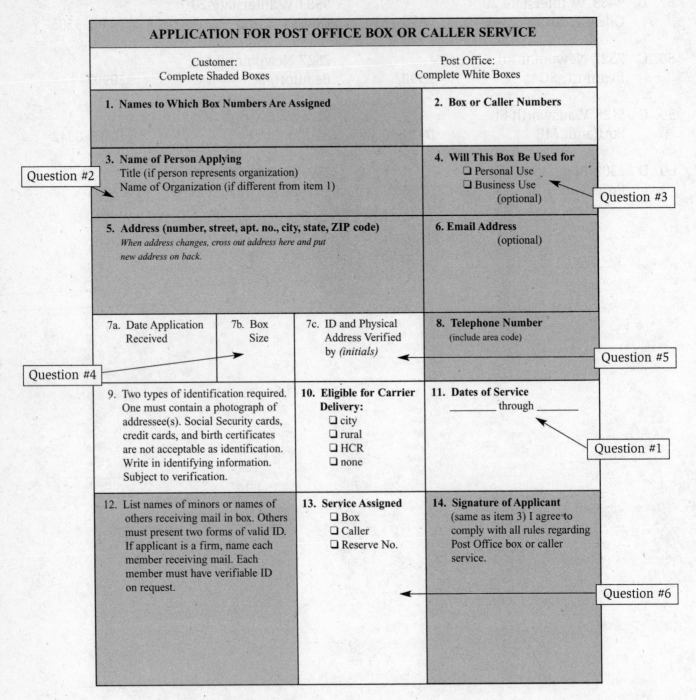

1. **A** Box 11 has space for two dates—beginning and ending.
2. **C** If an application is made by an organization with a name different from that in Box 1, the organization's name must be placed in Box 3.
3. **C** Box 4 has a check box for personal use.
4. **B** The only place in which box size is indicated is Box 7b.
5. **D** Box 7c requires only the initials of the verifier of the ID.
6. **D** "Caller" can be checked in Box 13.

MAILING PERMIT APPLICATION AND CUSTOMER PROFILE

1. Two types of identification are required. One must contain a photograph of the addressee(s). Social Security cards, credit cards, and birth certificates are unacceptable as identification. The agent must write in identifying information. Subject to verification.

> **Question #7**

1a. Enter the first ID number.

1b. Enter the second ID number.

Application Information
(please print or type)

2. Individual or Company Name	3. Date
4. Applicant's Signature	5. Email Address

6. Address (Street and number, apartment or suite number, city, state, ZIP Code)

7. Other Names Under Which Company Does Business (if applicable)	8. How Can We Contact You? 8a. ❑ Phone 8b. ❑ Email 8c. ❑ Mail
9. Contact Person	10. Telephone (include area code)

> **Question #8**

For Postal Service Use
Check Type of Permit/Authorization Requested
(do not fill in shaded boxes)

	Permit Number	Date Issued	Date Fee Paid	Date Canceled	Sample Approved
11. ❑ **Permit Imprint Authorization** (fee applies) 11f. ❑ First-Class Mail 11g. ❑ Standard Mail 11h. ❑ Package Services 11i. ❑ Company Permit	11a.	11b.	11c.	11d.	11e.
12. ❑ **Precanceled Stamp or Government Precanceled Stamped Envelope Authorization** (no fee)	12a.	12b.	12c.	12d.	12e.
13. ❑ **Notification to Present Metered Mail in Bulk** (no fee)	13a.	13b.	13c.	13d.	13e.
13f. ❑ First-Class Mail 13g. ❑ Standard Mail 13h. ❑ Package Services	13i.	13j.	13k.	13l.	13m.
14. ❑ **Business Reply Mail (BRM) Authorization** (fee applies)	14a.	14b.	14c.	14d.	14e.
15. ❑ **Merchandise Return Service (MRS) Authorization** (fee applies)	15a.	15b.	15c.	15d.	15e.

> **Question #11** (points to line 11h)
> **Question #10** (points to box 12c)
> **Question #9** (points to box 14c)

15f. Type of Application ❑ Initial ❑ Reapplication	15g. Return Location ❑ Single ❑ Multiple	15h. Advance Deposit Account ❑ Each Location ❑ Centralized

> **Question #12** (points to 15f)

---

7. **B** Box 1 indicates that a birth certificate is not acceptable ID, so answers A, C, and D cannot be right.

8. **C** Box 8 is titled "How Can We Contact You?" and there is a check box there labeled "Mail."

9. **D** Business Reply Mail is dealt with in Box 14, and the specific box for the date on which the fee is paid is Box 14c.

10. **B** The form says "do not fill in shaded boxes." So, of those boxes listed, you could fill in all of them *except* Box 12c, which is part of answer B.

11. **B** In Box 11, there is a line to check for Package Services, Line 11h.

12. **D** Two types of applications are listed in Box 15f, initial (meaning "first") and reapplication.

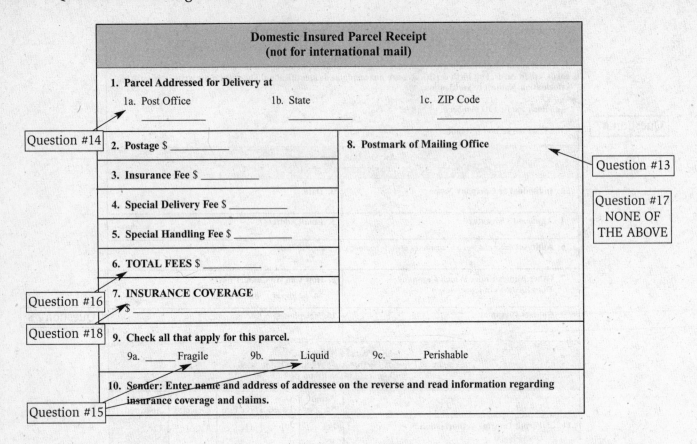

Domestic Insured Parcel Receipt
(not for international mail)

1. Parcel Addressed for Delivery at

    1a. Post Office   1b. State   1c. ZIP Code

Question #14

2. Postage $ _____   **8. Postmark of Mailing Office**

3. Insurance Fee $ _____

4. Special Delivery Fee $ _____

5. Special Handling Fee $ _____

6. TOTAL FEES $ _____

Question #16

7. INSURANCE COVERAGE

$ _____

Question #18

9. Check all that apply for this parcel.

    9a. _____ Fragile   9b. _____ Liquid   9c. _____ Perishable

10. **Sender: Enter name and address of addressee on the reverse and read information regarding insurance coverage and claims.**

Question #15

Question #13

Question #17
NONE OF
THE ABOVE

13. **D** Notice that the question says "Post Office from which the package is mailed." But Box 1 deals with the Post Office to which the package is "addressed for delivery at," that is, the place the package is being *sent*. The only box that would show the mailing Post Office is Box 8, where this office's postmark is placed.

14. **A** A dollar amount could not go anywhere in Box 1.

15. **B** Line 9a is for "Fragile" (a glass bottle would be fragile), and Line 9b is for "Liquid."

16. **C** $6.60 represents the "Total Fees" and would go in Box 6.

17. **D** The top of the form says "not for international mail." A package sent to Lisbon, Portugal would involve international mail, so the answer is D, None of the above.

18. **B** Insurance coverage is listed in Box 7.

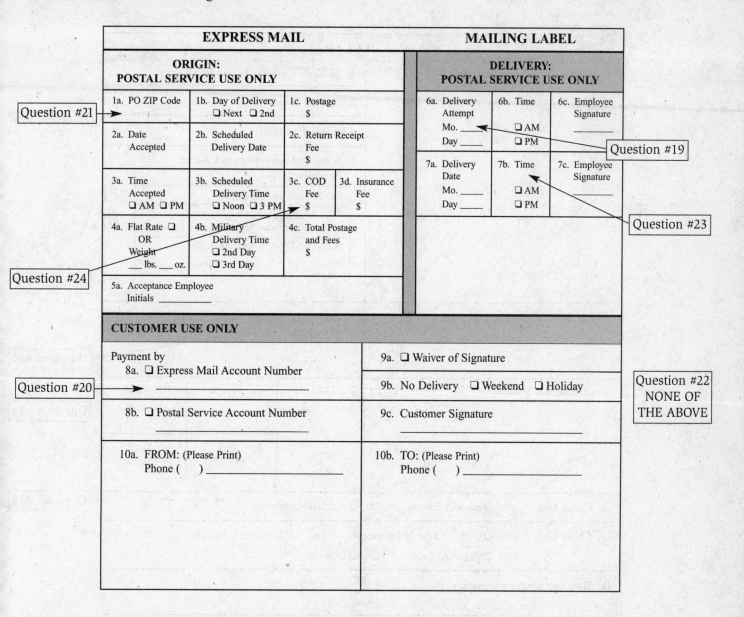

EXPRESS MAIL | **MAILING LABEL**

| ORIGIN: POSTAL SERVICE USE ONLY | | | DELIVERY: POSTAL SERVICE USE ONLY | | |

Question #21 →

1a. PO ZIP Code
1b. Day of Delivery ❏ Next ❏ 2nd
1c. Postage $

2a. Date Accepted
2b. Scheduled Delivery Date
2c. Return Receipt Fee $

3a. Time Accepted ❏ AM ❏ PM
3b. Scheduled Delivery Time ❏ Noon ❏ 3 PM
3c. COD Fee $
3d. Insurance Fee $

4a. Flat Rate ❏ OR Weight ___ lbs. ___ oz.
4b. Military Delivery Time ❏ 2nd Day ❏ 3rd Day
4c. Total Postage and Fees $

5a. Acceptance Employee Initials _____

6a. Delivery Attempt Mo. ___ Day ___
6b. Time ❏ AM ❏ PM
6c. Employee Signature _____

7a. Delivery Date Mo. ___ Day ___
7b. Time ❏ AM ❏ PM
7c. Employee Signature _____

Question #19

Question #23

Question #24

CUSTOMER USE ONLY

Payment by
8a. ❏ Express Mail Account Number
_____

Question #20 →

8b. ❏ Postal Service Account Number
_____

9a. ❏ Waiver of Signature

9b. No Delivery ❏ Weekend ❏ Holiday

9c. Customer Signature
_____

Question #22 NONE OF THE ABOVE

10a. FROM: (Please Print)
Phone ( ) _____

10b. TO: (Please Print)
Phone ( ) _____

19. **D** The date of a delivery attempt (rather than an actual delivery) can be listed in Box 6a.
20. **B** The Express Mail account number is entered in Box 8a.
21. **A** Only Box 1a cannot have a checkmark. It requires a ZIP code.
22. **D** The only box dealing with weekend delivery is Box 9b, but notice that the box is labeled "*No* Delivery." So the only answer possible here is D, None of the above.
23. **A** Box 7b asks for a time of delivery (and has boxes to check for "A.M." or "P.M.").
24. **B** The COD fee goes in Box 3c.

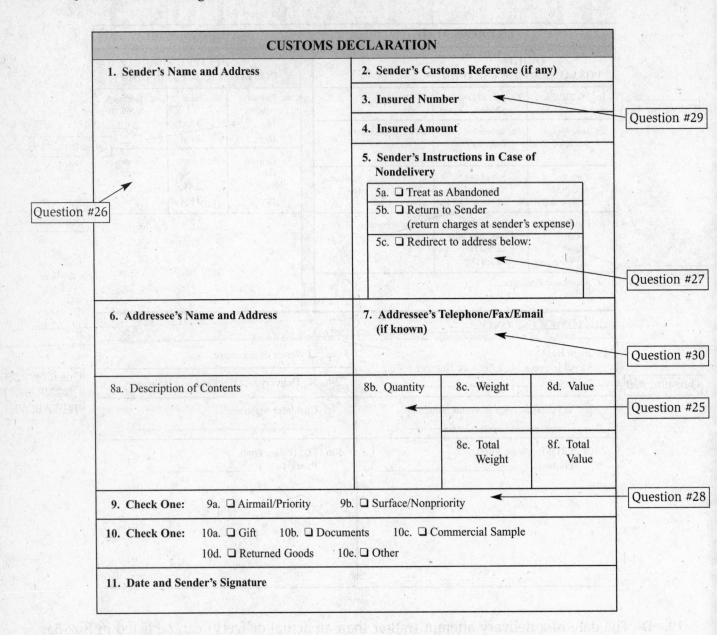

CUSTOMS DECLARATION

1. Sender's Name and Address

2. Sender's Customs Reference (if any)

3. Insured Number — Question #29

4. Insured Amount

5. Sender's Instructions in Case of Nondelivery

5a. ❏ Treat as Abandoned

5b. ❏ Return to Sender (return charges at sender's expense)

5c. ❏ Redirect to address below: — Question #27

Question #26

6. Addressee's Name and Address

7. Addressee's Telephone/Fax/Email (if known) — Question #30

8a. Description of Contents | 8b. Quantity — Question #25 | 8c. Weight | 8d. Value

8e. Total Weight | 8f. Total Value

9. Check One: 9a. ❏ Airmail/Priority   9b. ❏ Surface/Nonpriority — Question #28

10. Check One: 10a. ❏ Gift   10b. ❏ Documents   10c. ❏ Commercial Sample
10d. ❏ Returned Goods   10e. ❏ Other

11. Date and Sender's Signature

25. **C** You can list the quantity (number) of items in the package in Box 8b.
26. **A** Box 1 is for the sender's name and address, so "Inez Samuels," a name, would be correct for this box.
27. **B** Box 5c has the sender's instructions to "Redirect to address below."
28. **C** Line 9b can be checked for "Surface/Nonpriority."
29. **D** Box 3 is labeled "Insured Number." The only number given is in answer D.
30. **B** A dollar amount can't go in Box 7.

PRACTICE EXAMINATION 5

ANSWER SHEET FOR PRACTICE EXAMINATION 5

PART A: ADDRESS CHECKING

1. Ⓐ Ⓑ Ⓒ Ⓓ   16. Ⓐ Ⓑ Ⓒ Ⓓ   31. Ⓐ Ⓑ Ⓒ Ⓓ   46. Ⓐ Ⓑ Ⓒ Ⓓ
2. Ⓐ Ⓑ Ⓒ Ⓓ   17. Ⓐ Ⓑ Ⓒ Ⓓ   32. Ⓐ Ⓑ Ⓒ Ⓓ   47. Ⓐ Ⓑ Ⓒ Ⓓ
3. Ⓐ Ⓑ Ⓒ Ⓓ   18. Ⓐ Ⓑ Ⓒ Ⓓ   33. Ⓐ Ⓑ Ⓒ Ⓓ   48. Ⓐ Ⓑ Ⓒ Ⓓ
4. Ⓐ Ⓑ Ⓒ Ⓓ   19. Ⓐ Ⓑ Ⓒ Ⓓ   34. Ⓐ Ⓑ Ⓒ Ⓓ   49. Ⓐ Ⓑ Ⓒ Ⓓ
5. Ⓐ Ⓑ Ⓒ Ⓓ   20. Ⓐ Ⓑ Ⓒ Ⓓ   35. Ⓐ Ⓑ Ⓒ Ⓓ   50. Ⓐ Ⓑ Ⓒ Ⓓ
6. Ⓐ Ⓑ Ⓒ Ⓓ   21. Ⓐ Ⓑ Ⓒ Ⓓ   36. Ⓐ Ⓑ Ⓒ Ⓓ   51. Ⓐ Ⓑ Ⓒ Ⓓ
7. Ⓐ Ⓑ Ⓒ Ⓓ   22. Ⓐ Ⓑ Ⓒ Ⓓ   37. Ⓐ Ⓑ Ⓒ Ⓓ   52. Ⓐ Ⓑ Ⓒ Ⓓ
8. Ⓐ Ⓑ Ⓒ Ⓓ   23. Ⓐ Ⓑ Ⓒ Ⓓ   38. Ⓐ Ⓑ Ⓒ Ⓓ   53. Ⓐ Ⓑ Ⓒ Ⓓ
9. Ⓐ Ⓑ Ⓒ Ⓓ   24. Ⓐ Ⓑ Ⓒ Ⓓ   39. Ⓐ Ⓑ Ⓒ Ⓓ   54. Ⓐ Ⓑ Ⓒ Ⓓ
10. Ⓐ Ⓑ Ⓒ Ⓓ   25. Ⓐ Ⓑ Ⓒ Ⓓ   40. Ⓐ Ⓑ Ⓒ Ⓓ   55. Ⓐ Ⓑ Ⓒ Ⓓ
11. Ⓐ Ⓑ Ⓒ Ⓓ   26. Ⓐ Ⓑ Ⓒ Ⓓ   41. Ⓐ Ⓑ Ⓒ Ⓓ   56. Ⓐ Ⓑ Ⓒ Ⓓ
12. Ⓐ Ⓑ Ⓒ Ⓓ   27. Ⓐ Ⓑ Ⓒ Ⓓ   42. Ⓐ Ⓑ Ⓒ Ⓓ   57. Ⓐ Ⓑ Ⓒ Ⓓ
13. Ⓐ Ⓑ Ⓒ Ⓓ   28. Ⓐ Ⓑ Ⓒ Ⓓ   43. Ⓐ Ⓑ Ⓒ Ⓓ   58. Ⓐ Ⓑ Ⓒ Ⓓ
14. Ⓐ Ⓑ Ⓒ Ⓓ   29. Ⓐ Ⓑ Ⓒ Ⓓ   44. Ⓐ Ⓑ Ⓒ Ⓓ   59. Ⓐ Ⓑ Ⓒ Ⓓ
15. Ⓐ Ⓑ Ⓒ Ⓓ   30. Ⓐ Ⓑ Ⓒ Ⓓ   45. Ⓐ Ⓑ Ⓒ Ⓓ   60. Ⓐ Ⓑ Ⓒ Ⓓ

Remove answer sheet by cutting on dotted line

PART B: FORMS COMPLETION

1. Ⓐ Ⓑ Ⓒ Ⓓ   9. Ⓐ Ⓑ Ⓒ Ⓓ   17. Ⓐ Ⓑ Ⓒ Ⓓ   25. Ⓐ Ⓑ Ⓒ Ⓓ
2. Ⓐ Ⓑ Ⓒ Ⓓ   10. Ⓐ Ⓑ Ⓒ Ⓓ   18. Ⓐ Ⓑ Ⓒ Ⓓ   26. Ⓐ Ⓑ Ⓒ Ⓓ
3. Ⓐ Ⓑ Ⓒ Ⓓ   11. Ⓐ Ⓑ Ⓒ Ⓓ   19. Ⓐ Ⓑ Ⓒ Ⓓ   27. Ⓐ Ⓑ Ⓒ Ⓓ
4. Ⓐ Ⓑ Ⓒ Ⓓ   12. Ⓐ Ⓑ Ⓒ Ⓓ   20. Ⓐ Ⓑ Ⓒ Ⓓ   28. Ⓐ Ⓑ Ⓒ Ⓓ
5. Ⓐ Ⓑ Ⓒ Ⓓ   13. Ⓐ Ⓑ Ⓒ Ⓓ   21. Ⓐ Ⓑ Ⓒ Ⓓ   29. Ⓐ Ⓑ Ⓒ Ⓓ
6. Ⓐ Ⓑ Ⓒ Ⓓ   14. Ⓐ Ⓑ Ⓒ Ⓓ   22. Ⓐ Ⓑ Ⓒ Ⓓ   30. Ⓐ Ⓑ Ⓒ Ⓓ
7. Ⓐ Ⓑ Ⓒ Ⓓ   15. Ⓐ Ⓑ Ⓒ Ⓓ   23. Ⓐ Ⓑ Ⓒ Ⓓ
8. Ⓐ Ⓑ Ⓒ Ⓓ   16. Ⓐ Ⓑ Ⓒ Ⓓ   24. Ⓐ Ⓑ Ⓒ Ⓓ

PART C: CODING AND MEMORY
SECTION 1—CODING

1. Ⓐ Ⓑ Ⓒ Ⓓ   10. Ⓐ Ⓑ Ⓒ Ⓓ   19. Ⓐ Ⓑ Ⓒ Ⓓ   28. Ⓐ Ⓑ Ⓒ Ⓓ
2. Ⓐ Ⓑ Ⓒ Ⓓ   11. Ⓐ Ⓑ Ⓒ Ⓓ   20. Ⓐ Ⓑ Ⓒ Ⓓ   29. Ⓐ Ⓑ Ⓒ Ⓓ
3. Ⓐ Ⓑ Ⓒ Ⓓ   12. Ⓐ Ⓑ Ⓒ Ⓓ   21. Ⓐ Ⓑ Ⓒ Ⓓ   30. Ⓐ Ⓑ Ⓒ Ⓓ
4. Ⓐ Ⓑ Ⓒ Ⓓ   13. Ⓐ Ⓑ Ⓒ Ⓓ   22. Ⓐ Ⓑ Ⓒ Ⓓ   31. Ⓐ Ⓑ Ⓒ Ⓓ
5. Ⓐ Ⓑ Ⓒ Ⓓ   14. Ⓐ Ⓑ Ⓒ Ⓓ   23. Ⓐ Ⓑ Ⓒ Ⓓ   32. Ⓐ Ⓑ Ⓒ Ⓓ
6. Ⓐ Ⓑ Ⓒ Ⓓ   15. Ⓐ Ⓑ Ⓒ Ⓓ   24. Ⓐ Ⓑ Ⓒ Ⓓ   33. Ⓐ Ⓑ Ⓒ Ⓓ
7. Ⓐ Ⓑ Ⓒ Ⓓ   16. Ⓐ Ⓑ Ⓒ Ⓓ   25. Ⓐ Ⓑ Ⓒ Ⓓ   34. Ⓐ Ⓑ Ⓒ Ⓓ
8. Ⓐ Ⓑ Ⓒ Ⓓ   17. Ⓐ Ⓑ Ⓒ Ⓓ   26. Ⓐ Ⓑ Ⓒ Ⓓ   35. Ⓐ Ⓑ Ⓒ Ⓓ
9. Ⓐ Ⓑ Ⓒ Ⓓ   18. Ⓐ Ⓑ Ⓒ Ⓓ   27. Ⓐ Ⓑ Ⓒ Ⓓ   36. Ⓐ Ⓑ Ⓒ Ⓓ

SECTION 2—MEMORY

37. Ⓐ Ⓑ Ⓒ Ⓓ   46. Ⓐ Ⓑ Ⓒ Ⓓ   55. Ⓐ Ⓑ Ⓒ Ⓓ   64. Ⓐ Ⓑ Ⓒ Ⓓ
38. Ⓐ Ⓑ Ⓒ Ⓓ   47. Ⓐ Ⓑ Ⓒ Ⓓ   56. Ⓐ Ⓑ Ⓒ Ⓓ   65. Ⓐ Ⓑ Ⓒ Ⓓ
39. Ⓐ Ⓑ Ⓒ Ⓓ   48. Ⓐ Ⓑ Ⓒ Ⓓ   57. Ⓐ Ⓑ Ⓒ Ⓓ   66. Ⓐ Ⓑ Ⓒ Ⓓ
40. Ⓐ Ⓑ Ⓒ Ⓓ   49. Ⓐ Ⓑ Ⓒ Ⓓ   58. Ⓐ Ⓑ Ⓒ Ⓓ   67. Ⓐ Ⓑ Ⓒ Ⓓ
41. Ⓐ Ⓑ Ⓒ Ⓓ   50. Ⓐ Ⓑ Ⓒ Ⓓ   59. Ⓐ Ⓑ Ⓒ Ⓓ   68. Ⓐ Ⓑ Ⓒ Ⓓ
42. Ⓐ Ⓑ Ⓒ Ⓓ   51. Ⓐ Ⓑ Ⓒ Ⓓ   60. Ⓐ Ⓑ Ⓒ Ⓓ   69. Ⓐ Ⓑ Ⓒ Ⓓ
43. Ⓐ Ⓑ Ⓒ Ⓓ   52. Ⓐ Ⓑ Ⓒ Ⓓ   61. Ⓐ Ⓑ Ⓒ Ⓓ   70. Ⓐ Ⓑ Ⓒ Ⓓ
44. Ⓐ Ⓑ Ⓒ Ⓓ   53. Ⓐ Ⓑ Ⓒ Ⓓ   62. Ⓐ Ⓑ Ⓒ Ⓓ   71. Ⓐ Ⓑ Ⓒ Ⓓ
45. Ⓐ Ⓑ Ⓒ Ⓓ   54. Ⓐ Ⓑ Ⓒ Ⓓ   63. Ⓐ Ⓑ Ⓒ Ⓓ   72. Ⓐ Ⓑ Ⓒ Ⓓ

PART D: PERSONAL CHARACTERISTICS AND EXPERIENCE INVENTORY

(236 Questions—not included here)

ADDRESS CHECKING SAMPLE QUESTIONS

Look at the row of information for sample question 1, which is labeled "S1" below. Carefully but quickly compare the **List to Be Checked** with the **Correct List**. Then decide if there are **No Errors** (select A), an error in the **Address Only** (select B), an error in the **ZIP Code Only** (select C), or an error in **Both** the address and the ZIP code (select D). Record your response to the sample questions in the **Sample Answer Grid** below. Complete the other three samples given, S2, S3, and S4, and record your responses on the **Sample Answer Grid**.

A. No Errors	B. Address Only	C. ZIP Code Only	D. Both

Correct List

	Address	ZIP Code
S1.	432 Rosewood Ct. Pasadena, CA	91106
S2.	1977 Hully Street Austin, TX	78734-1141
S3.	648 Central Dr. New York, NY	10034
S4.	9812 Pine Ave. Chicago, IL	60467-5113

List to Be Checked

Address	ZIP Code
432 Rosewood Ct. Pasedena, CA	91106
1977 Holly Street Austin, TX	78734-1114
648 Central Dr. New York, NY	10054
9812 Pine Ave. Chicago, IL	60467-5113

Sample Answer Grid

S1.	Ⓐ	Ⓑ	Ⓒ	Ⓓ
S2.	Ⓐ	Ⓑ	Ⓒ	Ⓓ
S3.	Ⓐ	Ⓑ	Ⓒ	Ⓓ
S4.	Ⓐ	Ⓑ	Ⓒ	Ⓓ

Completed Sample Answer Grid

S1.	Ⓐ	●	Ⓒ	Ⓓ
S2.	Ⓐ	Ⓑ	Ⓒ	●
S3.	Ⓐ	Ⓑ	●	Ⓓ
S4.	●	Ⓑ	Ⓒ	Ⓓ

In sample 1, the address in the **List to Be Checked** shows Pasedena, but the **Correct List** shows Pasadena. So there is an error in the address. Since the Zip codes are exactly the same, the correct answer is **B—Address Only**.

In sample 2, the address in the **List to Be Checked** shows Holly Street, but the **Correct List** shows Hully Street. So there is an error in the address. The **List to Be Checked** also shows an error in the ZIP code. The last four numbers are 1114, and they are 1141 in the **Correct List**. Because there is an error in the address and in the ZIP code, the correct answer is **D—Both**.

In sample 3, the addresses in the **List to Be Checked** and the **Correct List** are exactly the same, but there is an error in the ZIP code on the **List to Be Checked**. The **List to Be Checked** shows 10054, but the **Correct List** shows 10034. So there is an error in the ZIP code. The correct answer is **C—ZIP Code Only**.

In sample 4, the addresses in the **List to Be Checked** and the **Correct List** are exactly the same. The ZIP codes are also exactly the same. So the correct answer is **A—No Errors**.

Now turn to the next page and begin the address checking test.

PART A: ADDRESS CHECKING

For the following 60 items, compare the address in the **Correct List** with the address in the **List to Be Checked**. Determine if there are **No Errors** (answer A), an error in the **Address Only** (answer B), an error in the **ZIP Code Only** (answer C), or an error in **Both** (answer D). Mark your answers in the Address Checking section of the answer sheet. You have 11 minutes to complete this test.

A. No Errors	B. Address Only	C. ZIP Code Only	D. Both

	Correct List		List to Be Checked	
	Address	*ZIP Code*	*Address*	*ZIP Code*
1.	6703 Trumbull St. Elizabeth, NJ	07201	6703 Trumbull St. Elizabeth, NJ	77201 C
2.	2255 Higher Ground Drive Winston Salem, NC	27127-4538	2255 Higher Ground Drive Winston Salem, NC	27127-5438 C
3.	1333 Gambusino Ave. El Paso, Texas	79938-2999	1313 Gambusino Ave. El Paso, Texas	B 79938-2999
4.	91745 Industrial Pkwy. Coulterville, CA	95311-5280	9175 Industrial Pkwy. Coulterville, CA	D 85311-5280
5.	3272 Rise Branch Rd. Rehoboth Beach, DE	19971	3272 Rise Branch Rd. Rehoboth Beach, DE	19971 A
6.	4203 Colchester Road Woodbridge, VA	22191-6109	4203 Colchester Road Woodbridge, VA	22191-6199 C
7.	4617 NW 100th Pl Ocala, Florida	34482	4617 NW 100th Pl Ocala, Florida	34482 A
8.	4617 Syringa Ln. Caldwell, ID	83605	4617 Syringe Ln. Caldwell, ID	83605 B
9.	6108 Edwards Rd. West Monroe, LA	71292	6108 Edwards Rd. West Monroe, LA	71292 A
10.	2966 E Grand Ave. Laramie, WY	82070-7626	2966 E Grand Dr. Laramie, WY	82070-7626 B
11.	2997 Seminole Ave. Knoxville, TN	37915-8641	2997 Seminole Ave. Knoxville, MN	37915-8641 B

	Correct List		**List to Be Checked**	
	Address	*ZIP Code*	*Address*	*ZIP Code*
12.	6006 Montgomery Ave. Apt. 273 Pittston, PA	18643	6006 Montgomery Ave. Apt. 273 Pittston, PA	38643 C
13.	Post Office Box 61539 Tallahassee, FL	32302-1539	Post Office Box 65193 Tallahassee, FL	32302-1539 B
14.	2910 Tabernash Drive Columbus, OH	43240	2910 Tabernash Drive Columbus, OH	43240 A
15.	291 Dartmoor Ct. Rocky Mount, NC	27803-6312	291 Dartmoor Ct. Rocky Mount, NC	27883-6312 C
16.	1359 Allview Ave. Norwalk, CT	06854-1134	1359 Allwood Ave. Norwalk, CT	06854-1134 B
17.	4702 W Conkling Ave. Middletown, NY	10940	4702 N Conklin Ave. Middletown, NY	10490 C X
18.	4975 38th St. San Diego, CA	92116-0835	4975 38th St. San Diego, CA	92616-0835 C
19.	3195 Wenonah Street Gadsden, AL	35903	3195 Wenonah Street Marsden, AL	35903 B
20.	31954 SE Frontage Rd. Joliet, IL	60436-4273	31954 SE Frontage Rd. Joliet, IL	60423-4273 C
21.	2012 Muncaster Mill Road Gaithersburg, MD	20877-1115	2012 Muncaster Mill Road Gaithersburg, MD	02877-1115 C
22.	6366 Staffordshire Dr. Cherry Hill, NJ	08003-0188	6366 Stafford Dr. Cherry Hill, NJ	08003-0188 B
23.	1443 Cranleigh Mews Nashua, NH	03063-0469	1443 Cranleigh News Nashua, NH	03363-0469 D
24.	8754 Brownell Pkwy. Vineyard Haven, MA	02568	8754 Brownell Pkwy. Vineyard Haven, MA	02568 A
25.	875 Princeton Mill Ct. Athens, Georgia	30606	578 Princeton Mill Ct. Athens, Georgia	30600 D

Correct List

	Address	ZIP Code
26.	2341 Longshanks Way Henderson, NV	89015
27.	3399 Lotus Garden Dr. Talofofo, GU	96930-2754
28.	9238 Summer Wynde Ct. Louisville, KY	40272-6798
29.	2020 Breckenridge Dr. Clinton Township, MI	48038
30.	2276 Brundin Ave. Chickasha, OK	73018
31.	24437 County Road 42 Bemidji, MN	56601-5402
32.	4950 Livengood Wy. Bend, Oregon	97701-2412
33.	5317 Magnolia Cv. Biloxi, MS	39532
34.	2860 Fomance Rd. Bethlehem, PA	18020-1475
35.	Rural Route 83 Cape Girardeau, MO	63701
36.	1619 Pommenville St. Pawtucket, RI	02861-3984
37.	3743 Randolph Ave. SE Huntsville, AL	35801-0841
38.	5769 Carolina Ridge Road Gaffney, SC	29341
39.	3769 Endicott Trl. Eden Prairie, MN	55347

List to Be Checked

Address	ZIP Code	
2341 Longshanks Way Cooperton, NV	89015	B
33399 Lotus Garden Dr. Talofofo, GU	96930-2754	B
9238 Summer Wynde Ct. Louisville, KY	40272-8798	C
2020 Breckenridge Dr. Clinton Township, MI	48038	A
2276 Brundin Dr. Chickasha, OK	73018	B
24437 County Road 42 Bemidji, MN	56601-5402	A
4950 Livengood Wy. Bend, Oregon	90901-2412	C
5317 Magnolia Ct. Biloxi, MS	39523	D
2860 Forman Rd. Bethlehem, PA	18020-1475	B
Rural Route 83 Cape Girardeau, MO	63701	A
1619 Pommenville St. Pawtucket, RI	90861-3984	C
3743 Randolph Ave. SE Huntsville, AL	35801-0841	A
5769 Carolina Ridge Road Gaffney, SC	29141	C
3679 Endicott Trl. Eden Prairie, MN	55347	B

Correct List

	Address	ZIP Code
40.	5234 Pheasant Holw. Denton, Texas	76207
41.	58741 Camp Creek Pkwy. SW Atlanta, GA	30331-1210
42.	48808 Cadillac Ext. Parkersburg, WV	26104-1243
43.	3654 Meetinghouse Rd. Chicopee, MA	01013
44.	1649 N Indiana Ave. West Bend, WI	53095
45.	8831 US Highway 43 Waterville, ME	04901-2496
46.	1872 Eastbrook Blvd. Winter Park, FL	32792-0504
47.	2118 Middleton Lane Silver City, NM	88061-6367
48.	6015 Cobblestone West Columbus, NE	68601
49.	1918 Abigails Way Fairfield, CT	06430-6151
50.	4080 Interlacken Drive Piedmont, WY	82933
51.	59944 N 95th St. Longmont, CO	80504
52.	7432 Langley Ave. San Lorenzo, NM	88041-0491
53.	3575 Autumnwood Dr. Sacramento, CA	95826-1495

List to Be Checked

Address	ZIP Code	
5234 Pleasant Holw. Denton, Texas	76207	X
58741 Camp Creek Pkwy. SW Atlas, GA	31331-1210	D
48808 Cadillac Ext. Parkersburg, WV	26140-1243	C
5654 Meetinghouse Rd. Chicopee, MA	01013	B
1649 W Indiana Ave. West Bend, WI	56045	D
8831 US Highway 43 Waterton, ME	04901-2496	B
1872 Eastbrook Blvd. Winter Park, FL	32792-0504	A
2118 Middleton Lane Silver City, NM	88061-6367	A
6015 Cobblestone West Columbus, NE	68600	C
1918 Abigails Way Fairfield, MT	06430-6161	D
4080 Interlacken Drive Peters, WY	82933	B
59444 N 95th St. Longmont, CO	80504	B
7432 Langley Ave. San Lorenzo, NM	88041-0491	A
3575 Autumnwood Dr. Sacramento, CA	95826-1585	C

Correct List		List to Be Checked	
Address	*ZIP Code*	*Address*	*ZIP Code*
54. 5914 Gunderman Road Ithaca, NY	14850-2314	5914 Gunnerman Road Ithaca, NY	14850-2314 *B*
55. 2950 S Enid Ave. Apt. MG Russellville, AR	72801	2950 S Enid Ave. Apt. MG Russellville, AR	32801 *C*
56. 2067 W Tamarack Rd. Spokane, WA	99224	2067 W Tamarind Rd. Spokane, WA	88224 *D*
57. 36488 93rd Ave. SE Minot, ND	58701-1870	36488 93rd Ave. SE Minot, ND	58701-1870 *A*
58. 3011 SE Browning Road Evansville, IN	47725-0622	3011 SE Brown Road Evansville, IN	47725-0622 *B*
59. 1479 Oberlin Ave. Lorain, OH	44053	1497 Oberlin Ave. Lorain, OH	44088 *X*
60. 245 Wilmett Ct. Bethesda, MD	20817-3989	245 Wilmett Ct. Bethesda, MD	20816-3989 *C*

PART B: FORMS COMPLETION

Look at this sample form and answer the two questions below it. Mark your answers in the sample answer grid that follows the questions.

Sample Form

1. First Name	2. Middle Name	3. Last Name
4. Street Address		
5. City	6. State	7. ZIP Code
8. Fee $ _____	9. Date 9a. Day _____ 9b. Month _____ 9c. Year _____	

S1. Which of these would be a correct entry for Box 6?
   A. "2542 Oak Avenue"
   B. "November"
   C. "$6.80"
   D. "Nevada"

S2. Where should the middle name be entered on the form?
   A. Box 1
   B. Box 2
   C. Box 3
   D. Box 4

Sample Answer Grid				
S1.	Ⓐ	Ⓑ	Ⓒ	Ⓓ
S2.	Ⓐ	Ⓑ	Ⓒ	Ⓓ

Completed Sample Answer Grid				
S1.	Ⓐ	Ⓑ	Ⓒ	●
S2.	Ⓐ	●	Ⓒ	Ⓓ

On the form, Box 6 is labeled "State." So the correct answer for sample question 1 is "D. Nevada," which is the only state listed among the answers. Box 2 is labeled "Middle Name," so the correct answer for sample question 2 is "B. Box 2." The completed sample answer grid above shows these correct answers filled in.

Directions: Each of the following forms is followed by questions based on that form. Each part of the form is labeled with a number or a number and a letter. You will have 15 minutes to complete the 30 questions in this section

Set 1: Forms Completion
Questions 1 through 6 are based on Form 1.

Form 1

Delivery Notice/Reminder/Receipt
1. Sorry we missed you.
1a. Today's Date _____   1b. Sender's Name _____
2. Delivery
2a. _____ We will redeliver the item   2b. _____ Please pick up the item at the Post Office.
3. Check type of item

3a. _____ Letter
   3b. _____ Large envelope, magazine, catalog, etc.
   3c. _____ Parcel
   3d. _____ Restricted Delivery
   3e. _____ Perishable Item
   3f. _____ Other:

4. If delivery confirmation is required, check type of mail service.

4a. _____ Express Mail
   4b. _____ Certified Mail
   4c. _____ Recorded Delivery
   4d. _____ Registered Mail
   4e. _____ Insured Mail
   4f. _____ Return Receipt
   4g. _____ Delivery Confirmation

5. If article requires payment check type(s) and note total payment amount.
5a. Postage Due _____   5b. COD _____   5c. Customs Fee _____   5d. Total Amount Due $ _____
6. Final Notice: Article will be returned to sender on this date: _____

1. This article will be returned to the sender on March 14. Where would you indicate this?
   A. Line 1a
   B. Line 2a
   C. Line 5d
   D. Box 6

2. What should the carrier do if the mail is a magazine with postage due?
   A. Make an entry in Line 3b, Line 5a, and Line 5d
   B. Make an entry in Line 3c and Line 5d
   C. Make an entry in Line 3b, Line 4d, and Line 5d
   D. Make an entry in Line 4d, Line 4e, and Line 5d

3. The COD for the mail is $87.25, and a customs fee for $12.50 is also due, for a total due of $99.75. Which of these amounts would be a correct entry for Line 5c?
   A. "$87.25"
   B. "$12.50"
   C. "$99.75"
   D. None of the above

4. The sender of the mail has requested a Return Receipt. Where would you indicate this?
   A. Line 1b
   B. Line 4c
   C. Line 4f
   D. Line 5a

5. If this item will be redelivered, where would this be indicated?
   A. Line 1a
   B. Line 2a
   C. Line 3a
   D. Line 4a

6. You could indicate the mail service requiring a delivery confirmation on all of the following EXCEPT which one?
   A. Line 3e
   B. Line 4e
   C. Line 4f
   D. Line 4g

Set 2: Forms Completion
Questions 7 through 12 are based on Form 2.

Form 2

Authorization to Hold Mail	
To Be Completed by Customer	*To Be Completed by Post Office*
Postmaster: Please hold mail for:	**7. Date Received**
1. Name (s)	**8. Clerk**
	9. Carrier
	10. Route Number
2. Address 2a. Street/apartment/suite number _____ 2b. City _____ 2c. State _____ 2d. ZIP Code _____	
3. Beginning Date	
4. Ending Date	
5. Instructions 5a. _____ Please deliver all accumulated mail and resume normal delivery on the ending date shown above. 5b. _____ I will pick up all accumulated mail when I return.	
6. Customer Signature _____	

7. The mail for both Vernon Jeffries and Debra Fleish is to be held. Where would this be indicated?
A. Box 1
B. Box 2
C. Box 5
D. None of the above

8. Dan Costas is the carrier for this customer, Vernon Jeffries. Where would Dan Costas's name be entered?
A. Box 1
B. Box 6
C. Box 8
D. Box 9

9. The customer should complete all of the following EXCEPT which one?
A. Line 2e
B. Box 4
C. Box 6
D. Box 10

10. Which of these would be a correct entry for Line 2b?
A. "66202"
B. "Taos"
C. "Arizona"
D. "8529 Prairie Road"

11. The mail for this customer will be held from August 10 to September 20. Where would the customer enter "August 10"?
A. Box 2
B. Box 3
C. Box 4
D. Box 7

12. The Post Office received this form from the customer on August 1. Where would this date be indicated?
A. Box 3
B. Box 4
C. Box 7
D. Box 10

Set 3: Forms Completion

Questions 13 through 18 are based on Form 3.

Form 3

DOMESTIC MAIL OR REGISTERED MAIL INQUIRY					
To Be Completed by Customer					

1. Mailer Information

1a. First Name	1b. Middle Initial	1c. Last Name

1d. Business Name
(use only if mailer is a company)

1e. Street Name
(number, street, suite/apartment number)

1f. City	1g. State	1h. ZIP Code

1i. Telephone Number (include area code)

2. Addressee Information

2a. First Name	2b. Middle Initial	2c. Last Name

2d. Business Name
(use only if addressee is a company)

2e. Street Name
(number, street, suite/apartment number)

2f. City	2g. State	2h. ZIP Code

2i. Telephone Number (include area code)

**3. Payment Assignment—
Alternate Payment Address**

3a. Who Is to Receive Payment?
(check one)
❑ Mailer   ❑ Addressee

3b. Street Name (if other than address above)
(number, street, suite/apartment number)

3c. City	3d. State	3e. ZIP Code

**4. Description of Lost or Damaged Article(s)—
Add Extra Sheets as Needed**

4a. Item No.	4b. Description of Article	4c. Value or Cost	4d. Purchase Date
First			
Second			
Third			
Fourth			

5. COD Amount to Be Remitted to Sender | **6. Total Amount Claimed for All Articles**

7. Certification and Signature

7a. Customer Submitting Claim: ❑ Mailer ❑ Addressee	7b. Signature of Customer Filing the Claim	7c. Date Signed (MM/DD/YYYY)

13. The American Camera Company sent this mail from Denver, Colorado, to Greta Berry, who lives in Nashville, Tennessee. Where should the name "Nashville" be entered?
    A. Box 1f
    B. Box 2f
    C. Box 2g
    D. Box 3b

14. Where would the customer enter the name of the mailer, American Camera Company?
    A. Box 1d
    B. Box 2a
    C. Box 2d
    D. Box 3a

15. Which of these would be a correct entry for Box 4e?
    A. "camera"
    B. "$537"
    C. "12/13/06"
    D. "1"

16. The mailer is to receive a COD amount of $500. Where would this amount be entered?
    A. Box 3a
    B. Box 4c
    C. Box 5
    D. Box 6

17. Which of these would be a correct entry for Box 7c?
    A. "$500"
    B. "12/13/06"
    C. A checkmark
    D. "12/13/2006"

18. The customer should complete all of the following EXCEPT which one?
    A. Box 3a
    B. Box 6
    C. Box 7a
    D. None of the above

Form 4

CERTIFICATE OF BULK MAILING

Mailer: Fill in this statement in ink. Affix meter stamp or uncanceled postage stamps covering fee in the block to the right.

1. **Meter stamp or postage in payment of fee must be affixed here and canceled by postmarking, including date.**

2. Fee for Certificate

2a. Up to 1,000 pieces	USE CURRENT RATE CHART
2b. For each additional 1,000 pieces or fraction	
2c. Duplicate copy of certificate	

3. Mailing Information

3a. Number of Identical Pieces	3b. Class of Mail	3c. Postage on Each	3d. Number of Pieces to the Pound	3e. Total Number of Pounds	3f. Total Postage Paid	3g. Fee Paid

4. Mailed For

5. Mailed By

Postmaster's Certificate

It is hereby certified that the above-described mailing has been received and the number of pieces and postage verified.

6. _____

(Signature of Postmaster or Designee)

19. There are 2,000 identical pieces of mail being sent, with 18 cents postage on each, with a total weight for the 2,000 pieces of mail of 126 pounds 6 ounces. Where would "18 cents" be entered?
    A. Box 2b
    B. Box 3a
    C. Box 3c
    D. Box 3f

20. There are 2,000 identical pieces of mail being sent, with 18 cents postage on each, with a total weight for the 2,000 pieces of mail of 126 pounds 6 ounces. Where would "2000" be entered?
    A. Box 2b
    B. Box 3a
    C. Box 3c
    D. Box 3f

21. Wesley Hunter is sending the mail for Big Boy Tire Company. Where would "Big Boy Tire Company" be entered?
    A. Box 1
    B. Box 4
    C. Box 5
    D. Box 6

22. Which of these would be a correct entry for Box 1?
    A. A meter stamp
    B. Postage
    C. A postmark
    D. All of the above

23. The Postmaster's Certificate certifies all of the following EXCEPT which one?
    A. The weight of the mail
    B. The number of pieces of the mail
    C. The postage of the mail
    D. That the mail has been received

24. Each pound of mail contains 16 pieces. Where would this be indicated?
    A. Line 2a
    B. Box 3a
    C. Box 3d
    D. Box 3e

Form 5

MAIL FORWARDING CHANGE OF ADDRESS ORDER		
1. Change of address for (check one) 1a. ❑ Individual 1b. ❑ Entire Family 1c. ❑ Business	**17. Official Use Only**	
	17a. Zone/Route ID Number	
2. Is this move temporary? (check one) 2a. ❑ Yes 2b. ❑ No	17b. Date Entered on Form 3982	
	17c. Clerk/Carrier Endorsement	
3. Start Date	**4. If the move is temporary, list date to discontinue forwarding.**	
5. Name 5a. Last Name	5b. First Name and Middle Initial	
6. If Business Move, Print Business Name		
PRINT OLD MAILING ADDRESS BELOW		
7. OLD Street Address or PO Box		
8. OLD City	**9. OLD State**	**10. OLD ZIP Code**
PRINT NEW MAILING ADDRESS BELOW		
11. NEW Street Address or PO Box		
12. NEW City	**13. NEW State**	**14. NEW ZIP Code**
15. Print and sign name: 15a. Print: _____ 15b. Sign: _____	**16. Date Signed**	

25. How would you indicate that Henry Slaughter, his wife, Wanda Slaughter, and their children will be moving?
   A. Enter a checkmark on Line 1a
   B. Enter a checkmark on Line 1b
   C. Enter several names in Box 5a
   D. Enter several names in Box 15

26. Which of these would be a correct entry for Box 4?
   A. "99577"
   B. "4/5/06"
   C. "688-698-3759"
   D. "649"

27. The customer is moving from 5309 Jackson Avenue to 6399 Jackson Avenue in the same city. Where would "5309" be entered?
   A. Box 7
   B. Box 10
   C. Box 11
   D. Box 14

28. The customer signed the form on May 4. Where would this be indicated?
   A. Box 3
   B. Box 4
   C. Box 16
   D. Box 17b

29. If information is entered in Box 6, which of the following also should be done?
   A. Enter a checkmark on Line 1c
   B. Enter a checkmark on Line 2b
   C. Enter a date in Box 4
   D. Leave Box 16 blank

30. Which of these would be a correct entry for Box 15?
   A. The printed name and signature of the clerk or carrier
   B. The name of the clerk or carrier and the application date
   C. The name of the customer and the application date
   D. The printed name and signature of the customer

PART C: CODING AND MEMORY

SECTION 1—CODING

Coding Exercise

Choose the correct delivery route, based on the Coding Guide, for each of the following 4 items and mark your answers on the answer sheet below. You have 2 minutes to complete this practice exercise. This exercise will not be scored.

CODING GUIDE

Address Range	Delivery Route
1771–3100 Summit Pass Hwy.	
450–1199 S Tripoli Expressway	A
1–499 Cotton Gin Ave.	
3101–7250 Summit Pass Hwy.	
500–2400 Cotton Gin Ave.	B
24000–57000 Rural Rt. 5	
80–370 Arcadia Dr.	C
1200–1799 S Tripoli Expressway	
All mail that doesn't fall in one of the address ranges listed above	D

	Address	Delivery Route
1.	540 S Tripoli Expressway	A B C D
2.	58360 Rural Rt. 5	A B C D
3.	911 Cotton Gin Ave.	A B C D
4.	3041 Summit Pass Hwy.	A B C D

Sample Answer Grid				
1.	Ⓐ	Ⓑ	Ⓒ	Ⓓ
2.	Ⓐ	Ⓑ	Ⓒ	Ⓓ
3.	Ⓐ	Ⓑ	Ⓒ	Ⓓ
4.	Ⓐ	Ⓑ	Ⓒ	Ⓓ

Completed Sample Answer Grid				
1.	●	Ⓑ	Ⓒ	Ⓓ
2.	Ⓐ	Ⓑ	Ⓒ	●
3.	Ⓐ	●	Ⓒ	Ⓓ
4.	●	Ⓑ	Ⓒ	Ⓓ

CODING TEST

Choose the correct delivery route, based on the Coding Guide, for each of the following 36 items (items 1 through 36) and mark your answers in the Coding section of the Answer Sheet. You have 6 minutes to complete this test.

CODING GUIDE

Address Range	Delivery Route
1771–3100 Summit Pass Hwy.	
450–1199 S Tripoli Expressway	A
1–499 Cotton Gin Ave.	
3101–7250 Summit Pass Hwy.	
500–2400 Cotton Gin Ave.	B
24000–57000 Rural Rt. 5	
80–370 Arcadia Dr.	C
1200–1799 S Tripoli Expressway	
All mail that doesn't fall in one of the address ranges listed above	D

Address	Delivery Route
1. 380 Cotton Gin Ave.	A B C D
2. 7248 Summit Pass Hwy.	A B C D
3. 751 S Tripoli Expressway	A B C D
4. 173 Arcadia Dr.	A B C D
5. 21007 Summit Pass Hwy.	A B C D
6. 442 Cotton Gin Ave.	A B C D
7. 3342 Summit Pass Hwy.	A B C D
8. 52839 Rural Rt. 5	A B C D
9. 274 Arcadia Dr.	A B C D
10. 866 S Tripoli Expressway	A B C D

Address	Delivery Route
11. 5260 Rural Rt. 5	A B C D
12. 549 Arcadia Dr.	A B C D
13. 7060 Summit Pass Hwy.	A B C D
14. 1343 Cotton Gin Ave.	A B C D
15. 29775 Rural Rt. 5	A B C D
16. 952 S Tripoli Expressway	A B C D
17. 55711 Rural Rt. 5	A B C D
18. 1454 S Tripoli Beltway	A B C D
19. 1904 Summit Pass Hwy.	A B C D
20. 2377 Cotton Gin Ave.	A B C D
21. 56000 Rural Rt. 5	A B C D
22. 7070 Summit Pass Hwy.	A B C D
23. 1033 S Tripoli Expressway	A B C D
24. 35232 Rural Rt. 15	A B C D
25. 3443 Summit Pass Hwy.	A B C D
26. 2750 Cotton Gin Ave.	A B C D
27. 1664 S Tripoli Expressway	A B C D
28. 2835 Summit Pass Hwy.	A B C D
29. 2102 Cotton Gin Ave.	A B C D
30. 4506 Summit Pass Hwy.	A B C D
31. 767 N Tripoli Expressway	A B C D
32. 120 Arcadia Dr.	A B C D
33. 333 Cotton Gin Ave.	A B C D
34. 45946 Rural Rt. 5	A B C D
35. 2276 S Tripoli Expressway	A B C D
36. 4953 Summit Pass Hwy.	A B C D

Memory Study Period 1
Use the time given to memorize the information in the following Coding Guide.

CODING GUIDE

Address Range	Delivery Route
1771–3100 Summit Pass Hwy.	
450–1199 S Tripoli Expressway	A
1–499 Cotton Gin Ave.	
3101–7250 Summit Pass Hwy.	
500–2400 Cotton Gin Ave.	B
24000–57000 Rural Rt. 5	
80–370 Arcadia Dr.	C
1200–1799 S Tripoli Expressway	
All mail that doesn't fall in one of the address ranges listed above	D

Memory Exercise

Choose the correct delivery route, based on your memory of the information in the Coding Guide, for each of the following 8 items and mark your answers on the answer sheet below. You have 90 seconds to complete this practice exercise. This exercise will not be scored.

Address	Delivery Route
1. 1744 S Tripoli Expressway	A B C D
2. 80 Arcadia Dr.	A B C D
3. 1778 Summer Pass Hwy.	A B C D
4. 12 Cotton Gin Ave.	A B C D
5. 379 Arcadia Dr.	A B C D
6. 4989 Summit Pass Hwy.	A B C D
7. 835 Cotton Gin Ave.	A B C D
8. 1024 S Tripoli Expressway	A B C D

Sample Answer Grid					
1.	Ⓐ	Ⓑ	Ⓒ	Ⓓ
2.	Ⓐ	Ⓑ	Ⓒ	Ⓓ
3.	Ⓐ	Ⓑ	Ⓒ	Ⓓ
4.	Ⓐ	Ⓑ	Ⓒ	Ⓓ
5.	Ⓐ	Ⓑ	Ⓒ	Ⓓ
6.	Ⓐ	Ⓑ	Ⓒ	Ⓓ
7.	Ⓐ	Ⓑ	Ⓒ	Ⓓ
8.	Ⓐ	Ⓑ	Ⓒ	Ⓓ

Completed Sample Answer Grid					
1.	Ⓐ	Ⓑ	●	Ⓓ
2.	Ⓐ	Ⓑ	●	Ⓓ
3.	Ⓐ	Ⓑ	Ⓒ	●
4.	●	Ⓑ	Ⓒ	Ⓓ
5.	Ⓐ	Ⓑ	Ⓒ	●
6.	Ⓐ	●	Ⓒ	Ⓓ
7.	Ⓐ	●	Ⓒ	Ⓓ
8.	●	Ⓑ	Ⓒ	Ⓓ

Memory Study Period 2

Use the time given to memorize the information in the following Coding Guide.

CODING GUIDE

Address Range	Delivery Route
1771–3100 Summit Pass Hwy.	
450–1199 S Tripoli Expressway	A
1–499 Cotton Gin Ave.	
3101–7250 Summit Pass Hwy.	
500–2400 Cotton Gin Ave.	B
24000–57000 Rural Rt. 5	
80–370 Arcadia Dr.	C
1200–1799 S Tripoli Expressway	
All mail that doesn't fall in one of the address ranges listed above	D

MEMORY TEST

Choose the correct delivery route, based on your memory of the information in the Coding Guide, for each of the following 36 items (items 37 through 72) and mark your answers in the Memory section of the Answer Sheet. You have 7 minutes to complete this test.

	Address	Delivery Route
37.	1969 Cotton Gin Ave.	A B C D
38.	7140 Summit Pass Hwy.	A B C D
39.	556 S Tripoli Expressway	A B C D
40.	272 Arcadia Dr.	A B C D
41.	3011 Summit Pass Hwy.	A B C D
42.	22346 Rural Rt. 5	A B C D
43.	1352 S Tripoli Expressway	A B C D
44.	22756 State Rt. 5	A B C D
45.	1478 S Tripoli Expressway	A B C D

	Address	Delivery Route			
46.	1887 Cotton Gin Ave.	A	B	C	D
47.	990 S Tripoli Expressway	A	B	C	D
48.	1912 Tripoli Expressway	A	B	C	D
49.	2775 Summit Pass Hwy.	A	B	C	D
50.	223 Arcadia Dr.	A	B	C	D
51.	55544 Rural Rt. 5	A	B	C	D
52.	854 Cotton Ave.	A	B	C	D
53.	6441 Summit Pass Hwy.	A	B	C	D
54.	644 S Tripoli Expressway	A	B	C	D
55.	9712 Summit Pass Hwy.	A	B	C	D
56.	549 S Tripoli Expressway	A	B	C	D
57.	320 Arcadia Dr.	A	B	C	D
58.	2974 Cotton Gin Ave.	A	B	C	D
59.	6092 Summit Pass Hwy.	A	B	C	D
60.	806 Cotton Gin Ave.	A	B	C	D
61.	1782 Summit Pass Hwy.	A	B	C	D
62.	400 Cotton Gin Ave.	A	B	C	D
63.	1001 S Tristate Expressway	A	B	C	D
64.	49372 Rural Rt. 5	A	B	C	D
65.	1061 Cotton Gin Ave.	A	B	C	D
66.	25252 Rural Rt. 5	A	B	C	D
67.	1636 S Tripoli Expressway	A	B	C	D
68.	334 Arcadia Ave.	A	B	C	D
69.	591 S Tripoli Expressway	A	B	C	D
70.	67900 Rural Rt. 5	A	B	C	D
71.	4633 Summit Pass Hwy.	A	B	C	D
72.	1697 S Tripoli Expressway	A	B	C	D

PART D: PERSONAL CHARACTERISTICS AND EXPERIENCE INVENTORY

On the actual exam, the next part that you would take is Part D: Personal Characteristics and Experience Inventory. This part of the exam is 90 minutes long and has 236 items. Because there is no particular advantage to practicing your responses on these statements and questions, no tests are given here for them.

Scoring and Explanations for Practice Examination 5

ANSWER KEY

Part A: Address Checking

1. C	11. B	21. C	31. A	41. D	51. B
2. C	12. C	22. B	32. C	42. C	52. A
3. B	13. B	23. D	33. D	43. B	53. C
4. D	14. A	24. A	34. B	44. D	54. B
5. A	15. C	25. D	35. A	45. B	55. C
6. C	16. B	26. B	36. C	46. A	56. D
7. A	17. D	27. B	37. A	47. A	57. A
8. B	18. C	28. C	38. C	48. C	58. B
9. A	19. B	29. A	39. B	49. D	59. D
10. B	20. C	30. B	40. B	50. B	60. C

Part B: Forms Completion

1. D	6. A	11. B	16. C	21. B	26. B
2. A	7. A	12. C	17. D	22. D	27. A
3. D	8. D	13. B	18. D	23. A	28. C
4. C	9. D	14. A	19. C	24. C	29. A
5. B	10. B	15. C	20. B	25. B	30. D

Part C: Coding Test

1. A	7. B	13. B	19. A	25. B	31. D
2. B	8. C	14. B	20. B	26. D	32. C
3. A	9. C	15. C	21. C	27. C	33. A
4. C	10. A	16. A	22. B	28. A	34. C
5. D	11. D	17. C	23. A	29. B	35. D
6. A	12. D	18. D	24. D	30. B	36. B

Part C: Memory Test

37. B	43. C	49. A	55. D	61. A	67. C
38. B	44. D	50. C	56. A	62. A	68. D
39. A	45. C	51. C	57. C	63. D	69. A
40. C	46. B	52. D	58. D	64. C	70. D
41. A	47. A	53. B	59. B	65. B	71. B
42. D	48. D	54. A	60. B	66. C	72. C

SCORING

Part A: Address Checking

Enter the number you got right: _____

Enter the number you got wrong
(not including those left blank): _____

Divide the number wrong by 3
(or multiply by 1/3): _____

Subtract this answer from the number right: - _____

Raw Score _____

Part B: Forms Completion

Enter the number you got right
(no penalty for guessing): Raw Score _____

Part C: Coding and Memory

Enter the number you got right: _____

Enter the number you got wrong
(not including those left blank): _____

Divide the number wrong by 3
(or multiply by 1/3): _____

Subtract this answer from the number right: - _____

Raw Score _____

Part D: Personal Characteristics and Experience Inventory

Scoring system not given.

Explanations

PART A: ADDRESS CHECKING

	Correct List		List to Be Checked	
	Address	*ZIP Code*	*Address*	*ZIP Code*
1. **C**	6703 Trumbull St. Elizabeth, NJ	**0**7201	6703 Trumbull St. Elizabeth, NJ	**7**7201
2. **C**	2255 Higher Ground Drive Winston Salem, NC	27127-**4538**	2255 Higher Ground Drive Winston Salem, NC	27127-**5438**
3. **B**	1**3**33 Gambusino Ave. El Paso, Texas	79938-2999	1**3**13 Gambusino Ave. El Paso, Texas	79938-2999
4. **D**	91**745** Industrial Pkwy. Coulterville, CA	**9**5311-5280	91**75** Industrial Pkwy. Coulterville, CA	**8**5311-5280
5. **A**	3272 Rise Branch Rd. Rehoboth Beach, DE	19971	3272 Rise Branch Rd. Rehoboth Beach, DE	19971
6. **C**	4203 Colchester Road Woodbridge, VA	22191-61**0**9	4203 Colchester Road Woodbridge, VA	22191-61**9**9
7. **A**	4617 NW 100th Pl Ocala, Florida	34482	4617 NW 100th Pl Ocala, Florida	34482
8. **B**	4617 Syring**a** Ln. Caldwell, ID	83605	4617 Syring**e** Ln. Caldwell, ID	83605
9. **A**	6108 Edwards Rd. West Monroe, LA	71292	6108 Edwards Rd. West Monroe, LA	71292
10. **B**	2966 E Grand **Ave.** Laramie, WY	82070-7626	2966 E Grand **Dr.** Laramie, WY	82070-7626
11. **B**	2997 Seminole Ave. Knoxville, **TN**	37915-8641	2997 Seminole Ave. Knoxville, **MN**	37915-8641
12. **C**	6006 Montgomery Ave. Apt. 273 Pittston, PA	**1**8643	6006 Montgomery Ave. Apt. 273 Pittston, PA	**3**8643
13. **B**	Post Office Box 6**1539** Tallahassee, FL	32302-1539	Post Office Box 6**5193** Tallahassee, FL	32302-1539
14. **A**	2910 Tabernash Drive Columbus, OH	43240	2910 Tabernash Drive Columbus, OH	43240

	Correct List		List to Be Checked	
	Address	ZIP Code	Address	ZIP Code

15. **C** 291 Dartmoor Ct.
Rocky Mount, NC   27803-6312   291 Dartmoor Ct.
Rocky Mount, NC   27883-6312

16. **B** 1359 All**view** Ave.
Norwalk, CT   06854-1134   1359 All**wood** Ave.
Norwalk, CT   06854-1134

17. **D** 4702 **W** Conklin**g** Ave.
Middletown, NY   10940   4702 **N** Conkli**n** Ave.
Middletown, NY   10490

18. **C** 4975 38th St.
San Diego, CA   92116-0835   4975 38th St.
San Diego, CA   92616-0835

19. **B** 3195 Wenonah Street
Gadsden, AL   35903   3195 Wenonah Street
Marsden, AL   35903

20. **C** 31954 SE Frontage Rd.
Joliet, IL   60436-4273   31954 SE Frontage Rd.
Joliet, IL   60423-4273

21. **C** 2012 Muncaster Mill Road
Gaithersburg, MD   **20**877-1115   2012 Muncaster Mill Road
Gaithersburg, MD   **02**877-1115

22. **B** 6366 Staffor**dshire** Dr.
Cherry Hill, NJ   08003-0188   6366 Staffor**d** Dr.
Cherry Hill, NJ   08003-0188

23. **D** 1443 Cranleigh **M**ews
Nashua, NH   03063-0469   1443 Cranleigh **N**ews
Nashua, NH   03**3**63-0469

24. **A** 8754 Brownell Pkwy.
Vineyard Haven, MA   02568   8754 Brownell Pkwy.
Vineyard Haven, MA   02568

25. **D** **875** Princeton Mill Ct.
Athens, Georgia   30606   **578** Princeton Mill Ct.
Athens, Georgia   3060**0**

26. **B** 2341 Longshanks Way
Henderson, NV   89015   2341 Longshanks Way
Cooperton, NV   89015

27. **B** **33**99 Lotus Garden Dr.
Talofofo, GU   96930-2754   **333**99 Lotus Garden Dr.
Talofofo, GU   96930-2754

28. **C** 9238 Summer Wynde Ct.
Louisville, KY   40272-**6**798   9238 Summer Wynde Ct.
Louisville, KY   40272-**8**798

	Address	ZIP Code	Address	ZIP Code
29. **A**	2020 Breckenridge Dr. Clinton Township, MI	48038	2020 Breckenridge Dr. Clinton Township, MI	48038
30. **B**	2276 Brundin **Ave.** Chickasha, OK	73018	2276 Brundin **Dr.** Chickasha, OK	73018
31. **A**	24437 County Road 42 Bemidji, MN	56601-5402	24437 County Road 42 Bemidji, MN	56601-5402
32. **C**	4950 Livengood Wy. Bend, Oregon	97701-2412	4950 Livengood Wy. Bend, Oregon	90901-2412
33. **D**	5317 Magnolia **Cv.** Biloxi, MS	39532	5317 Magnolia **Ct.** Biloxi, MS	39523
34. **B**	2860 **Fomance** Rd. Bethlehem, PA	18020-1475	2860 **Forman** Rd. Bethlehem, PA	18020-1475
35. **A**	Rural Route 83 Cape Girardeau, MO	63701	Rural Route 83 Cape Girardeau, MO	63701
36. **C**	1619 Pommenville St. Pawtucket, RI	**02**861-3984	1619 Pommenville St. Pawtucket, RI	**90**861-3984
37. **A**	3743 Randolph Ave. SE Huntsville, AL	35801-0841	3743 Randolph Ave. SE Huntsville, AL	35801-0841
38. **C**	5769 Carolina Ridge Road Gaffney, SC	29341	5769 Carolina Ridge Road Gaffney, SC	29141
39. **B**	3**769** Endicott Trl. Eden Prairie, MN	55347	3**679** Endicott Trl. Eden Prairie, MN	55347
40. **B**	5234 P**h**easant Holw. Denton, Texas	76207	5234 Pleasant Holw. Denton, Texas	76207
41. **D**	58741 Camp Creek Pkwy. SW **Atlanta,** GA	30331-1210	58741 Camp Creek Pkwy. SW **Atlas,** GA	31331-1210
42. **C**	48808 Cadillac Ext. Parkersburg, WV	261**04**-1243	48808 Cadillac Ext. Parkersburg, WV	261**40**-1243

	Correct List		**List to Be Checked**	
	Address	*ZIP Code*	*Address*	*ZIP Code*
43. **B**	**3**654 Meetinghouse Rd. Chicopee, MA	01013	**5**654 Meetinghouse Rd. Chicopee, MA	01013
44. **D**	1649 **N** Indiana Ave. West Bend, WI	5**3**095	1649 **W** Indiana Ave. West Bend, WI	5**6**0**4**5
45. **B**	8831 US Highway 43 Water**ville**, ME	04901-2496	8831 US Highway 43 Water**ton**, ME	04901-2496
46. **A**	1872 Eastbrook Blvd. Winter Park, FL	32792-0504	1872 Eastbrook Blvd. Winter Park, FL	32792-0504
47. **A**	2118 Middleton Lane Silver City, NM	88061-6367	2118 Middleton Lane Silver City, NM	88061-6367
48. **C**	6015 Cobblestone West Columbus, NE	6860**1**	6015 Cobblestone West Columbus, NE	6860**0**
49. **D**	1918 Abigails Way Fairfield, **CT**	06430-61**5**1	1918 Abigails Way Fairfield, **MT**	06430-61**6**1
50. **B**	4080 Interlacken Drive **Piedmont**, WY	82933	4080 Interlacken Drive **Peters**, WY	82933
51. **B**	59**9**44 N 95th St. Longmont, CO	80504	59**4**44 N 95th St. Longmont, CO	80504
52. **A**	7432 Langley Ave. San Lorenzo, NM	88041-0491	7432 Langley Ave. San Lorenzo, NM	88041-0491
53. **C**	3575 Autumnwood Dr. Sacramento, CA	95826-1**4**95	3575 Autumnwood Dr. Sacramento, CA	95826-1**5**85
54. **B**	5914 Gun**d**erman Road Ithaca, NY	14850-2314	5914 Gun**n**erman Road Ithaca, NY	14850-2314
55. **C**	2950 S Enid Ave. Apt. MG Russellville, AR	**7**2801	2950 S Enid Ave. Apt. MG Russellville, AR	**3**2801
56. **D**	2067 W Tamar**ack** Rd. Spokane, WA	**9**9224	2067 W Tamar**ind** Rd. Spokane, WA	**8**8224

	Correct List		**List to Be Checked**	
	Address	*ZIP Code*	*Address*	*ZIP Code*
57. **A**	36488 93rd Ave. SE		36488 93rd Ave. SE	
	Minot, ND	58701-1870	Minot, ND	58701-1870
58. **B**	3011 SE Brow**ning** Road		3011 SE Brow**n** Road	
	Evansville, IN	47725-0622	Evansville, IN	47725-0622
59. **D**	1**479** Oberlin Ave.		1**497** Oberlin Ave.	
	Lorain, OH	44053	Lorain, OH	440**88**
60. **C**	245 Wilmett Ct.		245 Wilmett Ct.	
	Bethesda, MD	20817-3989	Bethesda, MD	2081**6**-3989

PART B: FORMS COMPLETION

Set 1: Questions 1 through 6

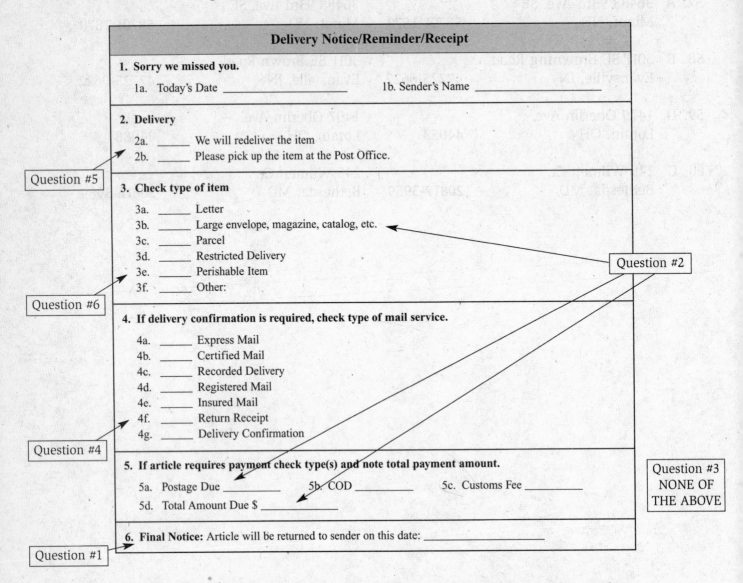

Question #5

Question #6

Question #4

Question #1

Delivery Notice/Reminder/Receipt

1. Sorry we missed you.

1a. Today's Date _____   1b. Sender's Name _____

2. Delivery

2a. _____ We will redeliver the item
2b. _____ Please pick up the item at the Post Office.

3. Check type of item

3a. _____ Letter
3b. _____ Large envelope, magazine, catalog, etc.
3c. _____ Parcel
3d. _____ Restricted Delivery
3e. _____ Perishable Item
3f. _____ Other:

4. If delivery confirmation is required, check type of mail service.

4a. _____ Express Mail
4b. _____ Certified Mail
4c. _____ Recorded Delivery
4d. _____ Registered Mail
4e. _____ Insured Mail
4f. _____ Return Receipt
4g. _____ Delivery Confirmation

5. If article requires payment check type(s) and note total payment amount.

5a. Postage Due _____   5b. COD _____   5c. Customs Fee _____
5d. Total Amount Due $ _____

6. Final Notice: Article will be returned to sender on this date: _____

Question #2

Question #3
NONE OF
THE ABOVE

1. **D** Box 6 provides a place for the date the article will be returned to the sender.
2. **A** Line 3b should be checked for "Large envelope, magazine, catalog, etc." "Postage Due" is checked on Line 5a, and the "Total Amount Due" should be filled in on Line 5d. So the correct answer is A.
3. **D** Line 5c requires a checkmark if there is a customs fee. No dollar amount should be entered on this line (the dollar amount goes on Line 5d). So the correct answer is D, None of the above.
4. **C** "Return Receipt" is indicated on Line 4f.
5. **B** Line 2a should be checked if the carrier will redeliver the item.
6. **A** Box 4 gives several types of mail service that could be checked if delivery confirmation is required. But Line 3e, answer A, is for perishable items and *wouldn't* be checked as a type of mail service.

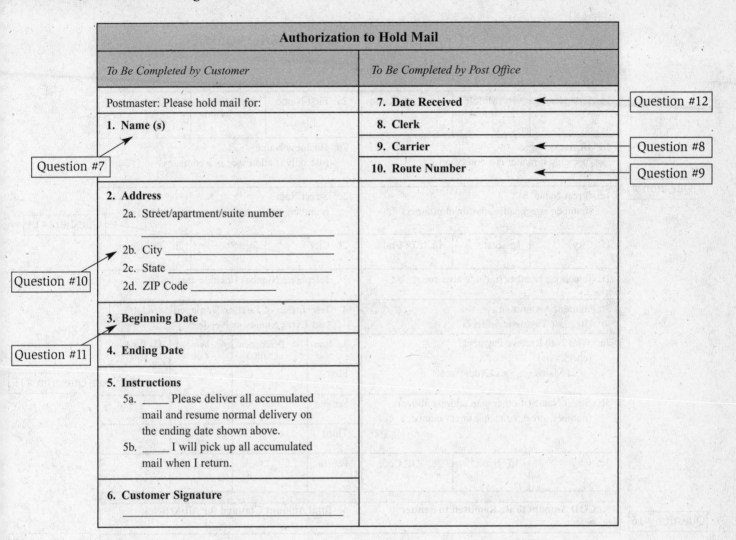

7. **A** Box 1 is labeled "Name(s)," indicating that more than one name can be entered here if more than one person's mail will be held.
8. **D** The carrier's name would be entered in Box 9.
9. **D** The right side of the form (Boxes 7 through 10) should be completed by the Post Office. So the customer would *not* complete Box 10.
10. **B** Line 2b is for a city name.
11. **B** August 10 would be the beginning date and would be entered in Box 3.
12. **C** Box 7 is labeled "Date Received."

DOMESTIC MAIL OR REGISTERED MAIL INQUIRY						
To Be Completed by Customer						

1. Mailer Information | **2. Addressee Information**

1a. First Name	1b. Middle Initial	1c. Last Name	2a. First Name	2b. Middle Initial	2c. Last Name

1d. Business Name
(use only if mailer is a company) | 2d. Business Name
(use only if addressee is a company)

Question #14

1e. Street Name
(number, street, suite/apartment number) | 2e. Street Name
(number, street, suite/apartment number)

Question #13

1f. City	1g. State	1h. ZIP Code	2f. City	2g. State	2h. ZIP Code

1i. Telephone Number (include area code) | 2i. Telephone Number (include area code)

**3. Payment Assignment—
Alternate Payment Address** | **4. Description of Lost or Damaged Article(s)—
Add Extra Sheets as Needed**

3a. Who Is to Receive Payment?
(check one)
❏ Mailer   ❏ Addressee

4a. Item No.	4b. Description of Article	4c. Value or Cost	4d. Purchase Date
First			

Question #15

3b. Street Name (if other than address above)
(number, street, suite/apartment number)

| Second | | | |
| Third | | | |

3c. City	3d. State	3e. ZIP Code

| Fourth | | | |

Question #16

5. COD Amount to Be Remitted to Sender   **6. Total Amount Claimed for All Articles**

7. Certification and Signature

Question #17

Question #18
NONE OF
THE ABOVE

| 7a. Customer Submitting Claim:

❏ Mailer   ❏ Addressee | 7b. Signature of Customer Filing the Claim | 7c. Date Signed
(MM/DD/YYYY) |
|---|---|---|

13. **B** "Nashville" would be entered under "Addressee Information," Box 2f.

14. **A** If the mailer is a company (a business), that name would be entered in Box 1d.

15. **C** Box 4e is for a purchase date.

16. **C** A COD amount would go in Box 5.

17. **D** Box 7c requires a date, but two answers here give a date. Notice, though, that this particular form asks for four digits for the year (YYYY), so the correct answer is D.

18. **D** This entire form is for the customer to complete. Notice that the top of the form says "To Be Completed by Customer." So the answer is D, None of the above.

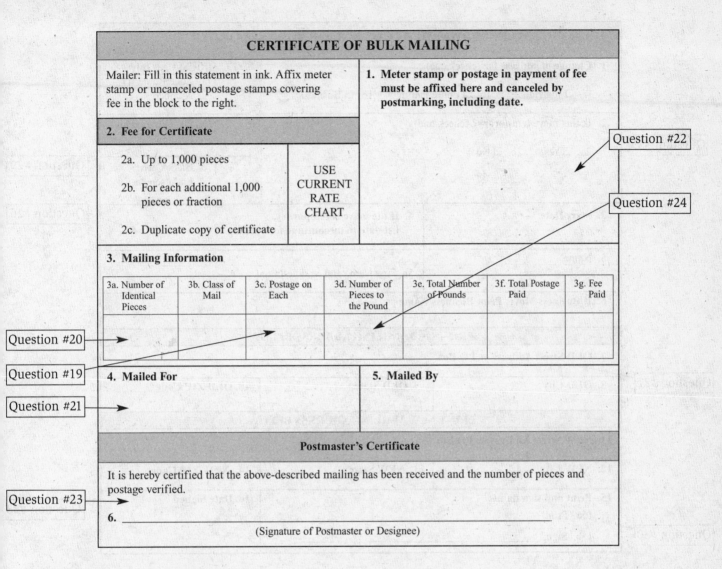

CERTIFICATE OF BULK MAILING

Mailer: Fill in this statement in ink. Affix meter stamp or uncanceled postage stamps covering fee in the block to the right.

1. **Meter stamp or postage in payment of fee must be affixed here and canceled by postmarking, including date.**

Question #22

Question #24

2. Fee for Certificate

2a. Up to 1,000 pieces

2b. For each additional 1,000 pieces or fraction

2c. Duplicate copy of certificate

USE CURRENT RATE CHART

3. Mailing Information

3a. Number of Identical Pieces	3b. Class of Mail	3c. Postage on Each	3d. Number of Pieces to the Pound	3e. Total Number of Pounds	3f. Total Postage Paid	3g. Fee Paid

Question #20

Question #19

4. Mailed For

5. Mailed By

Question #21

Postmaster's Certificate

It is hereby certified that the above-described mailing has been received and the number of pieces and postage verified.

Question #23

6. _____

(Signature of Postmaster or Designee)

19. **C** Each piece of mail takes 18 cents postage. Box 3c is labeled "Postage on Each."
20. **B** There are 2,000 identical pieces of mail. Box 3a is labeled "Number of Identical Pieces."
21. **B** "Big Boy Tire Company" would be entered in Box 4 because Hunter is sending the mail *for* this company.
22. **D** All of these items, a meter stamp, postage, and a postmark, could go in Box 1.
23. **A** The Postmaster's Certificate certifies that the mail has been received, as well as the number of pieces and the postage. It *doesn't* certify the weight.
24. **C** Box 3d is labeled "Number of Pieces to the Pound."

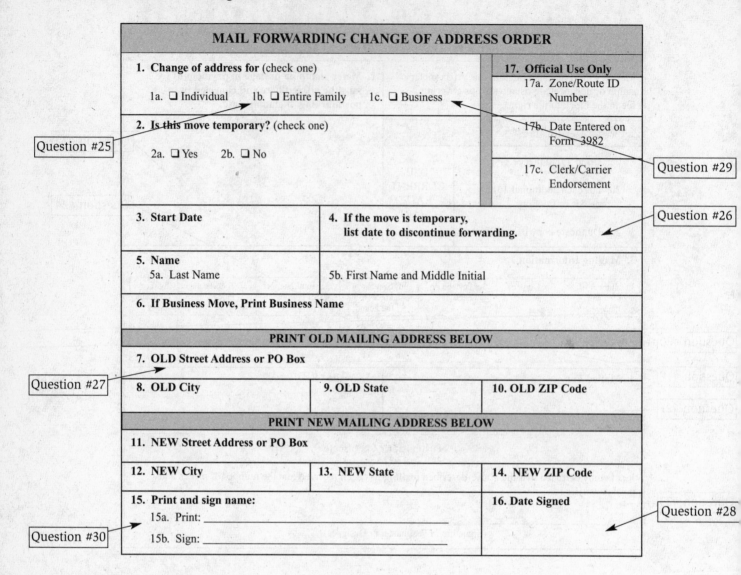

25. **B** The whole family is moving, so Line 1b should be checked.
26. **B** Box 4 lists a date if the move is temporary.
27. **A** 5309 is the old street number, which should go in Box 7.
28. **C** Box 16 is for entry of the date the form is signed.
29. **A** Box 6 is filled in only if a business (rather than an individual) is moving. If this is a business move, then Box 1c will have to be checked also.
30. **D** Box 15 is for the customer's name, both signed and printed (the Post Office entries are only in Box 17).

PRACTICE EXAMINATION 6

ANSWER SHEET FOR PRACTICE EXAMINATION 6

PART A: ADDRESS CHECKING

1. Ⓐ Ⓑ Ⓒ Ⓓ   16. Ⓐ Ⓑ Ⓒ Ⓓ   31. Ⓐ Ⓑ Ⓒ Ⓓ   46. Ⓐ Ⓑ Ⓒ Ⓓ
2. Ⓐ Ⓑ Ⓒ Ⓓ   17. Ⓐ Ⓑ Ⓒ Ⓓ   32. Ⓐ Ⓑ Ⓒ Ⓓ   47. Ⓐ Ⓑ Ⓒ Ⓓ
3. Ⓐ Ⓑ Ⓒ Ⓓ   18. Ⓐ Ⓑ Ⓒ Ⓓ   33. Ⓐ Ⓑ Ⓒ Ⓓ   48. Ⓐ Ⓑ Ⓒ Ⓓ
4. Ⓐ Ⓑ Ⓒ Ⓓ   19. Ⓐ Ⓑ Ⓒ Ⓓ   34. Ⓐ Ⓑ Ⓒ Ⓓ   49. Ⓐ Ⓑ Ⓒ Ⓓ
5. Ⓐ Ⓑ Ⓒ Ⓓ   20. Ⓐ Ⓑ Ⓒ Ⓓ   35. Ⓐ Ⓑ Ⓒ Ⓓ   50. Ⓐ Ⓑ Ⓒ Ⓓ
6. Ⓐ Ⓑ Ⓒ Ⓓ   21. Ⓐ Ⓑ Ⓒ Ⓓ   36. Ⓐ Ⓑ Ⓒ Ⓓ   51. Ⓐ Ⓑ Ⓒ Ⓓ
7. Ⓐ Ⓑ Ⓒ Ⓓ   22. Ⓐ Ⓑ Ⓒ Ⓓ   37. Ⓐ Ⓑ Ⓒ Ⓓ   52. Ⓐ Ⓑ Ⓒ Ⓓ
8. Ⓐ Ⓑ Ⓒ Ⓓ   23. Ⓐ Ⓑ Ⓒ Ⓓ   38. Ⓐ Ⓑ Ⓒ Ⓓ   53. Ⓐ Ⓑ Ⓒ Ⓓ
9. Ⓐ Ⓑ Ⓒ Ⓓ   24. Ⓐ Ⓑ Ⓒ Ⓓ   39. Ⓐ Ⓑ Ⓒ Ⓓ   54. Ⓐ Ⓑ Ⓒ Ⓓ
10. Ⓐ Ⓑ Ⓒ Ⓓ   25. Ⓐ Ⓑ Ⓒ Ⓓ   40. Ⓐ Ⓑ Ⓒ Ⓓ   55. Ⓐ Ⓑ Ⓒ Ⓓ
11. Ⓐ Ⓑ Ⓒ Ⓓ   26. Ⓐ Ⓑ Ⓒ Ⓓ   41. Ⓐ Ⓑ Ⓒ Ⓓ   56. Ⓐ Ⓑ Ⓒ Ⓓ
12. Ⓐ Ⓑ Ⓒ Ⓓ   27. Ⓐ Ⓑ Ⓒ Ⓓ   42. Ⓐ Ⓑ Ⓒ Ⓓ   57. Ⓐ Ⓑ Ⓒ Ⓓ
13. Ⓐ Ⓑ Ⓒ Ⓓ   28. Ⓐ Ⓑ Ⓒ Ⓓ   43. Ⓐ Ⓑ Ⓒ Ⓓ   58. Ⓐ Ⓑ Ⓒ Ⓓ
14. Ⓐ Ⓑ Ⓒ Ⓓ   29. Ⓐ Ⓑ Ⓒ Ⓓ   44. Ⓐ Ⓑ Ⓒ Ⓓ   59. Ⓐ Ⓑ Ⓒ Ⓓ
15. Ⓐ Ⓑ Ⓒ Ⓓ   30. Ⓐ Ⓑ Ⓒ Ⓓ   45. Ⓐ Ⓑ Ⓒ Ⓓ   60. Ⓐ Ⓑ Ⓒ Ⓓ

PART B: FORMS COMPLETION

1. Ⓐ Ⓑ Ⓒ Ⓓ   9. Ⓐ Ⓑ Ⓒ Ⓓ   17. Ⓐ Ⓑ Ⓒ Ⓓ   25. Ⓐ Ⓑ Ⓒ Ⓓ
2. Ⓐ Ⓑ Ⓒ Ⓓ   10. Ⓐ Ⓑ Ⓒ Ⓓ   18. Ⓐ Ⓑ Ⓒ Ⓓ   26. Ⓐ Ⓑ Ⓒ Ⓓ
3. Ⓐ Ⓑ Ⓒ Ⓓ   11. Ⓐ Ⓑ Ⓒ Ⓓ   19. Ⓐ Ⓑ Ⓒ Ⓓ   27. Ⓐ Ⓑ Ⓒ Ⓓ
4. Ⓐ Ⓑ Ⓒ Ⓓ   12. Ⓐ Ⓑ Ⓒ Ⓓ   20. Ⓐ Ⓑ Ⓒ Ⓓ   28. Ⓐ Ⓑ Ⓒ Ⓓ
5. Ⓐ Ⓑ Ⓒ Ⓓ   13. Ⓐ Ⓑ Ⓒ Ⓓ   21. Ⓐ Ⓑ Ⓒ Ⓓ   29. Ⓐ Ⓑ Ⓒ Ⓓ
6. Ⓐ Ⓑ Ⓒ Ⓓ   14. Ⓐ Ⓑ Ⓒ Ⓓ   22. Ⓐ Ⓑ Ⓒ Ⓓ   30. Ⓐ Ⓑ Ⓒ Ⓓ
7. Ⓐ Ⓑ Ⓒ Ⓓ   15. Ⓐ Ⓑ Ⓒ Ⓓ   23. Ⓐ Ⓑ Ⓒ Ⓓ
8. Ⓐ Ⓑ Ⓒ Ⓓ   16. Ⓐ Ⓑ Ⓒ Ⓓ   24. Ⓐ Ⓑ Ⓒ Ⓓ

PART C: CODING AND MEMORY
SECTION 1—CODING

1. Ⓐ Ⓑ Ⓒ Ⓓ   10. Ⓐ Ⓑ Ⓒ Ⓓ   19. Ⓐ Ⓑ Ⓒ Ⓓ   28. Ⓐ Ⓑ Ⓒ Ⓓ
2. Ⓐ Ⓑ Ⓒ Ⓓ   11. Ⓐ Ⓑ Ⓒ Ⓓ   20. Ⓐ Ⓑ Ⓒ Ⓓ   29. Ⓐ Ⓑ Ⓒ Ⓓ
3. Ⓐ Ⓑ Ⓒ Ⓓ   12. Ⓐ Ⓑ Ⓒ Ⓓ   21. Ⓐ Ⓑ Ⓒ Ⓓ   30. Ⓐ Ⓑ Ⓒ Ⓓ
4. Ⓐ Ⓑ Ⓒ Ⓓ   13. Ⓐ Ⓑ Ⓒ Ⓓ   22. Ⓐ Ⓑ Ⓒ Ⓓ   31. Ⓐ Ⓑ Ⓒ Ⓓ
5. Ⓐ Ⓑ Ⓒ Ⓓ   14. Ⓐ Ⓑ Ⓒ Ⓓ   23. Ⓐ Ⓑ Ⓒ Ⓓ   32. Ⓐ Ⓑ Ⓒ Ⓓ
6. Ⓐ Ⓑ Ⓒ Ⓓ   15. Ⓐ Ⓑ Ⓒ Ⓓ   24. Ⓐ Ⓑ Ⓒ Ⓓ   33. Ⓐ Ⓑ Ⓒ Ⓓ
7. Ⓐ Ⓑ Ⓒ Ⓓ   16. Ⓐ Ⓑ Ⓒ Ⓓ   25. Ⓐ Ⓑ Ⓒ Ⓓ   34. Ⓐ Ⓑ Ⓒ Ⓓ
8. Ⓐ Ⓑ Ⓒ Ⓓ   17. Ⓐ Ⓑ Ⓒ Ⓓ   26. Ⓐ Ⓑ Ⓒ Ⓓ   35. Ⓐ Ⓑ Ⓒ Ⓓ
9. Ⓐ Ⓑ Ⓒ Ⓓ   18. Ⓐ Ⓑ Ⓒ Ⓓ   27. Ⓐ Ⓑ Ⓒ Ⓓ   36. Ⓐ Ⓑ Ⓒ Ⓓ

SECTION 2—MEMORY

37. Ⓐ Ⓑ Ⓒ Ⓓ   46. Ⓐ Ⓑ Ⓒ Ⓓ   55. Ⓐ Ⓑ Ⓒ Ⓓ   64. Ⓐ Ⓑ Ⓒ Ⓓ
38. Ⓐ Ⓑ Ⓒ Ⓓ   47. Ⓐ Ⓑ Ⓒ Ⓓ   56. Ⓐ Ⓑ Ⓒ Ⓓ   65. Ⓐ Ⓑ Ⓒ Ⓓ
39. Ⓐ Ⓑ Ⓒ Ⓓ   48. Ⓐ Ⓑ Ⓒ Ⓓ   57. Ⓐ Ⓑ Ⓒ Ⓓ   66. Ⓐ Ⓑ Ⓒ Ⓓ
40. Ⓐ Ⓑ Ⓒ Ⓓ   49. Ⓐ Ⓑ Ⓒ Ⓓ   58. Ⓐ Ⓑ Ⓒ Ⓓ   67. Ⓐ Ⓑ Ⓒ Ⓓ
41. Ⓐ Ⓑ Ⓒ Ⓓ   50. Ⓐ Ⓑ Ⓒ Ⓓ   59. Ⓐ Ⓑ Ⓒ Ⓓ   68. Ⓐ Ⓑ Ⓒ Ⓓ
42. Ⓐ Ⓑ Ⓒ Ⓓ   51. Ⓐ Ⓑ Ⓒ Ⓓ   60. Ⓐ Ⓑ Ⓒ Ⓓ   69. Ⓐ Ⓑ Ⓒ Ⓓ
43. Ⓐ Ⓑ Ⓒ Ⓓ   52. Ⓐ Ⓑ Ⓒ Ⓓ   61. Ⓐ Ⓑ Ⓒ Ⓓ   70. Ⓐ Ⓑ Ⓒ Ⓓ
44. Ⓐ Ⓑ Ⓒ Ⓓ   53. Ⓐ Ⓑ Ⓒ Ⓓ   62. Ⓐ Ⓑ Ⓒ Ⓓ   71. Ⓐ Ⓑ Ⓒ Ⓓ
45. Ⓐ Ⓑ Ⓒ Ⓓ   54. Ⓐ Ⓑ Ⓒ Ⓓ   63. Ⓐ Ⓑ Ⓒ Ⓓ   72. Ⓐ Ⓑ Ⓒ Ⓓ

PART D: PERSONAL CHARACTERISTICS AND EXPERIENCE INVENTORY

(236 Questions—not included here)

ADDRESS CHECKING SAMPLE QUESTIONS

Look at the row of information for sample question 1, which is labeled "S1" below. Carefully [and]
quickly compare the **List to Be Checked** with the **Correct List**. Then decide if there are **No Erro[rs]**
(select A), an error in the **Address Only** (select B), an error in the **ZIP Code Only** (select C), [or]
an error in **Both** the address and the ZIP code (select D). Record your response to the sample que[s-]
tions in the **Sample Answer Grid** below. Complete the other three samples given, S2, S3, and S4
and record your responses on the **Sample Answer Grid**.

A. No Errors	B. Address Only	C. ZIP Code Only	D. Both

<table>
<tr><th colspan="3">Correct List</th><th colspan="3">List to Be Checked</th></tr>
<tr><td></td><td>Address</td><td>ZIP Code</td><td></td><td>Address</td><td>ZIP Code</td></tr>
<tr><td>S1.</td><td>432 Rosewood Ct.
Pasadena, CA</td><td>91106</td><td></td><td>432 Rosewood Ct.
Pasedena, CA</td><td>91106</td></tr>
<tr><td>S2.</td><td>1977 Hully Street
Austin, TX</td><td>78734-1141</td><td></td><td>1977 Holly Street
Austin, TX</td><td>78734-1114</td></tr>
<tr><td>S3.</td><td>648 Central Dr.
New York, NY</td><td>10034</td><td></td><td>648 Central Dr.
New York, NY</td><td>10054</td></tr>
<tr><td>S4.</td><td>9812 Pine Ave.
Chicago, IL</td><td>60467-5113</td><td></td><td>9812 Pine Ave.
Chicago, IL</td><td>60467-5113</td></tr>
</table>

Sample Answer Grid				
S1.	Ⓐ	Ⓑ	Ⓒ	Ⓓ
S2.	Ⓐ	Ⓑ	Ⓒ	Ⓓ
S3.	Ⓐ	Ⓑ	Ⓒ	Ⓓ
S4.	Ⓐ	Ⓑ	Ⓒ	Ⓓ

Completed Sample Answer Grid				
S1.	Ⓐ	●	Ⓒ	Ⓓ
S2.	Ⓐ	Ⓑ	Ⓒ	●
S3.	Ⓐ	Ⓑ	●	Ⓓ
S4.	●	Ⓑ	Ⓒ	Ⓓ

In sample 1, the address in the **List to Be Checked** shows Pasedena, but the **Correct List**
shows Pasadena. So there is an error in the address. Since the Zip codes are exactly the same, the
correct answer is **B—Address Only**.

In sample 2, the address in the **List to Be Checked** shows Holly Street, but the **Correct List**
shows Hully Street. So there is an error in the address. The **List to Be Checked** also shows an error
in the ZIP code. The last four numbers are 1114, and they are 1141 in the **Correct List**. Because
there is an error in the address and in the ZIP code, the correct answer is **D—Both**.

In sample 3, the addresses in the **List to Be Checked** and the **Correct List** are exactly the
same, but there is an error in the ZIP code on the **List to Be Checked**. The **List to Be Checked**
shows 10054, but the **Correct List** shows 10034. So there is an error in the ZIP code. The correct
answer is **C—ZIP Code Only**.

In sample 4, the addresses in the **List to Be Checked** and the **Correct List** are exactly the
same. The ZIP codes are also exactly the same. So the correct answer is **A—No Errors**.

Now turn to the next page and begin the address checking test.

PART A: ADDRESS CHECKING

For the following 60 items, compare the address in the **Correct List** with the address in the **List to Be Checked**. Determine if there are **No Errors** (answer A), an error in the **Address Only** (answer B), an error in the **ZIP Code Only** (answer C), or an error in **Both** (answer D). Mark your answers in the Address Checking section of the answer sheet. You have 11 minutes to complete this test.

A. No Errors	B. Address Only	C. ZIP Code Only	D. Both

Correct List		List to Be Checked	
Address	ZIP Code	Address	ZIP Code
1. 1974 Kamana Rd. Apple Valley, CA	92307-7676	1974 Karmina Rd. Apple Valley, CA	93307-7676 _D_
2. 5854 Merriline Ave. Utica, New York	13502-2573	5854 Merriline Ave. Utica, New York	13502-6473 _C_
3. 3631 98th Way Sebastian, FL	32958-5600	3631 98th Way Sebastian, FL	32958-5660 _C_
4. 287 Laurelridge Pl. Grants Pass, OR	97526	287 Laurelridge Pl. Grants Pass, OR	97526 _A_
5. 3111 W Wimbledon Dr. Charleston, SC	29412-8327	3111 W Wimbledon Dr. Charleston, SC	24912-8327 _C_
6. 69614 Hoskinson Pkwy. Glen Ellyn, IL	60137	69614 Hoskinson Pkwy. Glenn Ellen, IL	60137 _A_
7. 5561 53rd Pl. Apt. 243D Hyattsville, MD	20781	5561 53rd Pl. Apt. 243D Hyattsville, ND	20781 _B_
8. 75317 County Rd. 4302 Greenville, TX	75401-3572	75317 County Rd. 4302 Greenville, TX	75411-3572 _C_
9. 68910 Fort Emory Rd. Petersburg, VA	23803	68910 Fort Emory Dr. Petersburg, VA	23803 _A_
10. 5080 Club View Drive Milwaukee, WI	53209-5865	5080 Club View Drive Milwaukee, WI	53209-5865 _A_
11. 440 Stonegate Ct. York, PA	17404	640 Stonegate Ct. York, PA	27404 _D_

	Correct List		**List to Be Checked**	
	Address	ZIP Code	Address	ZIP Code
12.	3396 Moorefield Rd. Springfield, OH	45502	3396 Mooreford Rd. Springfield, OH	45052 *D*
13.	4333 Maryknoll Dr. E Rochester, MI	48309-0279	4333 Maryknoll Rd. E Rochester, MI	48309-6279 *D*
14.	5230 Craftsland Ln. NE Palm Bay, FL	32905-0018	5230 Craftsland Ln. NE Palm Bay, FL	83905-0018 *C*
15.	5440 Flora Vista Pl. Danville, CA	94526	5440 Flora Vista Pl. Denton, CA	94526 *B*
16.	826 1st St. Wharf New Orleans, LA	70130-1060	882 1st St. Wharf New Orleans, LA	70130-1060 *B*
17.	2115 E 20th St. Far Rockaway, NY	11693	2115 E 20th St. Far Rockaway, NY	11396 *C*
18.	4187 Price Ave. Cincinnati, OH	45205-2662	4187 Price Ave. Cincinnati, OH	45205-2662 *A*
19.	2686 Howe Pond Rd. Readsboro, Vermont	05350-5378	2686 Howe Point Rd. Readsboro, Vermont	05850-5378 *D*
20.	2487 Mcleod Road Bellingham, WA	98225-2773	2487 Mcleod Road Bellingham, WA	98225-2773 *A*
21.	3116 Morgan Ave. S Longmeadow, MA	01106	3116 Morgan Ave. S Longmeadow, MA	01006 *C*
22.	7687 Farabaugh Ln. Pueblo, CO	81005	7687 Farabaugh Ln. Pueblo, CO	81005 *A*
23.	8724 Groveside Ave. Whittier, CA	90604	8724 Groveside Ave. Whittier, CA	90640 *C*
24.	2604 E Lakeview Ter. Springdale, AR	72764-2442	2604 E Lakeview Ter. Springdale, AR	*C* 73764-2442
25.	2279 Jonathan Ave. Lithonia, GA	30058-9839	2279 Johnson Ave. Lithonia, GA	*D* 60058-9839

	Correct List		List to Be Checked	
	Address	*ZIP Code*	**Address**	*ZIP Code*
26.	22403 3 Oaks Rd. Crystal Lake, IL	60014-3073	22403 3 Oaks Rd. Crystal Lake, IL	60014-3073 *A*
27.	2349 S 167th Avenue Cir. Papillion, NE	68135	2349 S 167th Avenue Ct. Papillion, NE	68135 *B*
28.	2916 County Road 1764 Farmington, NM	87401	29116 County Road 1764 Farmington, NM	87403 *D*
29.	1012 Terrytown Dr. Apt. 43 Rear McKeesport, PA	15135-0266	1012 Terry Dr. Apt. 43 Rear McKeesport, PA	15135-0266 *B*
30.	2760 Marabou Mills Way Indianapolis, IN	46214	2760 Marabou Mills Way Indianapolis, IN	46214 *A*
31.	2143 Clemence St. Cranston, RI	02920	2143 Clemence St. Cranston, RI	93920 *C*
32.	2183 Alton Park Blvd. Chattanooga, TN	37410-8578	2183 Alton Park Blvd. Chattanooga, TN	37410-8758 *C*
33.	10316 Rural Route 19 Leander, TX	78641-0496	10316 Rural Road 19 Leander, TX	78641-0496 *AB*
34.	5713 W 2280 S Salt Lake City, UT	84119-5529	5713 N 2280 S Salt Lake City, UT	84119-5529 *B*
35.	2832 Teresita Way Frederiksted, VI	00840	2832 Teresita Way Frederiksted, VI	09840 *C*
36.	8543 Cumberland Dr. Somerset, KY	42503	8543 Cumberland Dr. Somerton, KY	45503 *D*
37.	3931 Freeman Park Yarmouth, Maine	04096-3707	3931 Freedman Park Yarmouth, Maine	04096-3707 *B*
38.	5324 Schubert Pl. Morgantown, WV	26505-0346	5324 Schubert Pl. Morgantown, WV	26285-0346 *C*
39.	4827 N Winnifred Rd. Brockton, MA	02301	4827 N Winnifred Rd. Brockton, MA	02301 *A*

	Correct List			List to Be Checked	
	Address	*ZIP Code*		*Address*	*ZIP Code*
40.	P.O. Box 7305F Danbury, CT	06810		P.O. Box 7305F Danbury, CT	06896 C
41.	20977 Telegraph Road Wilmington, Delaware	19804		2097 Telegraph Road Wilmington, Delaware	19834 D
42.	1908 Rhodes Pt. Road Mcfadden, WY	82083-5696		1908 Rhodes Pt. Road Mcfadden, WY	C 62063-5696
43.	2648 NE Pollard St. Lees Summit, MO	64086-5500		2648 SE Pollack St. Lees Summit, MO	D 64006-5500
44.	7946 N 124th St. Ct. W Wichita, KS	67223-3679		7946 N 124th St. Ct. W Wichita, KS	A 67223-3679
45.	5104 Haynes Haven Lane Murfreesboro, TN	37129		5104 Haynes Haven Lane Murfreesboro, TN	37219 C
46.	4307 Mulligan Mile Rapid City, SD	57702-3422		4607 Mulligan Mile Rapid City, SD	X 57702-3442 B
47.	3674 Grandview Dr. Owensboro, KY	42303		3674 Grandview Ter. Owensboro, KY	42303 B
48.	44591 Highway Y Holly Springs, MS	38635		44591 Highway Y Holly Hills, MS	38335 D
49.	11857 Old Federal Rd. SE Cleveland, TN	37323-6265		11857 Old Federal Rd. SE Cleveland, OH	X 37323-6265 A
50.	9481 Parish Parc Dr. Summerville, SC	29485-3399		9481 Parish Parc Dr. Summerville, SC	29485-3399 A
51.	391 S Hubbard Court Westland, MI	48186		391 S Hubble Court Westland, MI	48186 B
52.	3912 Letsch Rd. Waterloo, IA	50701-3155		3912 Letsch Rd. Waterloo, IA	50701-3154 C
53.	4788 N Williamsburg Ln. Pocatello, Idaho	83204-3041		4788 N Williamsburg Ln. Pocatello, Idaho	83204-3041 A

	Correct List		**List to Be Checked**	
	Address	*ZIP Code*	*Address*	*ZIP Code*
54.	4637 Rd. 135-3 Winnemucca, NV	89445	4637 Rt. 135-3 Winnemucca, NV	84445 *D*
55.	9805 E Durham Crossing Stone Mountain, GA	30083-2807	9850 E Durham Crossing Stone Mountain, GA	30083-2807 *B*
56.	4187 Crimson Rd. Toms River, NJ	08755-5709	4187 Crimson Rd. Toms River, NC	08555-5709 *C*
57.	1723 S 600th St. N Anderson, Indiana	46011-0870	1723 S 600th St. N Anderson, Indiana	46011-0870 *A*
58.	5770 Hammerlee Rd. Glen Burnie, MD	21060	5770 Hammerlee Rd. Glen Burnie, MD	31060 *C*
59.	9775 Bell Meade Road Statesville, NC	28625-6132	9775 Bell Meade Road Statesville, NC	28625-6122 *C*
60.	1826 Timberline Dr. Stillwater, OK	74074	1826 Timberlake Dr. Stillwater, OK	74074 *A*

PART B: FORMS COMPLETION

Look at this sample form and answer the two questions below it. Mark your answers in the sample answer grid that follows the questions.

Sample Form

1. First Name	2. Middle Name	3. Last Name
4. Street Address		
5. City	6. State	7. ZIP Code
8. Fee $ _____	9. Date 9a. Day _____ 9b. Month _____ 9c. Year _____	

S1. Which of these would be a correct entry for Box 6?
    A. "2542 Oak Avenue"
    B. "November"
    C. "$6.80"
    D. "Nevada"

S2. Where should the middle name be entered on the form?
    A. Box 1
    B. Box 2
    C. Box 3
    D. Box 4

Sample Answer Grid				
S1.	Ⓐ	Ⓑ	Ⓒ	Ⓓ
S2.	Ⓐ	Ⓑ	Ⓒ	Ⓓ

Completed Sample Answer Grid				
S1.	Ⓐ	Ⓑ	Ⓒ	●
S2.	Ⓐ	●	Ⓒ	Ⓓ

On the form, Box 6 is labeled "State." So the correct answer for sample question 1 is "D. Nevada," which is the only state listed among the answers. Box 2 is labeled "Middle Name," so the correct answer for sample question 2 is "B. Box 2." The completed sample answer grid above shows these correct answers filled in.

Directions: Each of the following forms is followed by questions based on that form. Each part of the form is labeled with a number or a number and a letter. You will have 15 minutes to complete the 30 questions in this section

Set 1: Forms Completion
Questions 1 through 6 are based on Form 1.

Form 1

DOMESTIC RETURN RECEIPT	
SENDER: Complete this section	**CARRIER:** Complete this section on delivery
1. Article Addressed to: 　1a.　Name _____ 　1b.　Street _____ 　1c.　City _____ 　1d.　State _____ 　1e.　ZIP Code _____	**4. Signature of receiver of mail:** 　　X _____
	5. This signature is that of (check one) 　5a. Addressee ___ 　5b. Addressee's Agent ___
2. Service Type Requested: 　2a.　Certified Mail _____ 　2b.　Registered Mail _____ 　2c.　Insured Mail _____ 　2d.　Express Mail _____ 　2e.　C.O.D. _____	**6. Is delivery address different from Item 1?** 　　6a. Yes _____　　6b. No _____
	7. If "Yes" is checked in Box 6, enter 　　delivery address below.
3. Restricted Delivery 　(Extra Fee) 　3a. Yes _____　3b. No _____	

1. Which of these would be a correct entry for Line 1b?
   A. "Brenda Curry"
   B. "72 Eastwood Road"
   C. "Arizona"
   D. "85218"

2. Which of these would be a correct entry for Box 7?
   A. "72 Eastwood Road"
   B. "Arizona"
   C. "85218"
   D. All of the above

3. If the person signing for the mail, Amanda Soukup, is not the addressee, Brenda Curry, where would you indicate this?
   A. Box 1
   B. Box 2
   C. Box 5
   D. Box 6

4. Where would the entry "Arizona" be correct?
   A. Line 1c
   B. Line 1d
   C. Line 2a
   D. Box 4

5. You could correctly enter a checkmark on all of the following EXCEPT which one?
   A. Line 1e
   B. Line 2e
   C. Line 3b
   D. Line 6b

6. If Line 6b is checked, what should be done in Box 7?
   A. Enter the delivery address
   B. Leave the box blank
   C. Enter a checkmark
   D. Enter a signature

Form 2

STAMP VENDING MACHINE REIMBURSEMENT REQUEST

For Customer Use

1. **Customer Information:**

   1a. Name _____

   1b. Address _____

   _____

   _____

   1c. Daytime Phone Number (include area code) _____

2. **Loss Information:**

   2a. Amount of Loss $_____ 2b. Date of Loss _____ 2c. Time of Loss

   ❑ AM

   ❑ PM

3. **Machine Information:** Machine ID (6-digit number on front of vending machine) _____

4. **Occurrence Information:** What Happened? (circle all that apply)

   4a. Did not receive product

   4b. Incorrect change given

   4c. Did not register/jammed

   4d. No change given

   4e. No credit shown

   4f. Money not returned

   4g. Currency lost

   4h. Coin lost

   4i. Credit/debit lost

   4j. Other (enter in "Comments")

5. **Comments:** (optional)

For Postal Service Use

6. **Paid by**	7. **Date**

8. **Action Taken** (circle one)

   8a. Paid   8b. Not Paid

9. **Sales and Services Associate Signature** _____

---

7. Which of these would be a correct entry for Line 2a?
   A. "Michael Marx"
   B. "$5.00"
   C. "593 Rachel Road"
   D. A checkmark

8. Which of these would be a correct entry for Line 4h?
   A. "$5.00"
   B. "50 cents"
   C. A circle
   D. A checkmark

9. Where would the entry "Michael Marx" be correct?
   A. Line 1a
   B. Line 1b
   C. Box 5
   D. Box 8

10. Where should the amount of money the customer lost be entered?
   A. Line 1c
   B. Line 2a
   C. Box 6
   D. Box 8

11. Alan Nadimi, the Postal Service employee, paid Michael Marx, the customer, $5.00 on April 27. Where should "Alan Nadimi" be entered?
   A. Line 1a
   B. Box 5
   C. Box 6
   D. Box 7

12. How would the customer indicate that his dollar bill was shredded when it was returned by the machine?
   A. Enter the information on Line 2b
   B. Enter the information on Line 4b
   C. Enter the information on Line 4h
   D. Enter the information in Box 5

Set 3: Forms Completion

Questions 13 through 18 are based on Form 3.

Form 3

COD
Copy 1: Delivery Unit

Delivery Employee: Remove Copies 1 (Delivery Unit Copy) and 2 (Mailer's Copy) at Time of Delivery.

Collect the amount shown below if customer pays by CHECK made payable to the mailer.	Collect the amount shown below if customer pays in CASH (includes money order fee or fees).
1. Check Amount $	**2. Cash** Amount $

3a. ❑ Registered Mail	3b. ❑ Express Mail	3c. ❑ Form 3849-D Requested
4. Date of Mailing	**5. ❑ Remit COD Charges to Sender via Express Mail**	

6. From:	7. To:

8. Delivered By	9. Date Delivered	10. Check Number
11. Date Payment Sent to Mailer	**12. Date Form 3849-D Sent**	**13. Money Order Number(s)**

DO NOT allow the recipient to examine the contents before payment.
DO NOT deliver this article until payment is collected.
If payment is by check, enter check number above.
Have customer sign Form 3849.

13. Which of these would be a correct entry for Box 3a?
    A. "$64.50"
    B. "6/6/06"
    C. "Joseph Ostransky"
    D. A checkmark

14. Which of the following would be a correct entry for Box 6?
    A. "64.50"
    B. "6/6/06"
    C. "Joseph Ostransky"
    D. A checkmark

15. The COD was delivered to Anna Wilkerson, and the payment was sent to the sender, Joseph Ostransky, on June 6, 2006. Where would "June 6, 2006" be entered?
    A. Box 4
    B. Box 5
    C. Box 11
    D. Box 12

16. Where would you indicate that the COD amount should be sent by Express Mail?
    A. Box 1
    B. Box 3b
    C. Box 4
    D. Box 5

17. Where would you indicate that the COD was delivered by Postal Service employee Ricardo Prado?
    A. Box 6
    B. Box 7
    C. Box 8
    D. Box 11

18. The delivery employee should do all of the following EXCEPT which one?
    A. Deliver the article only after payment is collected
    B. Collect the amount in Box 1 if the customer pays in cash
    C. Have the customer sign Form 3849-D if it has been requested
    D. Include fees in the amount collected in cash

Set 4: Forms Completion

Questions 19 through 24 are based on Form 4.

Form 4

APPLICATION FOR POST OFFICE BOX OR CALLER SERVICE	
Customer: Complete Shaded Boxes	Post Office: Complete White Boxes
1. Names to Which Box Numbers Are Assigned	2. Box or Caller Numbers
3. Name of Person Applying Title (if person represents organization) Name of Organization (if different from item 1)	4. Will This Box Be Used for ❏ Personal Use ❏ Business Use (optional)
5. Address (number, street, apt. no., city, state, ZIP code) *When address changes, cross out address here and put* *new address on back.*	6. Email Address (optional)

7a. Date Application Received	7b. Box Size	7c. ID and Physical Address Verified by *(initials)*	8. Telephone Number (include area code)
9. Two types of identification required. One must contain a photograph of addressee(s). Social Security cards, credit cards, and birth certificates are not acceptable as identification. Write in identifying information. Subject to verification.	10. Eligible for Carrier Delivery: ❏ city ❏ rural ❏ HCR ❏ none		11. Dates of Service _____ through _____
12. List names of minors or names of others receiving mail in box. Others must present two forms of valid ID. If applicant is a firm, name each member receiving mail. Each member must have verifiable ID on request.	13. Service Assigned ❏ Box ❏ Caller ❏ Reserve No.		14. Signature of Applicant (same as item 3) I agree to comply with all rules regarding Post Office box or caller service.

19. You could enter a checkmark in each of the following EXCEPT which?
   A. Box 4
   B. Box 10
   C. Box 13
   D. Box 14

20. Which of these would be a correct entry for Box 5?
   A. "870 Cove Lane"
   B. "Acme Painting Company"
   C. "Alice Voorhees"
   D. A checkmark

21. Which of these would be a correct entry for Box 10?
   A. A list of names
   B. A driver's license number
   C. A signature
   D. A checkmark

22. Which of the following should be completed by Post Office employees?
   A. Box 3 and Box 7
   B. Box 7a and Box 13
   C. Box 8 and Box 9
   D. Box 12 and Box 13

23. In which of these is entry of information optional?
   A. Box 1 and Box 2
   B. Box 2 and Box 4
   C. Box 4 and Box 6
   D. Box 6 and Box 11

24. Ten employees will be receiving mail in this Post Office box, which is assigned to Acme Painting Company. Where should the employees' names be entered?
   A. Box 1
   B. Box 3
   C. Box 9
   D. Box 12

Form 5

MAILING PERMIT APPLICATION AND CUSTOMER PROFILE

1. Two types of identification are required. One must contain a photograph of the addressee(s). Social Security cards, credit cards, and birth certificates are unacceptable as identification. The agent must write in identifying information. Subject to verification.

1a. Enter the first ID number.

1b. Enter the second ID number.

Application Information
(please print or type)

2. Individual or Company Name	3. Date
4. Applicant's Signature	5. Email Address

6. Address (Street and number, apartment or suite number, city, state, ZIP Code)

7. Other Names Under Which Company Does Business (if applicable)	8. How Can We Contact You? 8a. ❏ Phone 8b. ❏ Email 8c. ❏ Mail
9. Contact Person	10. Telephone (include area code)

For Postal Service Use
Check Type of Permit/Authorization Requested
(do not fill in shaded boxes)

	Permit Number	Date Issued	Date Fee Paid	Date Canceled	Sample Approved
11. ❏ **Permit Imprint Authorization** (fee applies) 11f. ❏ First-Class Mail 11g. ❏ Standard Mail 11h. ❏ Package Services 11i. ❏ Company Permit	11a.	11b.	11c.	11d.	11e.
12. ❏ **Precanceled Stamp or Government Precanceled Stamped Envelope Authorization** (no fee)	12a.	12b.	12c.	12d.	12e.
13. ❏ **Notification to Present Metered Mail in Bulk** (no fee)	13a.	13b.	13c.	13d.	13e.
13f. ❏ First-Class Mail 13g. ❏ Standard Mail 13h. ❏ Package Services	13i.	13j.	13k.	13l.	13m.
14. ❏ **Business Reply Mail (BRM) Authorization** (fee applies)	14a.	14b.	14c.	14d.	14e.
15. ❏ **Merchandise Return Service (MRS) Authorization** (fee applies)	15a.	15b.	15c.	15d.	15e.

15f. Type of Application ❏ Initial ❏ Reapplication	15g. Return Location ❏ Single ❏ Multiple	15h. Advance Deposit Account ❏ Each Location ❏ Centralized

25. Where would the date this Mailing Permit Application was made be entered?
    A. Box 3
    B. Box 11a
    C. Box 11c
    D. Box 14b

26. The Permit Imprint Authorization was canceled on August 15, 2006. Where would this date be entered?
    A. Box 11b
    B. Box 11d
    C. Box 12b
    D. Box 12d

27. Where would you indicate that the fee has been paid for Merchandise Return Service?
    A. Box 11c
    B. Box 14b
    C. Box 15b
    D. Box 15c

28. J & C Refrigeration Services has applied for the permit and has designated an employee, Diane Summers, as the person to be contacted by the Post Office. Where would "Diane Summers" be entered?
    A. Box 2
    B. Box 3
    C. Box 9
    D. Box 10

29. How would you indicate that Notification to Present Metered Mail in Bulk has been issued for standard mail?
    A. Check Box 11 and Box 11g
    B. Check Box 13 and Box 13g
    C. Check Box 13 and Box 14
    D. Check Box 14 and Box 15

30. Returned mail will go only to J & C Refrigeration's central office address. Where would you indicate this?
    A. Box 6
    B. Box 7
    C. Box 15f
    D. Box 15g

PART C: CODING AND MEMORY

SECTION 1—CODING

Coding Exercise

Choose the correct delivery route, based on the Coding Guide, for each of the following 4 items and mark your answers on the answer sheet below. You have 2 minutes to complete this practice exercise. This exercise will not be scored.

CODING GUIDE

Address Range	Delivery Route
2301–2800 Hoffman Hollow Expressway 29–99 Jefferson Ct.	A
11500–19550 Silver Sands Blvd. 2801–3900 Hoffman Hollow Expressway 100–350 Jefferson Ct.	B
400–1530 E Monteverde Trnpk. 1–899 Carpenter Way 19551–33439 Silver Sands Blvd.	C
All mail that doesn't fall in one of the address ranges listed above	D

	Address	Delivery Route
1.	399 Jefferson Ct.	A B C D
2.	2744 Hoffman Hollow Expressway	A B C D
3.	13515 Silver Sands Blvd.	A B C D
4.	1060 E Monteverde Trnpk.	A B C D

Sample Answer Grid				
1.	Ⓐ	Ⓑ	Ⓒ	Ⓓ
2.	Ⓐ	Ⓑ	Ⓒ	Ⓓ
3.	Ⓐ	Ⓑ	Ⓒ	Ⓓ
4.	Ⓐ	Ⓑ	Ⓒ	Ⓓ

Completed Sample Answer Grid				
1.	Ⓐ	Ⓑ	Ⓒ	●
2.	●	Ⓑ	Ⓒ	Ⓓ
3.	Ⓐ	●	Ⓒ	Ⓓ
4.	Ⓐ	Ⓑ	●	Ⓓ

CODING TEST

Choose the correct delivery route, based on the Coding Guide, for each of the following 36 items (items 1 through 36) and mark your answers in the Coding section of the Answer Sheet. You have 6 minutes to complete this test.

CODING GUIDE

Address Range	Delivery Route
2301–2800 Hoffman Hollow Expressway 29–99 Jefferson Ct.	A
11500–19550 Silver Sands Blvd. 2801–3900 Hoffman Hollow Expressway 100–350 Jefferson Ct.	B
400–1530 E Monteverde Trnpk. 1–899 Carpenter Way 19551–33439 Silver Sands Blvd.	C
All mail that doesn't fall in one of the address ranges listed above	D

	Address	Delivery Route
1.	662 Carpenter Way	A B (C) D
2.	85 Jefferson Ct.	(A) B C D
3.	961 E Montevideo Trnpk.	A B (C) D
4.	15 Carpenter Way	A B (C) D
5.	3691 Hoffman Hollow Expressway	A (B) C D
6.	20991 Silver Sands Blvd.	A B (C) D
7.	14000 Silver Sands Blvd.	A (B) C D
8.	111 Jefferson Ct.	A (B) C D
9.	23000 Hoffman Hollow Expressway	A B (C) (D)
10.	38 Jefferson Ct.	(A) B C D

308

	Address	Delivery Route
11.	2750 Silver Sands Blvd.	A B C D
12.	3419 Hoffman Hollow Expressway	A B C D
13.	2775 Hoffman Hollow Expressway	A B C D
14.	899 Jefferson Ct.	A B C D
15.	1519 E Monteverde Trnpk.	A B C D
16.	22 Carpenter Way	A B C D
17.	47 Jefferson Ct.	A B C D
18.	2423 Hoffman Hollow Expressway	A B C D
19.	12195 Silver Sands Blvd.	A B C D
20.	1188 E Monteverde Trnpk.	A B C D
21.	2378 Hoffman Hollow Expressway	A B C D
22.	43427 Silver Sands Blvd.	A B C D
23.	272 Carpenter Lane	A B C D
24.	462 E Monteverde Trnpk.	A B C D
25.	3575 Hoffman Hollow Expressway	A B C D
26.	52 Jefferson Ct.	A B C D
27.	18643 Silver Sands Blvd.	A B C D
28.	2594 Hoffman Hollow Expressway	A B C D
29.	20200 Silver Sands Dr.	A B C D
30.	639 Carpenter Way	A B C D
31.	3692 Hoffman Hollow Expressway	A B C D
32.	1599 Carpenter Way	A B C D
33.	299 Jefferson Ct.	A B C D
34.	776 E Monteverde Trnpk.	A B C D
35.	2662 Hoffman Hills Expressway	A B C D
36.	75 Jefferson Ct.	A B C D

SECTION 2—MEMORY

Memory Study Period 1

Use the time given to memorize the information in the following Coding Guide.

CODING GUIDE

Address Range	Delivery Route
2301–2800 Hoffman Hollow Expressway	
29–99 Jefferson Ct.	A
11500–19550 Silver Sands Blvd.	
2801–3900 Hoffman Hollow Expressway	B
100–350 Jefferson Ct.	
400–1530 E Monteverde Trnpk.	
1–899 Carpenter Way	C
19551–33439 Silver Sands Blvd.	
All mail that doesn't fall in one of the address ranges listed above	D

Memory Exercise

Choose the correct delivery route, based on your memory of the information in the Coding Guide, for each of the following 8 items and mark your answers on the answer sheet below. You have 90 seconds to complete this practice exercise. This exercise will not be scored.

Address	Delivery Route
1. 181 Jefferson Ct.	A B C D
2. 3386 Hoffman Hollow Expressway	A B C D
3. 10732 Silver Sands Blvd.	A B C D
4. 958 Carpenter Way	A B C D
5. 2494 Hoffman Hollow Expressway	A B C D
6. 15054 Silver Sands Blvd.	A B C D
7. 2496 Hoffman Hollow Expressway	A B C D
8. 29637 Silver Sands Blvd.	A B C D

Sample Answer Grid		Completed Sample Answer Grid	
1.	Ⓐ Ⓑ Ⓒ Ⓓ	1.	Ⓐ ● Ⓒ Ⓓ
2.	Ⓐ Ⓑ Ⓒ Ⓓ	2.	Ⓐ ● Ⓒ Ⓓ
3.	Ⓐ Ⓑ Ⓒ Ⓓ	3.	Ⓐ Ⓑ Ⓒ ●
4.	Ⓐ Ⓑ Ⓒ Ⓓ	4.	Ⓐ Ⓑ Ⓒ ●
5.	Ⓐ Ⓑ Ⓒ Ⓓ	5.	● Ⓑ Ⓒ Ⓓ
6.	Ⓐ Ⓑ Ⓒ Ⓓ	6.	Ⓐ ● Ⓒ Ⓓ
7.	Ⓐ Ⓑ Ⓒ Ⓓ	7.	● Ⓑ Ⓒ Ⓓ
8.	Ⓐ Ⓑ Ⓒ Ⓓ	8.	Ⓐ Ⓑ ● Ⓓ

Memory Study Period 2

Use the time given to memorize the information in the following Coding Guide.

CODING GUIDE

Address Range	Delivery Route
2301–2800 Hoffman Hollow Expressway 29–99 Jefferson Ct.	A
11500–19550 Silver Sands Blvd. 2801–3900 Hoffman Hollow Expressway 100–350 Jefferson Ct.	B
400–1530 E Monteverde Trnpk. 1–899 Carpenter Way 19551–33439 Silver Sands Blvd.	C
All mail that doesn't fall in one of the address ranges listed above	D

MEMORY TEST

Choose the correct delivery route, based on your memory of the information in the Coding Guide, for each of the following 36 items (items 37 through 72) and mark your answers in the Memory section of the Answer Sheet. You have 7 minutes to complete this test.

	Address	Delivery Route
37.	2790 Hoffman Hollow Expressway	A B C D
38.	161 Jackson Ct.	A B C D
39.	649 Monteverde Trnpk.	A B C D
40.	588 Carpenter Way	A B C D
41.	17878 Silver Sands Blvd.	A B C D
42.	2325 Hoffman Hollow Expressway	A B C D
43.	1384 E Monteverde Trnpk.	A B C D
44.	41 Jefferson Ct.	A B C D
45.	2999 Hoffman Hollow Expressway	A B C D

	Address	Delivery Route
46.	2103 Hoffman Hollow Expressway	A B C D
47.	12456 Silver Sands Blvd.	A B C D
48.	373 Carpenter Way	A B C D
49.	1444 E Monteverde Trnpk.	A B C D
50.	2315 Hoffman Hollow Expressway	A B C D
51.	77 Jefferson Ct.	A B C D
52.	16309 Silver Strand Blvd.	A B C D
53.	329 Jefferson Ct.	A B C D
54.	699 Carpenteria Dr.	A B C D
55.	2725 Hoffman Hollow Expressway	A B C D
56.	920 E Monteverde Trnpk.	A B C D
57.	3837 Hoffman Hollow Expressway	A B C D
58.	405 Jefferson Ct.	A B C D
59.	2665 Hoffman Hollow Expressway	A B C D
60.	17542 Silver Sands Blvd.	A B C D
61.	292 Jefferson Ct.	A B C D
62.	659 Carpenter Way	A B C D
63.	2555 Hoffman Hollow Expressway	A B C D
64.	418 E Monteverde Trnpk.	A B C D
65.	193 Jefferson Ct.	A B C D
66.	363887 Silver Sands Blvd.	A B C D
67.	299 E Monteverde Trnpk.	A B C D
68.	3097 Hoffman Hollow Expressway	A B C D
69.	496 Carpenter Way	A B C D
70.	36 Jefferson Ct.	A B C D
71.	1237 E Monteverde Trnpk.	A B C D
72.	12986 Silver Sands Blvd.	A B C D

PART D: PERSONAL CHARACTERISTICS AND EXPERIENCE INVENTORY

On the actual exam, the next part that you would take is Part D: Personal Characteristics and Experience Inventory. This part of the exam is 90 minutes long and has 236 items. Because there is no particular advantage to practicing your responses on these statements and questions, no tests are given here for them.

Scoring and Explanations for Practice Examination 6

ANSWER KEY

Part A: Address Checking

1. D	11. D	21. C	31. C	41. D	51. B
2. C	12. D	22. A	32. C	42. C	52. C
3. C	13. D	23. C	33. B	43. D	53. A
4. A	14. C	24. C	34. B	44. A	54. D
5. C	15. B	25. D	35. C	45. C	55. B
6. B	16. B	26. A	36. D	46. D	56. D
7. B	17. C	27. B	37. B	47. B	57. A
8. C	18. A	28. D	38. C	48. D	58. C
9. B	19. D	29. B	39. A	49. B	59. C
10. A	20. A	30. A	40. C	50. A	60. B

Part B: Forms Completion

1. B	6. B	11. C	16. D	21. D	26. B
2. D	7. B	12. D	17. C	22. B	27. D
3. C	8. C	13. D	18. B	23. C	28. C
4. B	9. A	14. C	19. D	24. D	29. B
5. A	10. B	15. C	20. A	25. A	30. D

Part C: Coding Test

1. C	7. B	13. A	19. B	25. B	31. B
2. A	8. B	14. D	20. C	26. A	32. D
3. D	9. D	15. C	21. A	27. B	33. B
4. C	10. A	16. C	22. D	28. A	34. C
5. B	11. D	17. A	23. D	29. D	35. D
6. C	12. B	18. A	24. C	30. C	36. A

Part C: Memory Test

37. A	43. C	49. C	55. A	61. B	67. D
38. D	44. A	50. A	56. C	62. C	68. B
39. D	45. B	51. A	57. B	63. A	69. C
40. C	46. D	52. D	58. D	64. C	70. A
41. B	47. B	53. B	59. A	65. B	71. C
42. A	48. C	54. D	60. B	66. D	72. B

SCORING

Part A: Address Checking

Enter the number you got right: _____

Enter the number you got wrong
(not including those left blank): _____

Divide the number wrong by 3
(or multiply by 1/3): _____

Subtract this answer from the number right: - _____

Raw Score _____

Part B: Forms Completion

Enter the number you got right
(no penalty for guessing): Raw Score _____

Part C: Coding and Memory

Enter the number you got right: _____

Enter the number you got wrong
(not including those left blank): _____

Divide the number wrong by 3
(or multiply by 1/3): _____

Subtract this answer from the number right: - _____

Raw Score _____

Part D: Personal Characteristics and Experience Inventory

Scoring system not given.

Explanations

PART A: ADDRESS CHECKING

	Correct List		List to Be Checked	
	Address	*ZIP Code*	*Address*	*ZIP Code*
1. D	1974 **Kamana** Rd. Apple Valley, CA	92307-7676	1974 **Karmina** Rd. Apple Valley, CA	93307-7676
2. C	5854 Merriline Ave. Utica, New York	13502-**2**573	5854 Merriline Ave. Utica, New York	13502-**6**473
3. C	3631 98th Way Sebastian, FL	32958-56**00**	3631 98th Way Sebastian, FL	32958-56**60**
4. A	287 Laurelridge Pl. Grants Pass, OR	97526	287 Laurelridge Pl. Grants Pass, OR	97526
5. C	3111 W Wimbledon Dr. Charleston, SC	2**9**412-8327	3111 W Wimbledon Dr. Charleston, SC	2**4**912-8327
6. B	69614 Hoskinson Pkwy. Glen Ellyn, IL	60137	69614 Hoskinson Pkwy. **Glenn Ellen**, IL	60137
7. B	5561 53rd Pl. Apt. 243D Hyattsville, **MD**	20781	5561 53rd Pl. Apt. 243D Hyattsville, **ND**	20781
8. C	75317 County Rd. 4302 Greenville, TX	754**0**1-3572	75317 County Rd. 4302 Greenville, TX	754**1**1-3572
9. B	68910 Fort Emory **Rd.** Petersburg, VA	23803	68910 Fort Emory **Dr.** Petersburg, VA	23803
10. A	5080 Club View Drive Milwaukee, WI	53209-5865	5080 Club View Drive Milwaukee, WI	53209-5865
11. D	**4**40 Stonegate Ct. York, PA	**1**7404	**6**40 Stonegate Ct. York, PA	**2**7404
12. D	3396 Moore**field** Rd. Springfield, OH	455**02**	3396 Moore**ford** Rd. Springfield, OH	450**52**
13. D	4333 Maryknoll **Dr.** E Rochester, MI	48309-**0**279	4333 Maryknoll **Rd.** E Rochester, MI	48309-**6**279
14. C	5230 Craftsland Ln. NE Palm Bay, FL	**3**2905-0018	5230 Craftsland Ln. NE Palm Bay, FL	**8**3905-0018

		Correct List		**List to Be Checked**	
		Address	*ZIP Code*	*Address*	*ZIP Code*
15.	B	5440 Flora Vista Pl. **Danville,** CA	94526	5440 Flora Vista Pl. **Denton,** CA	94526
16.	B	**826** 1st St. Wharf New Orleans, LA	70130-1060	**882** 1st St. Wharf New Orleans, LA	70130-1060
17.	C	2115 E 20th St. Far Rockaway, NY	11**693**	2115 E 20th St. Far Rockaway, NY	11**396**
18.	A	4187 Price Ave. Cincinnati, OH	45205-2662	4187 Price Ave. Cincinnati, OH	45205-2662
19.	D	2686 Howe **Pond** Rd. Readsboro, Vermont	05**3**50-5378	2686 Howe **Point** Rd. Readsboro, Vermont	05**8**50-5378
20.	A	2487 Mcleod Road Bellingham, WA	98225-2773	2487 Mcleod Road Bellingham, WA	98225-2773
21.	C	3116 Morgan Ave. S Longmeadow, MA	01**1**06	3116 Morgan Ave. S Longmeadow, MA	01**0**06
22.	A	7687 Farabaugh Ln. Pueblo, CO	81005	7687 Farabaugh Ln. Pueblo, CO	81005
23.	C	8724 Groveside Ave. Whittier, CA	9060**4**	8724 Groveside Ave. Whittier, CA	9064**0**
24.	C	2604 E Lakeview Ter. Springdale, AR	7**2**764-2442	2604 E Lakeview Ter. Springdale, AR	7**3**764-2442
25.	D	2279 **Jonathan** Ave. Lithonia, GA	**3**0058-9839	2279 **Johnson** Ave. Lithonia, GA	**6**0058-9839
26.	A	22403 3 Oaks Rd. Crystal Lake, IL	60014-3073	22403 3 Oaks Rd. Crystal Lake, IL	60014-3073
27.	B	2349 S 167th Avenue **Cir.** Papillion, NE	68135	2349 S 167th Avenue **Ct.** Papillion, NE	68135
28.	D	29**1**6 County Road 1764 Farmington, NM	8740**1**	29**11**6 County Road 1764 Farmington, NM	8740**3**

		Address	ZIP Code	Address	ZIP Code
29.	B	1012 Terry**town** Dr. Apt. 43 Rear McKeesport, PA	15135-0266	1012 Terr**y** Dr. Apt. 43 Rear McKeesport, PA	15135-0266
30.	A	2760 Marabou Mills Way Indianapolis, IN	46214	2760 Marabou Mills Way Indianapolis, IN	46214
31.	C	2143 Clemence St. Cranston, RI	**02**920	2143 Clemence St. Cranston, RI	**93**920
32.	C	2183 Alton Park Blvd. Chattanooga, TN	37410-**8578**	2183 Alton Park Blvd. Chattanooga, TN	37410-**8758**
33.	B	10316 Rural **Route** 19 Leander, TX	78641-0496	10316 Rural **Road** 19 Leander, TX	78641-0496
34.	B	5713 **W** 2280 S Salt Lake City, UT	84119-5529	5713 **N** 2280 S Salt Lake City, UT	84119-5529
35.	C	2832 Teresita Way Frederiksted, VI	**0**0840	2832 Teresita Way Frederiksted, VI	**0**9840
36.	D	8543 Cumberland Dr. Somer**set**, KY	42503	8543 Cumberland Dr. Somer**ton**, KY	45503
37.	B	3931 Free**m**an Park Yarmouth, Maine	04096-3707	3931 Free**dm**an Park Yarmouth, Maine	04096-3707
38.	C	5324 Schubert Pl. Morgantown, WV	26**505**-0346	5324 Schubert Pl. Morgantown, WV	26**285**-0346
39.	A	4827 N Winnifred Rd. Brockton, MA	02301	4827 N Winnifred Rd. Brockton, MA	02301
40.	C	P.O. Box 7305F Danbury, CT	068**10**	P.O. Box 7305F Danbury, CT	068**96**
41.	D	20977 Telegraph Road Wilmington, Delaware	19804	2097 Telegraph Road Wilmington, Delaware	19834
42.	C	1908 Rhodes Pt. Road Mcfadden, WY	**82083**-5696	1908 Rhodes Pt. Road Mcfadden, WY	**62063**-5696

	Correct List		List to Be Checked	
	Address	ZIP Code	Address	ZIP Code

43. D 2648 NE Pollard St.
Lees Summit, MO — 64086-5500 | 2648 SE Pollack St. Lees Summit, MO — 64006-5500

44. A 7946 N 124th St. Ct. W
Wichita, KS — 67223-3679 | 7946 N 124th St. Ct. W Wichita, KS — 67223-3679

45. C 5104 Haynes Haven Lane
Murfreesboro, TN — 37129 | 5104 Haynes Haven Lane Murfreesboro, TN — 37219

46. D 4307 Mulligan Mile
Rapid City, SD — 57702-3422 | 4607 Mulligan Mile Rapid City, SD — 57702-3442

47. B 3674 Grandview **Dr.**
Owensboro, KY — 42303 | 3674 Grandview **Ter.** Owensboro, KY — 42303

48. D 44591 Highway Y
Holly **Springs,** MS — 38635 | 44591 Highway Y Holly **Hills,** MS — 38335

49. B 11857 Old Federal Rd. SE
Cleveland, **TN** — 37323-6265 | 11857 Old Federal Rd. SE Cleveland, **OH** — 37323-6265

50. A 9481 Parish Parc Dr.
Summerville, SC — 29485-3399 | 9481 Parish Parc Dr. Summerville, SC — 29485-3399

51. B 391 S Hubb**ard** Court
Westland, MI — 48186 | 391 S Hubb**le** Court Westland, MI — 48186

52. C 3912 Letsch Rd.
Waterloo, IA — 50701-3155 | 3912 Letsch Rd. Waterloo, IA — 50701-3154

53. A 4788 N Williamsburg Ln.
Pocatello, Idaho — 83204-3041 | 4788 N Williamsburg Ln. Pocatello, Idaho — 83204-3041

54. D 4637 **Rd.** 135-3
Winnemucca, NV — 89445 | 4637 **Rt.** 135-3 Winnemucca, NV — 84445

55. B 9805 E Durham Crossing
Stone Mountain, GA — 30083-2807 | 9850 E Durham Crossing Stone Mountain, GA — 30083-2807

56. D 4187 Crimson Rd.
Toms River, **NJ** — 08755-5709 | 4187 Crimson Rd. Toms River, **NC** — 08555-5709

		Correct List		List to Be Checked	
		Address	*ZIP Code*	*Address*	*ZIP Code*
57.	**A**	1723 S 600th St. N Anderson, Indiana	46011-0870	1723 S 600th St. N Anderson, Indiana	46011-0870
58.	**C**	5770 Hammerlee Rd. Glen Burnie, MD	**2**1060	5770 Hammerlee Rd. Glen Burnie, MD	**3**1060
59.	**C**	9775 Bell Meade Road Statesville, NC	28625-61**3**2	9775 Bell Meade Road Statesville, NC	28625-61**2**2
60.	**B**	1826 Timber**line** Dr. Stillwater, OK	74074	1826 Timber**lake** Dr. Stillwater, OK	74074

PART B: FORMS COMPLETION

Set 1: Questions 1 through 6

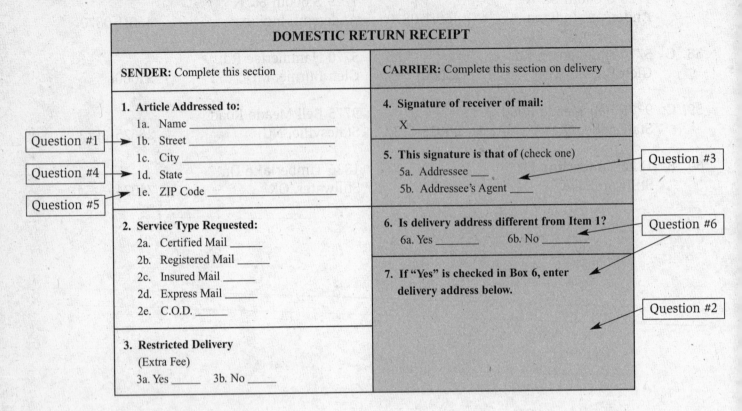

1. **B** Line 1b is for the street address.
2. **D** Box 7 is for a delivery address. Answers A, B, and C could all be part of such an address, so the correct answer is D, All of the above.
3. **C** In Box 5 you can indicate that the person signing for the mail is not the addressee, but the addressee's agent.
4. **B** "Arizona," a state name, would go on Line 1d. (It could also go in Box 7, but Box 7 isn't given as an answer choice.)
5. **A** You couldn't correctly put a checkmark on Line 1e, which requires a ZIP code.
6. **B** If Line 6b is checked, that indicates that the delivery address is *not* different from Item 1, and so you would leave Box 7 blank.

STAMP VENDING MACHINE REIMBURSEMENT REQUEST	

For Customer Use

1. Customer Information:

Question #9

   1a. Name _____

   1b. Address _____

                       _____

                       _____

   1c. Daytime Phone Number (include area code) _____

2. Loss Information:

Question #7

Question #10

   2a. Amount of Loss $_____   2b. Date of Loss _____   2c. Time of Loss

                                                                    ❑ AM

                                                                   ❑ PM

3. Machine Information: Machine ID (6-digit number on front of vending machine) _____

4. Occurrence Information: What Happened? (circle all that apply)

   4a. Did not receive product   4f. Money not returned

   4b. Incorrect change given   4g. Currency lost   Question #8

   4c. Did not register/jammed   4h. Coin lost ◄

   4d. No change given   4i. Credit/debit lost

   4e. No credit shown   4j. Other (enter in "Comments")

5. Comments: (optional)

Question #12

For Postal Service Use

6. Paid by	**7. Date**

Question #11

8. Action Taken (circle one)

   8a. Paid   8b. Not Paid

9. Sales and Services Associate Signature _____

  7. **B** Line 2a is for the dollar amount of the loss.

  8. **C** Items in Box 4 should be circled, including Line 4h.

  9. **A** A name could go on Line 1a.

10. **B** The amount of loss goes on Line 2a.

11. **C** The space for the name of the employee who paid this claim is Box 6.

12. **D** There are no items in Box 4 that specifically mention shredding (or otherwise destroy-ing) a bill. So the customer would circle Line 4j ("Other"), which is not one of the answers, and enter this information in Box 5, "Comments."

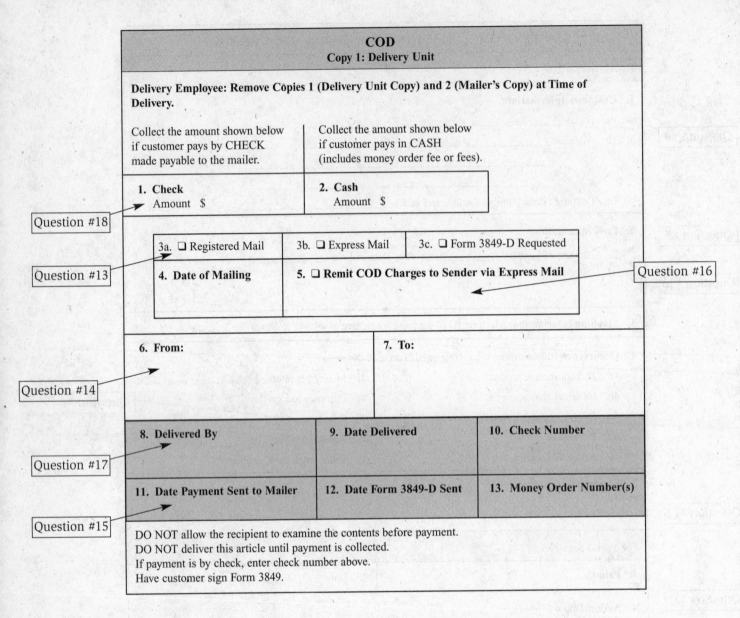

13. **D** Box 3a should be checked if this delivery is by Registered Mail.
14. **C** Box 6 is for the name and address of the sender.
15. **C** The date the payment is sent to the sender (the mailer) is entered in Box 11.
16. **D** If the COD amount is to be sent to the sender by Express Mail, that is indicated in Box 5.
17. **C** The name of the Postal Service delivery employee goes in Box 8.
18. **B** At both the top and the bottom of the form are instructions for the delivery employee. That employee should do all of these things *except* B. The employee should collect the amount shown in Box 1 only if the customer pays by *check,* not with cash.

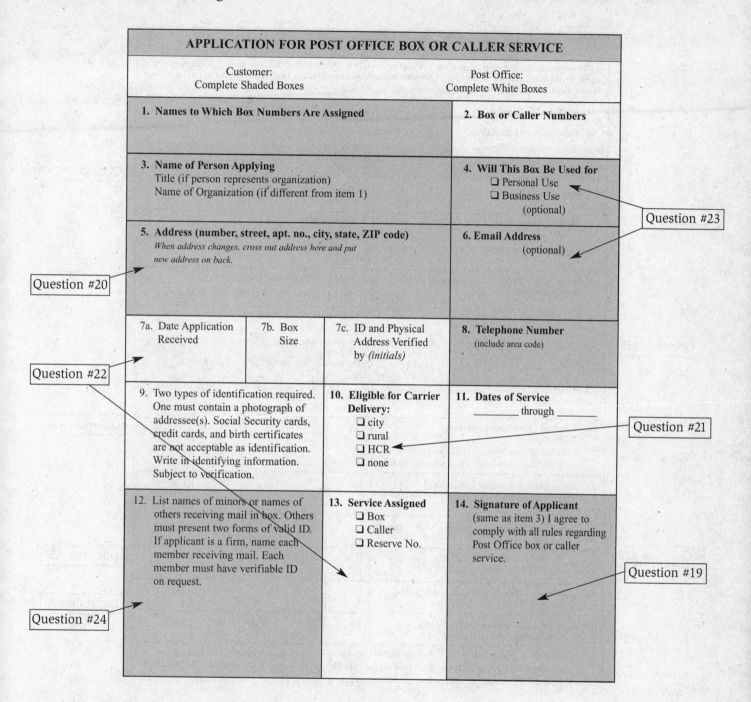

APPLICATION FOR POST OFFICE BOX OR CALLER SERVICE

Customer:
Complete Shaded Boxes

Post Office:
Complete White Boxes

1. **Names to Which Box Numbers Are Assigned**

2. **Box or Caller Numbers**

3. **Name of Person Applying**
Title (if person represents organization)
Name of Organization (if different from item 1)

4. **Will This Box Be Used for**
❑ Personal Use
❑ Business Use
(optional)

Question #23

5. **Address (number, street, apt. no., city, state, ZIP code)**
*When address changes, cross out address here and put
new address on back.*

6. **Email Address**
(optional)

Question #20

7a. Date Application
Received

7b. Box
Size

7c. ID and Physical
Address Verified
by *(initials)*

8. **Telephone Number**
(include area code)

Question #22

9. Two types of identification required.
One must contain a photograph of
addressee(s). Social Security cards,
credit cards, and birth certificates
are not acceptable as identification.
Write in identifying information.
Subject to verification.

10. **Eligible for Carrier
Delivery:**
❑ city
❑ rural
❑ HCR
❑ none

11. **Dates of Service**
_____ through _____

Question #21

12. List names of minors or names of
others receiving mail in box. Others
must present two forms of valid ID.
If applicant is a firm, name each
member receiving mail. Each
member must have verifiable ID
on request.

13. **Service Assigned**
❑ Box
❑ Caller
❑ Reserve No.

14. **Signature of Applicant**
(same as item 3) I agree to
comply with all rules regarding
Post Office box or caller
service.

Question #19

Question #24

19. **D** Box 14 requires a signature, *not* a checkmark.
20. **A** Box 5 is for an address. Choice A is the only answer with part of an address.
21. **D** A checkmark is placed in Box 10 to indicate the type of carrier delivery.
22. **B** Notice that at the top of the form are the instructions "Post Office: Complete White Boxes." Of the combinations given, only answer B would include two white boxes.
23. **C** Both Box 4 and Box 6 indicate that the information here is optional.
24. **D** The names of those who will get mail in this Post Office box, other than the applying person or firm, should be listed in Box 12.

MAILING PERMIT APPLICATION AND CUSTOMER PROFILE

1. Two types of identification are required. One must contain a photograph of the addressee(s). Social Security cards, credit cards, and birth certificates are unacceptable as identification. The agent must write in identifying information. Subject to verification.

1a. Enter the first ID number.

1b. Enter the second ID number.

Application Information
(please print or type)

2. Individual or Company Name	3. Date
4. Applicant's Signature	5. Email Address
6. Address (Street and number, apartment or suite number, city, state, ZIP Code)	
7. Other Names Under Which Company Does Business (if applicable)	8. How Can We Contact You? 8a. ❑ Phone 8b. ❑ Email 8c. ❑ Mail
9. Contact Person	10. Telephone (include area code)

Question #25 → (Box 3 Date)

Question #28 → (Box 9 Contact Person)

For Postal Service Use
Check Type of Permit/Authorization Requested
(do not fill in shaded boxes)

	Permit Number	Date Issued	Date Fee Paid	Date Canceled	Sample Approved
11. ❑ **Permit Imprint Authorization** (fee applies) 11f. ❑ First-Class Mail 11g. ❑ Standard Mail 11h. ❑ Package Services 11i. ❑ Company Permit	11a.	11b.	11c.	11d.	11e.
12. ❑ **Precanceled Stamp or Government Precanceled Stamped Envelope Authorization** (no fee)	12a.	12b.	12c.	12d.	12e.
13. ❑ **Notification to Present Metered Mail in Bulk** (no fee)	13a.	13b.	13c.	13d.	13e.
13f. ❑ First-Class Mail 13g. ❑ Standard Mail 13h. ❑ Package Services →	13i.	13j.	13k.	13l.	13m.
14. ❑ **Business Reply Mail (BRM) Authorization** (fee applies)	14a.	14b.	14c.	14d.	14e.
15. ❑ **Merchandise Return Service (MRS) Authorization** (fee applies)	15a.	15b.	15c.	15d.	15e.

15f. Type of Application ❑ Initial ❑ Reapplication	15g. Return Location ❑ Single ❑ Multiple	15h. Advance Deposit Account ❑ Each Location ❑ Centralized

Question #26 → (Box 11d)

Question #29 → (Box 13)

Question #27 → (Box 15c)

Question #30 → (Box 15g)

25. **A** The date this application was made should be entered in Box 3.

26. **B** The Permit Imprint Authorization is in Box 11. The date of cancellation of this permit is in Box 11d, answer B.

27. **D** To indicate that the fee has been paid for Merchandise Return Service, you would enter the date of payment in Box 15c.

28. **C** The contact person's name goes in Box 9.

29. **B** To indicate both that Notification to Present Metered Mail in Bulk has been issued and that it has been issued for standard mail, you would check both Box 13 and Box 13g.

30. **D** Returned mail is mentioned only in Box 15g. There you can check either a single or a multiple location.

ARE YOU READY?

1. Make sure that you know when and where you are taking the test. Be familiar with the test location. Know how to get there, where to park, and if there's a parking fee.
2. Spend the week before the test working on building your speed and on a general review of test-taking strategies and techniques.
3. Don't cram the night before the exam. It's usually a waste of time!
4. If you normally eat breakfast or lunch, eat a nourishing meal before the exam.
5. Arrive in plenty of time at the testing site.
6. Remember to bring the proper materials: identification, admission ticket, three or four correctly sharpened number two pencils, a good eraser, and a watch.
7. Dress comfortably. Wear layers of clothing so that you can adjust to the temperature of the room (taking a sweater off if it's too hot or putting one on if it's too cold).
8. Start off crisply with confidence. Don't get stuck on one question.
9. Know the guessing strategies and penalties (if there are any) for each specific question type. On Parts A and C there is a penalty for guessing, so guess only if you can eliminate one or more choices. On Part B there is no penalty for guessing, so always fill in an answer.
10. Be familiar with the directions for each section.
11. Know the time constraints—how fast you'll have to work to complete the section. Remember, many of the sections require you to work very quickly.
12. Use a positive approach. The key to getting a top score is working quickly and accurately.

More Civil Service Test Prep Help from Barron's

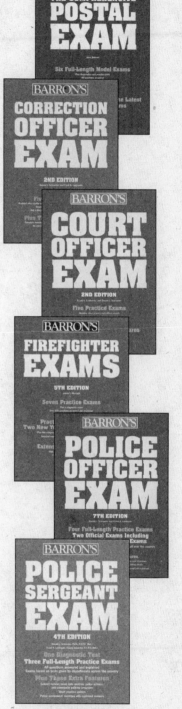